Le Pavillon

MENU

Déjeuner

Jambon de Bayonne 2.25	Melon 1.50	Grapefruit .90
Caviar Malossol 7.50	Pate Maison 3.50	Foie Gras Truffé 5.00
Saumon Fumé 2.75	Cherrystone 1.25	Anguille Fumée 2.25
Cocktails: Shrimps 2.50		Crab Meat 3.00

Oeufs

Omelette Pavillon 4.75	Omelette aux Champignons 3.25	Poché Mornay 3.00
Poché Bourguignonne 3.00	Brouillés aux Foies de Volaille 3.25	Froid à la Gelée 1.25

Plats du Jour

MOUSSAKA D'AGNEAU PAVILLON 5.50

VOLAILLE POÊLÉE AU AROMATES (P. P.) 5.00

NOIX DE VEAU FERMIÈRE 4.25

STEAK AU POIVRE. CÉLERI BRAISÉ 7.50

FOIE DE VEAU AU BACON 4.00

PIGEON GRILLÉ. POMMES SOUFFLEES 5.00

SOLE IMPORTÉE VÉRONIQUE 6.50

TRUITE SAUTE NORMANDIE 4.50

Légumes

Haricots Verts au Beurre 1.50	Epinards à la Crème 1.50	Courgettes Provençale 1.50
Céleris au Jus 2.00	Petits Pois Française 1.50	Carottes au Beurre 1.50

Entremets

Patisserie Pavillon 2.00	Soufflée Tous Parfums 3.00	Crêpes Pavillon 3.00
Macedoine de Fruits aux Liqueurs 2.50	Coupe aux Marrons 1.75	Pêche Melba 2.50

Glaces: Vanille 1.00   Chocolat 1.00   Framboise 1.00   Moka 1.00   Citron 1.00   Fraise 1.00

Café .70   Demi-Tasse .60   Bread and Butter .75

A Chef's Tale

A Chef's Tale

A MEMOIR OF FOOD, FRANCE

AND AMERICA

BY Pierre Franey

WITH RICHARD FLASTE

AND BRYAN MILLER

ALFRED A. KNOPF · NEW YORK · 1994

THIS IS A BORZOI BOOK
PUBLISHED BY ALFRED A. KNOPF, INC.

Library of Congress Cataloging-in-Publication Data
Franey, Pierre.
A chef's tale: a memoir of food, France
and America / by Pierre Franey with
Richard Flaste and Bryan Miller.— 1st ed.
p. cm.
Includes index.
ISBN 0-394-58600-X
1. Franey, Pierre. 2. Cooks—France—Biography.
3. Cooks—United States—Biography.
I. Flaste, Richard. II. Miller, Bryan. III. Title.
TX649.F74A3 1994
641.5'092—dc20 [B] 93-24991 CIP

Manufactured in the United States of America
FIRST EDITION

For my parents

CONTENTS

ACKNOWLEDGMENTS

As I HAVE RELATED the story of my life here, I find that many important friends who supported me and about whom I care deeply never made it into the narrative itself. The ones I want to mention especially are: Sam Aaron, Roger Fessaguet, Joe Baum, Clorinda Gorman, Lauren Jarret, Charles Pinsky, Michel Roux, Andre Soltner, Sirio Maccioni, Velma Cannon, Jean-Claude Baker, Paul Damaz, Louis Daniel, Michel Lopez, Andre Mailhan, Kay and Warner LeRoy, Marc Sarrazin, Robert Meyzen, Fred Decré, Jean-Paul Picot, Camille Dulac and Daniel Boulud.

In writing this memoir with recipes, the tasks were divided: for the narrative section my coauthor was Richard Flaste and for the recipes it was Bryan Miller, both close associates of long-standing. At every step along the way, from shaping the tone to creating the book's appearance, the guiding hand was my trusted editor of many years, Jonathan Segal.

A Chef's Tale

*The Franey family, circa
1932. I'm kneeling next to
the dog.*

Homecoming

T HE VILLAGE of St. Vinnemer, 160 miles from Paris in the hills of Burgundy, has not changed much. There were 398 residents during my childhood in the 1920s, and there are 390 or so now. The Parisians have discovered it, of course, and use it as a country escape on weekends. But the people, the values, the rituals, are more or less as they always were. Not long ago, on a visit from the United States, I was just outside delightful little St. Vinnemer, just a few miles away at the farm my brother Michel owns in Sambourg. Undaunted by modernity, he goes about life with the profound reverence for tradition and for food that marks the region generally. Michel and his wife, Françoise, knew I was coming to hunt and to visit, so I could pretty well guess what kind of meal they would be serving to celebrate my arrival.

Even the humblest farm family in France has mastered the age-old skills for marvelous cooking, and I was not only certain that those skills would be evident, but that they would be evident in particular dishes, a very particular meal, resplendent yet without pretension. Just before I arrived, Michel, I could be certain, would go down to the river for his favorite fish, pike (he admires it for, among other things, its size; I refer to it as "the turkey of river fish"), a voracious predator that can live for many years as it grows ever larger.

Michel would be hoping for an impressive big one, perhaps ten pounds or more. This was not because little fish are wanting in flavor; it was because the bigger fish seem so much more celebratory. The fish would be baked and stuffed with a few sprigs of thyme and a bay leaf or two, and around it would be sprinkled shallots and Chablis (not a bad Chablis, either, since—contrary to a widely held view—it always makes sense to cook with a decent wine if you expect it to enhance the food).

The dish would contain mushrooms, too—chanterelles that my brother and his wife like to gather out back and present as the delicate homegrown gift they are. I knew Michel would do the baking in the same wood-burning oven he has always used. Although there is no particular culinary advantage to such an oven—other than that it forces the cook to keep his focus a little sharper than it might otherwise be, moderating the heat just so—it is a rustic reminder that the past will not be relinquished easily around here.

Even though it is a simple, tried-and-true preparation, the baked pike always has about it an ineffable elegance. In the preparation, the pike, a sweet and moderately firm fish, is baked along with the shallots and wine until it is half-done, then at this advanced stage and no sooner, so they will not lose all of their firmness in the cooking, the mushrooms are added. Butter is whisked into the pan at the very end, and in an instant one has a beurre blanc, a white butter sauce, infused both with the wine and with the overtones of the fish itself, a smooth sauce given texture and contrast by the chanterelles.

But the pike is just one course. Françoise always keeps two roosters on the farm poised for one of these occasions to be stewed in wine. And then there would be a mousse served with brioche. (That dessert combination was a familiar one in my family. We never wanted to serve mousse alone because it was too monotonous; it required the firmness of the rich bread to lend counterpoint to the softness of the pudding. All good cooking from peasant to haute cuisine must never lose sight of the need for complementary textures.)

When I arrived at Michel's old stone farmhouse and was served precisely that meal, it didn't strike me as lamentably predictable but rather an assertion of affection, an understanding of the role food plays in our expression of ourselves, an extension of ourselves, really. It made me very happy. When I tasted that tender pike in my brother's century-old home, its aroma and flavor were all that was necessary to set loose in my mind a rush of images of childhood and growing up in St. Vinnemer.

It is literally possible for a single taste of some beloved dish to evoke a lifetime of relationships and experiences. At that moment, because of the pike, the memories were especially of my father, a dignified and reserved man, yet generous and warm, who taught all of us how to fish and also how to engage the land on its own terms so that we could nourish it as it nourished us.

We lived in a culture immersed in food, after all. The village of St. Vinnemer, seen as a whole, was a superbly efficient food-producing organism. The water, the fields, the forests, each contributed to the great variety of foods available in this one little place.

Food production and preparation went beyond playing necessary and social roles in our lives. They were spiritual and central. Every day of my childhood I was responsible for some aspect of food gathering or preparation. This was true even when I was as young as three or four years old. My mother or grandmother would assign me to gather beans or peppers, or to harvest the cherries for preserving. Maybe I would be the one to sugar the fruit before it was jarred and steamed. I would certainly be the one to hang around, like a pleading pet, so that I could get to eat the scraps—the extra bits of baked dough, the excess cherries. They called me Pierre Le Gourmand, and very early on they said I was bound to be a chef one day (I suppose they imagined I would become less gluttonous and more discriminating, with the appropriate tutoring). In fact, there was little else I ever imagined that I would be, and Burgundy was one of the best places on earth to start.

When I try to distinguish the food of Burgundy from that of the rest of France, I think first about the abundance of it. Nowhere I have ever been, in France or anywhere else, provides such dazzling variety at one's doorstep: freshwater fish, game, wild mushrooms, snails and frogs, beef and pork and rabbit, vegetables and fruits that have never been compromised by technology. In a place of such natural riches, we had the luxury to cultivate nuances in our food that would contribute to an endless sense of adventure.

Cheese, for one, varies in flavor from town to town and from hillside to valley, depending on the grass or the herbs or the hay the cows eat. And then, of course, there is the wine. It is wine that must be credited for the great stews such as beef Burgundy and coq au vin. But it is also wine that is responsible for the light sauces that characterize Burgundian cooking (and not the sauces inspired, say, by the cream of Normandy). These light wine-based sauces are the very ones that have achieved such current popularity beyond France.

Fertile Burgundy was lying in wait until the lessons learned there could be taken up by the rest of the world. American cooks today struggle to undo the culinary damage of modern processing as they strive to move closer once again to the sources of their food. Here, in late-twentieth-century America, one sees the Burgundian contribution in recipes and techniques, certainly, and also in a growing respect for the food itself, for nature.

If I can tell you about my childhood close to the soil in St. Vinnemer, and about my subsequent years in America, I believe it will explain so much, not just about how one cook made his way, but also about deeply held values and standards in cooking and how they came to be welcomed and embraced in kitchens far beyond my rustic Burgundy. One thing is for certain: in St. Vinnemer, we, even the humblest of us, ate well.

"PIERRE, come on let's go!" My father was calling. He was the mayor of St. Vinnemer then—and a blacksmith besides—austere looking and muscular, with big hands. I was eight years old and eager. "We've got to set those nets."

It was nearly dusk, and we were going fishing. The river was just a short walk from the house, but we were heading a mile upstream, and rather than walk we jumped into the big yellow Citroën to save time. We were on our way to catch not pike but trout, as noble a specimen as we could, to serve for the department deputy who would be arriving the next day with his wife and his secretary. At the riverside, my father pulled the little flat-bottomed boat from where it was tethered beneath my grandfather's apple trees, and I fetched the pole I had hidden just up the riverbank. It was my job to pole the boat to one of my father's favorite spots. (Everyone had a favorite spot in the river, of course; my suspicion is that they were all equally good.)

The river, l'Armançon, was full of rocks and vegetation. As the trout moved in their early evening journeys, they would seek out the runs where the water rushed past the weeds and around the rocks. It was in one such run that we would set our first net, an *araignée*, or spider. Each had weights to hold the bottom down and floats to hold the top up. If you returned to find that a float had been pulled beneath the surface, you would know a fish had been snared.

We had several nets of different lengths, but each one was designed to let a large trout's head, but not the rest of its body, pass through; then the trout could not go forward or backward. When trout cannot move, they cannot breathe, and they die. But the cold water would keep any that we caught fresh until the early morning, when we would return. It was important that the trout we took with us be netted well: if it had

been unfortunate enough to get tangled in the net or if it had pushed itself too far through a hole, some of its moist, protective coating would be scraped off, making it more likely that the trout

My father Aristide, with his Citroën

would dry and spoil quickly. Fresh trout must gleam with moisture, even hours after they have been caught. As an extra measure of protection, I learned to cover the fish with wet river weeds, even for the brief journey back to the house.

Thanks to my father, I was an accomplished fisherman at the age of eight. I even knew how to catch a trout with my bare hands. It was easy: In the warmth of the day, the trout lie in wait at the edge of the weeds, hoping some morsels—worms, flies—will come floating past. If you hold your hand with thumb and index finger spread to form a "C" and then slide your hand over a trout's body from the tail toward its head, you can grab it at the gills. This was so simple and involved so little challenge to either party that it was illegal. Netting a fish was all right, but grabbing it as it peacefully contemplated its next meal must have seemed somehow unforgivable to the rule makers.

Whenever we went on one of these excursions at dusk to trap trout for guests the next day, the excitement and the anticipation practically undid me. This was the case as the deputy's visit grew near. My brother Jacques, one year older, and I shared the same bed, and we were agitated through the night. At first light, we heard father stirring in the other room. We didn't want to keep him waiting, so we pulled on our sweaters, got into the shorts all French boys wore at the time and darted out to the Citroën. As it turned out, this time the catch was fine, with several trout, weighing more than six pounds, waiting for us in the river.

We had our centerpiece; a great relief. Bragging about the size of the fish brought to the table is a major part of French village life. The trout was to be poached and served lukewarm with a mustard-herb mayonnaise (I don't remember exactly, but certainly the mayonnaise contained tarragon and chervil). The fact that it was lukewarm rather than hot or cold meant that the flesh would be at its very best, still soft with warmth but not hardened by chill. It was also convenient to serve it this way, since my mother could make it early and let it rest in the cooking liquid, the court bouillon, until it was to be presented. The rest of the meal was traditional as well: *pâté en croûte,* sausage, a roast and a salad (dandelion on this occasion), cheese, wine and dessert. The roast was a leg of lamb, a gigot (see recipe page 209), served with the French beans called flageolets.

The beans had been soaked overnight and then boiled with onion, cloves, carrot and a bouquet garni of parsley, thyme and bay leaf. The thyme and bay leaf, more than any other ingredients, signal French cooking for me. Their flavors are distinct and yet they meld with the others so that the cook, like the chemist blending a perfume, creates something that is not dominated by one or another of the ingredients but is instead an expression of the harmony of all of them. The beans, scented in this way, would be served alongside the gigot, which would have its own light pan gravy.

There was always mustard on the table. Mustard seeds may have been known to the ancient Egyptians and to the Romans, but it was in Burgundy that mustard found the soil most to its liking, and the city of Dijon, producing many thousands of tons yearly, became the world's mustard center. This is a mustard given bite by the addition of the juice of unripe grapes. It was, and is, a good deal tarter than the "Dijon" mustard produced in America. It is also a smooth sauce, not the grainy mustard sometimes sold today under the Dijon name (the grainy variety comes from a different town, Meaux, and is more properly called *moutarde de Meaux*).

My father, traveling through Dijon, would always bring home mustard. For the children of St. Vinnemer, an afternoon snack was simply mustard smeared on bread. We even ate French fries with mustard (as the Belgians do). And mustard turned up throughout our cooking and eating: as a condiment and as an ingredient, a major contributor to the typical full-bodied flavors of Burgundy. It was mustard, of course, that provided the bite of the vinaigrette that usually dressed our salads. But beyond the flavor it supplies, mustard adds texture and fullness because the ground mustard seeds act much the way flour does, as a thickener and as an emulsifying agent.

It may sound strange, but the one mustard application that never entered the minds of Burgundians was its placement on sausages—the tartness, it seemed, would fight the smokiness of the sausage. (When I first arrived in America as a young adult and saw how everyone smeared mustard on hot dogs, I was puzzled, but then I understood— that yellow, sweeter mustard truly does go better with sausages.)

For the dandelion salad we would be serving during the deputy's visit, my father sent me out to the fields in search of the dandelions growing in mole mounds. Moles have the useful habit of kicking soil over the sprouting dandelions, and those plants that never see the sun, although they still grow, will grow with white stems, not green. The white-stemmed dandelion has more sweetness to it, tasting something like an endive.

The cheese and the wine were obtained during my father's travels in the area immediately surrounding St. Vinnemer. In addition to serving as the town's mayor, and operating his blacksmith shop, he sold McCormick Deering farm equipment throughout the region. It was the latter responsibility that took him to Beaujolais, where he would buy *crottins* of soft goat cheese, and to the Grand Cru Chablis vineyards just fifteen miles away. With fish, we only drank Chablis, which we would serve this day of the deputy's visit. Chablis is dry and crisp, not fruity, and for poached trout there is nothing as good. Dessert was a *mousse au chocolat* (see recipe page 241) and the meringues called *oeufs à la neige* (see recipe page 242).

When the deputy, his wife and his secretary pulled up in their auto, we were ready. There was never any panic in my house. Roles were as well established as they are on the battlefield. The men wore suits and ties; the boys wore woolen shorts, long socks, double-breasted jackets with the collars of the white shirts neatly arranged over the lapels of the jackets. The women were in long, dark dresses. As the meal got under-

The three Franey brothers—
Michel, me and Jacques—
dressed for a holiday

way, Father stationed himself at the head of the table, where he received
each of the dishes that might need to be apportioned and then served,
as the guests passed their plates toward him. He was a master carver. I
couldn't take my eyes off him. How carefully and stubbornly he carved!
No one could rush him. When the trout arrived, he removed the skin
and placed a boneless portion of the fish on each plate.

And throughout the meal there was political talk. My father was the
town's spokesman, and the deputy a man of such great influence that he
was in a position to arrange for piped water to come finally to St. Vinnemer. The talk and the eating went on and on. When the meal was
over, four or five hours later, people could hardly stand or walk. Public
water lines eventually did make it to St. Vinnemer; such is the power of
a good meal.

ST. VINNEMER is the sort of place that will be familiar to anyone
who has visited a small village in many regions of France. Weathered,
low buildings of stucco and stone, often accented with green shutters,

My grandparents Emile and Marie, keepers of one of the locks on the Burgundy canal, with my mother

line narrow streets. Some of the streets, running up the hill from the valley, are so narrow that three people walking abreast will fill them. It was on the hillside that my maternal grandfather and grandmother lived. Grandfather had once tended the canal below, maintaining its locks and the greenery alongside it. Today, the primary function of the canal, which connects the Seine and the Rhône rivers, is to pose for the tourists. But then it was a vital commercial artery, with twenty-five to fifty barges a day moving slowly through its locks. One might be carrying some prosaic material like the cement needed for construction, while another might be transporting an ethereal Burgundian red wine.

In 1920, before I was born, Grandfather retired from his work on the canal, but he never actually left it. He simply moved from the lockhouse to his place on the hill, living on a small pension. Standing in front of his house, he could see the canal and the river behind it. He could see the railroad tracks where trains, most notably the legendary *Train Bleu*, raced from Paris to Lyons. (I would watch the Train Bleu a few years later, focused entirely on the dining car; I could see the chefs through the steamed windows, their toques high, and I so wanted to be like them one day.) Behind the tracks was the main road to the French Riviera. From grandfather's house the whole fertile valley could be seen, the fields for wheat and those for sugar beets, the vineyards on the hills and the fruit trees along the canal.

My parents, my brothers and I lived close to the center of town. The house—a small complex of buildings and gardens, actually—was, like so many French homes, exceedingly efficient. Downstairs were the bedrooms and the *salle à manger,* which was antique filled and rarely used, except when guests came. We spent most of our time upstairs, in the big kitchen that merged into the living room.

In the vegetable garden we grew lettuce, carrots, tomatoes, parsley and other herbs. A stone trough stood there like a monument. My father used the solar-warmed stone to take the chill out of the frigid well water before watering the garden. It was in this garden that I learned to turn the earth by hand, and to this day I prefer a spade to a tiller, which tends to go too deep. We kept chickens and ducks alongside the garden. The barn housed the rabbits and the pigs, which were fed on potato peelings and refuse (we wasted nothing, ever). Mushrooms grew in the cool cellar, where carrots, cabbage and potatoes, as well as barrels of wine, were stored. I used to play in the hayloft. And in the yard outside the barn, greylag geese would chase me, hissing and nipping at my legs as I laughed.

Down the slope a bit were some fruit trees. My paternal grandmother had her own house next to ours. Her husband had died before I was born, and she lived alone. She had two of her own gardens next to the house for carrots, spinach and other vegetables and additional gardens elsewhere in town. This was not unusual in those days. The village was peppered with small, privately owned gardens, each with its individual personality. They were all positioned to bask in the southern light, but some were more open than others, some more sheltered, some higher and thus cooler. The result of so many microclimates could affect lives in the most peculiar ways. For instance, since my grandfather's garden was more sheltered than my uncle's, grandfather always got the first lettuce of the season, and he, of course, would brag about it.

In such surroundings, we all came to be on intimate terms with the food we ate. Each season, even each change in the weather, might alter how we would think about our sustenance. If it rained one day in the spring my father and one or another of the children might go off into

My father and mother after their wedding, 1918

the nearby vineyards to collect snails, which had climbed the vines in the rain to feed on the grape leaves. The Burgundian snails are reputedly the best on earth, black and succulent. But they are not to be eaten immediately after they are taken in the spring. Instead they are placed in a box until their winter hibernation, when they seal their shells with a thin excreted film, and in so doing cleanse themselves and become more tender and flavorful. Months after we collected the snails, we could begin to eat them—a long wait, but then we would enjoy them all winter. (See recipe page 183.)

The rabbits we raised would be used according to their age. The young ones would be roasted (with thyme, bay leaf, shallots and a touch of butter, which was expensive and sparingly used) or sautéed in lard along with vegetables, herbs and wine or stock. The older rabbits were saved for stew, the *civet de lapin* (see recipe page 186).

Living among farm animals, one becomes inured to the more brutal aspects of killing and processing. I will never forget the first chicken I killed. I was seven or eight and had watched many times as my grand-mother did the deed, always sitting. She would hold the chicken by its wings, its body tangled up in her lap in the folds of her dress, and, with a scissors, she would snip an artery under the tongue, which paralyzed the animal, and would bleed it to death. The blood, with the addition of some vinegar, was collected to be used in coq au vin (see recipe page 187); only in Burgundy is the blood still added, the one true coq au vin today, I believe. This day, my grandmother urged, "Now, Pierre, you do it." I approached a chicken warily, held it in my lap as best I could but botched the job; the animal leaped off my lap and ran around the kitchen, while my own blood seemed to drain away. I have since gotten better at it.

Besides the coq au vin, the most celebrated way of preparing chicken in Burgundy—and this may surprise you—was to poach it (a term that suggests simmering rather than boiling). It has the remarkable advantage of cooking the food at exactly 212 degrees and so is a gentle, yet penetrating, process that can coddle a delicate piece of fish or, through lengthy cooking, tenderize the toughest cut of meat without drying it out. Poaching also creates a broth in the process, so that the cook is left with the base for a sauce or a soup.

We never tired of poached chicken (see recipe page 188), preparing it often for guests and for the family, too. In fact, it was a poached chicken that I prepared for the family when, as a teenager, I returned home for the first time after embarking on a restaurant apprenticeship. The technique is just about the same every time: the chicken is simmered with carrots, leeks, celery, a bay leaf, thyme and parsley. Rice is cooked separately, using some of the liquid from the chicken's pot. Then you make a roux of butter and flour and add some of the cooking liquid to it, maybe a touch of nutmeg. The chicken is served on the rice with the sauce over it.

It's called *poule au riz* (*poule* is a hen, *poulet* a rooster). Usually, one uses a big old hen of five or six pounds and simmers it for a couple of hours. The trick is to make it tender, but not so that it is falling off the bones, so you are able to slice the chicken neatly, every part of it, even the meat from the legs. Generally, we would remove the skin because it was too tough and place it in the oven for a half hour to drain away all the fat, then eat it as crackling.

We often had a pot-au-feu (see page 152), boiled meats and vegetables, simmering all day long, especially in the winter. In his later years my grandfather—and this always struck me as sad—would sit by the woodstove adjusting the fire for hours on end to keep it soft and steady. Generally, we ate less beef than other meats because we produced none of our own. Instead we bought the consistently magnificent beef from the butcher who came through the town in his horse-drawn wagon. In Burgundy the finest beef cattle in France, the Charolais steer, are raised. The flavor of this meat doubtless contributed to the fame of beef Burgundy, a wine-rich stew, which was well known in the United States even before America's wider familiarity with French food.

Although the milk cows of the region were renowned, too, milk was rarely treated as a drink in Burgundy, usually appearing only in café au lait in the morning. (To this day, my wife, Betty, insists that the reason Frenchmen grew so much taller in the postwar years than they had before was that they finally discovered milk.) There was always water and wine on the table, but the notion that French children guzzle wine from birth is simply untrue. As a child of two or three, I had water with a drop—literally a drop—of wine in it. And throughout my childhood I would never drink wine straight. This was true of some adults, too. My mother always drank one-quarter cup of wine to three-quarters water. I first tasted pure wine when I was fifteen or sixteen. This routine dilution of wine may strike some people as blasphemy or something slightly less horrid, but the fact is that we drank, even in the heart of Burgundy, very ordinary wine from day to day. (Good bottled wine was reserved for important occasions when guests visited.) The water, in any event, was always spectacular, coming as it did from a spring so pure that it was said to guarantee women perfect pregnancies.

St. Vinnemer

2

Reverence and the River

DAILY LIFE for me was highly routinized. After school, which ended at 4:00 p.m., I had to do my homework. If I—or any of the kids in the family—seemed laggard, my mother would wave her *martinet* around and swat at our ankles, although she almost never actually hit us. Homework done, I would have chores to perform: work in the blacksmith shop, keeping the flies from irritating the horses, or maybe repairing the chicken coops. If the daylight held until I had finished my work, I would run for my fishing rod and head for l'Armançon or the Burgundy Canal.

For an officially landlocked people, we had lives suffused with the beauty and the fruits of the water. The river ran alongside the canal, which was built to take advantage of the river's water. While l'Armançon might rise and fall with the season, lock supervisors had to keep the canal at a constant depth to accommodate barges, so the canal would drain water from the river as needed. Most of the barges were pulled by horses, but sometimes, especially if a fellow was less than prosperous, he would pull his barge himself. The barges might bring charcoal or gravel to the town and pick up its sugar beets to transport them thirty-five miles for processing in a factory in Brinon.

Merchants would glide into town, and if they wished to stay overnight, they had to obtain the permission of my father, who, wearing his mayoralty hat, would allow them to stay if their papers were in order. I remember particularly the man-drawn barge called the *bateau vaisselle*, meaning that it purveyed anything needed in serving food, such as utensils or pots. Once or twice a year, we would receive advance word that the *bateau vaisselle* was in the next village, and people would rush to the canal far ahead of its arrival. In time, a man would come

In costume for a play (I'm at right), *with my friends Hubert Meurgey* (center) *and Guy Mignard*

trudging alongside the canal, his barge in the water behind him, with his pottery, glass, plates, all of it sturdily made to last.

But the canal and the river lured my friends and me, not so much because of the commerce, but because of the fish that lived beneath the surface. The river was alive with pike, pickerel, bream and perch, stocked by the government, and everyone, even the kids, needed a license to fish there. We were very serious about our fishing. My buddies Hubert, Guy and Marcel and I might spend hours just gathering and preparing our bait. Sandworms would be fine for some smaller fish, and to collect them, we would walk down the road alongside the canal to a stream called le Rue. Right by the *lavoir,* the spot where the townspeople washed their clothes, were large rocks, and under them we found the sandworms. There were also worms called *traîne-bûches* that lived inside little tubes of sand with which they attached themselves to a rock or a branch in the water. But our greatest energies went into the capture of the small fish known in English as whitebait, in French, *veron.* This was an excellent bait for the pike in the river (the *veron* were not bad deep-fried, either).

To catch the *veron,* we chiseled a hole in the concave bottom of a wine bottle and then plugged the top of the bottle with a potato. We carved ridges in the potato so that air could escape from the bottle while water filled it, and it sank. Inside the bottle was a bit of bread. The *veron,*

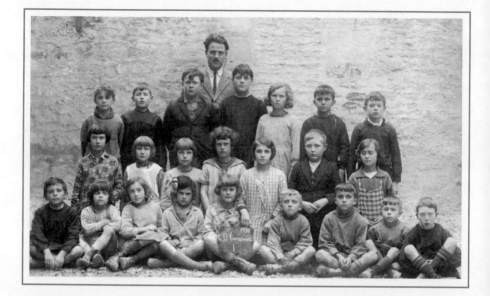

swimming upstream, would enter but could not go into reverse to leave. Once every day or so we came by and collected them. These little fish would, with great efficiency, lure river pike of six to eight pounds and perhaps three feet in length to my hook. I would sit on the tree-shaded riverbank with

My school class, circa 1929. I'm in the first row, third from right; Michel is fourth from right; and Jacques is standing at the far left of the top row.

my rod carefully braced by a branch shoved into the ground. I could daydream there for hours. When the float on the line was yanked downward, my adrenaline would surge and I would lurch for the rod.

If the notion struck me, I would fish in the canal rather than the river. There, smaller fish—perch, whitefish, catfish—could be caught with great regularity. An ideal lure for perch was a kernel of wheat, which, when poached, opens like popcorn and can be placed on a hook.

I might catch as many as five fish after school, clean them on the spot and bring them home for my mother to cook. By the time I was eight, I was capable of cooking the fish myself, dredging them in salt, pepper and flour, sautéing them in butter in a black steel pan and then browning more butter—with lemon juice added—to pour over them at the end. It is the classic French presentation called meunière (see recipe page 164). The term, which means "in the manner of a miller's wife," derives from the flour coating. It is the flour, of course, that seals the fish, but perhaps the most important stage in preparing a perfect meunière is browning the butter at the end. You remove the butter that the fish cooked in, wipe the pan and add fresh butter, agitating the pan rapidly so that the butter solids brown lightly and thoroughly but do not burn (the fact that they can burn relatively easily is the reason that, when butter is to be used in high-heat cooking, it is often gently melted and the solids skimmed away, yielding clarified butter).

When that light-brown color has been achieved, the butter has a delightful nutty flavor, and when lemon juice is incorporated, mere cooked butter becomes a sauce of true delicacy and richness. The meunière process and similar preparations are invaluable for everything from chicken breasts to calf's liver. At the time I was employing this method, of course, the process itself was not something I thought much about; I just wanted to be sure that the wonderful fish I had brought home would be treated with all the competence a young boy could muster.

On Sunday, when we would all pack into the big Citroën, it was more often than not to head for some distant river. What picnic days these could be! All of my life I have adored picnics: at the beach, in the woods, at the riverside. The organizers of a picnic do what every good restaurateur and home cook understands well: they create atmosphere to enhance the food. No need for some painted landscape at this meal—we are inside the landscape. There was, for instance, a meadow not far from St. Vinnemer that I will always remember because every year our family held a picnic there, just as the lilies of the valley began to bloom.

Picnics also gave my brothers and me the chance to engage in the activities we enjoyed most, fishing and trapping. At one river near Avallon we caught crayfish: we would take a bundle of thorned twigs from the prunelle bush and hide chicken necks in them as bait; the little crayfish would get in but could not get out, and in one bundle there might be twenty-four to thirty of them trapped.

We would boil them right there, with a bit of thyme, a bay leaf and salt, let them cool to lukewarm, and eat them with mayonnaise (we always traveled with mayonnaise, which resists spoilage because of the vinegar in it). To accompany the crayfish we often prepared a cucumber or potato salad. Perhaps we would have a roasted chicken, or some fish caught from the river and sautéed over a freshly built fire. And there was always the most perfect picnic food of all, *pâté en croûte*. When you think about it, this is a pâté that comes already packed for the picnic journey, in its own crust. No need for a heavy terrine or crock—just wrap it up and take it along.

Picnics were our excuse to eat *pâté en croûte,* but portability was not the only reason we craved it as we did. These pâtés are a study in French artistry. It's not just the flavor of the forcemeat spiked with cognac or wine, but also the symphony of textures. First you hit the crunch of the crust, then quickly glide through the layer of aspic and on into the meat, with its own varying textures and additions—rabbit or ham, pistachios or truffles. (See page 205 for a simpler Country Pâté recipe.)

Kneeling in my father's blacksmith shop. One of my jobs was to keep the forge hot by pumping the bellows.

THE WATERWAYS were the scene of some of our greatest family dramas, too. I remember most vividly one evening when my mother and father were quarreling. Father was a ladies' man. Everyone in town knew it, but said nothing, of course. My mother knew, but never talked about it. Until this bitter fight.

We heard Father as he strode out of the house and slammed the door. Then we saw Mother run toward the canal, evidently intent on drowning herself. "No, Mama, don't do it!" Jacques and I were shouting as we ran behind her. We grabbed her before she could take the plunge. To this day I do not know if she really meant to do herself in, nor do I know if she could have succeeded in that placid canal, even with the most dedicated of intentions. In any event, peace returned to our home, and

My father in 1918

once again no one talked about our father's mortifyingly obvious tendency to covet other women; silence seemed to protect the harmony.

But then none of us was entirely free of sin. A transgression of my own, committed when I was five, has stayed with me ever since. It, too, is linked to the water, taking place among the fruit trees on the canal bank. One of my grandfather's passions was the creation of pear alcohol, an eau-de-vie. He routinely examined the pear trees by the canal, and when a new pear struck him as promising, he would place a bottle over it while it was still small enough to fit inside and secure the bottle to the limb with wire. Then when the pear was fully grown inside the bottle, he removed them both from the tree and filled the bottle with homemade alcohol, which he prepared by allowing fruit to decompose and ferment in a barrel and then cooking the fermented fruit in a still to extract the alcohol. (Illegal though it was to sell homemade alcohol, he had been making alcohol for years and sometimes selling it, especially in the halcyon days just after World War I, when thirsty American soldiers filled the village, awaiting their orders to go home.) This rather raw drink is not enhanced or changed by the pear, except for the ornamental role the fruit plays, but the pear will be preserved in the bottle for as long as the alcohol is there.

On a beautiful but fateful sunny day, I saw one of these perfectly shaped pears, yellow and ripe and full in a bottle on a tree. I was hungry (I was always hungry then, even when sated from a meal), so I took a rock and hurled it at the bottle, shattering it. Without compunction, I ate the pear.

I no longer remember how my grandfather discovered my transgression; I only remember what he did. He barred me from his house forever ("Go away, you little thief; I never want to see you again"), and he named me Voleur de Poire, Thief of the Pear.

After about two months I was allowed to return to Grandfather's house, but he never again would call me Pierre, always Voleur de Poire. Even when I returned from the United States many years later, in 1939, bearing gifts (the colorful tobacco tins he liked to collect), he refused to forget. I walked into his house and proffered the tins, but there was no hello from the frail little man wearing his Greek fisherman's cap, no welcome home and no "Thank you, Pierre."

"Ah," he said, "Voleur de Poire returns." I was so hurt. He was a terribly stubborn man. He died a few years later, at eighty-five, never having entered an automobile, finding cars to be unnatural, crazy contraptions. He almost always dressed the same way, in corduroy pants, wooden shoes (Burgundians wear them just as the Dutch do) and his Greek cap, indoors and out, to cover his baldness. But I loved him always, as stubborn in my affection as he was in his grudge.

MY BROTHER and I suffered other, less traumatic mishaps among the fruit trees. On a strip of land along the river, Grandfather had planted apple trees that produced huge red fruit every year. It was the kids' job to climb the trees and bring the apples down unbruised. Before ascending, we would carefully tuck our shirts into our pants and then drop the fruit down our shirts, using them as soft baskets to hold several apples at a time, while our hands remained free. Adults would direct us through the trees—"Pick that one, pick that one," we were told constantly as we slowly worked our way through the branches.

On a day when my brother, either through laziness or optimism, allowed his shirt to become too heavy with fruit, his shirt pulled free of his pants, and apples fell in an avalanche. "Imbécile" came the call from the ground. Grandfather was angry again, but it wasn't a total loss. Normally, from the beginning of September through the end of October, the apples would be laid out on straw in the attic, where the autumn temperature was ideal for preserving them, cool but not freezing. Then in the winter they would be moved to the cellar, so they would not freeze when the temperature fell. But the bruised apples never made it; instead, they were headed directly into alcohol or a tart or a compote. Some of my favorite apple dishes derive from an apple compote, actually what is generally thought of as applesauce. Puff pastry filled with applesauce—it's called a *chausson*—is a wonderful creation. No, the bruising of apples that day was hardly a tragedy, except in Jacques's self-esteem.

My fondest memories of the fruit trees we tended center on the women of the family. My paternal grandmother and I made frequent grafting trips into the woods. We would, for example, take cuttings from the live branches of some of her healthiest cherry trees and go off in search of wild cherry trees. We would make an incision in the wild tree and insert the limb of the domestic tree, secure it neatly with wire and, we hoped, alter its genetic makeup forever. When we returned, many months later, if the graft had taken and the wild cherries were now the much-admired Bing cherries so frequently used in pies (see recipe page 243), we would uproot the newly domesticated tree and take it to one of Grandmother's plots. We did this not just with cherries but with pears, plums and apples, too.

In early May, our attention was briefly focused on the linden trees along the canal, which were in bloom just for a few days. The linden perfumed the air, and since I have been in the United States, I have never experienced anything like that fragrance, those scented days. We attempted to take the flowers—to be dried and brewed as tea—in great quantity at exactly the right time, when they were advanced enough to be fragrant, but not so advanced that they were beginning to form seeds.

I would climb the tree and cut any branch that was particularly heavy with blossoms and then bring the branches to my mother, who laid the blossoms out on a sheet in the sun; she would dry the whole flower. Whenever rain came during these days, Mother leaped into action, gathering up the blossoms in the sheets and taking them out again

when the sun returned. We drank linden tea all year long, and occasionally mixed in mint leaves we had dried for a bright drink even in the
darkest months.

In the wintertime when the canal and river were iced over and the
trees were bare, we still had plenty of the fruits of summer, but none of
the fish. So every week I would go to the railroad station by bicycle to
meet the train from Boulogne-sur-Mer on the English Channel. There
I might pick up salt cod, which could be rinsed free of salt and then
poached in milk to keep it white and served with vegetables and garlic
mayonnaise. In the cool weather the mayonnaise might be held for as
much as a week, a central part of a cuisine that developed in the absence
of refrigeration. (Cheese, after all, is simply preserved milk, and
escabeche is fish cooked in hot vinegar, which prevents its spoilage;
food like this turned out to be so fine that it survived the arrival of
refrigeration.)

The train also carried sole, whiting and mussels, although we never
knew exactly what would be arriving in the box with our name on it.
Our family had something of a contract with the fish merchant—we
paid a set fee every winter and he delivered a box of whatever was the
freshest fish. So it was always something of a surprise package, one
more of the small touches (food oriented, of course) that made life so
exhilarating, even in a rural village and even in the wintertime. No matter what we received, we were always deeply grateful for it, responding
emotionally, I think, the way Northerners in America do when they
clap their hands to see a winter gift of oranges from a grandmother living in Florida. The fresh fish allowed us to feel, there in cold and damp
Burgundy, like we were dining in sunny, coastal Marseilles.

I BAKE BREAD almost daily. Inexperienced cooks often find bread
baking difficult and anxiety producing, but when you've done it often,
the act is comforting, warm in a spiritual sense (besides bringing a
pleasant aroma and heat to a cold house). The technique, moreover, is
not difficult to master, and once you've learned it, the bread will nearly
always be perfect, with a thin, crisp crust and a tender center (see recipe
page 232). When I cut my bread, I always cut it right side up. This has
to do with reverence. My father taught me never to treat bread disre-
spectfully, but if he hadn't I would have learned it sooner or later just by
growing up in St. Vinnemer. Bread was not just a staple but, as it is in

many other cultures—only more so in Burgundy, I think—part of our fondest rituals. We revered St. Eloi, the saint of bread, and every winter we joyfully engaged in a ceremony in his honor.

Two of the townspeople, dressed in their finest, would meet at the chestnut tree that stood in the center of the village, assigned to carry a freshly cut evergreen tree. Others carried loaves of bread or brioche rounds encircling their arms like great bangles. Then we would parade with our tree and our bread through the village to the church, where paper flowers were placed on the tree and the priest blessed the bread. Each of us would take a slice home.

Pork was another basic food that brought out the festive in us, if not the sacred. When my father determined that he was ready to slaughter one of our pigs—always in the fall because the cool weather of winter would allow for months of safe storage—we would summon friends and relatives from all around. One of us would go to the single telephone in town and instruct Madame la Téléphoniste (the operator stationed at the phone) to place one call after the other. "I want to call Mrs. So-and-So," you'd say, and she would make the call, then you would step into the cubicle to speak.

The slaughter of the pig was always an exercise in great frugality and invention in which nearly every part of the animal was put to use. The long bristles on the pig's back, for instance, were shaved off with a razor and saved to use in brushes. Every bit of the meat and the blood was employed in one preparation or another. And the pig's products were eaten in a specified order. The preparations that might spoil quickly were eaten first. Thus one pig would inspire an initial feast and then feed a family, off and on, until spring.

A major participant was one Monsieur Ménétrier, a man of tremendous girth who owned a tobacco shop near the church in the village. He was a superb maker of sausages, particularly the boudin (blood sausage) and the andouille (tripe sausage). A single pig yielded about twenty feet of the boudin, created from blood, leeks, onion, garlic, caul fat and spices stuffed into meticulously cleaned casings. It would all be wound carefully on layers of straw that prevented the sausages from sticking to each other, the way pieces of paper now are used to separate processed-cheese slices.

We would also immediately prepare a huge stew from the lungs and neck meat, along with wine and some of the blood. This is called *la gruyotte*. Because neither the stew nor the boudin contained ingredients that stored well, they would be eaten in the first two days after the slaughter of the pig. So would the liver pâté. The day of the pig's demise, many people would be needed for the process—the butchering and the cooking.

Everything to be cured would be placed in fifteen-gallon earthenware crocks in the cellar. The spareribs would go on top, since they required less curing time and would be eaten first (a smaller piece of meat is permeated by the cure faster than a larger one); the ham would go on the bottom. The spareribs, by the way, were not barbecued, a delightful preparation of which we were completely ignorant. Instead they were prepared in a deep pot with cabbage, carrots, potatoes, onions and leeks and served with mustard and cornichons. Hearty country cooking, certainly, and you still see spareribs served this way all over France.

To cure the sections of the pig, we rubbed the meat with salt and pepper and garlic. Everybody had his own way in this, too. My uncle Francis would massage the meat for hours with salt, pepper, thyme and bay leaves. Some people would remove mineral deposits that accumulated on the stone in the cellar, a mysterious white substance, and rub it into the meat. The substance must have had nitrites in it because it kept the meat red, but none of us understood much about such chemical additives then.

In the days to come, culinary possibilities offered by this one pig would continue to seem infinite. The shoulders might be used for a roast (see recipe page 206). A rillettes (pork spread) would be made from fat and shredded meat. There might be a *côte de porc charcutière,* a classic pork chop, which involved sautéing the chop and then serving it in a sauce made pungent by mustard and cornichons. Everybody made his own cornichons, using some variation on a basic recipe, curing the gherkins in a brine with tarragon, peppercorns, cloves, thyme, bay leaves and allspice. Once the fat was removed and the pan deglazed (a liquid such as wine is added to dissolve the food particles adhering to the pan) for the sauce, the fat would be saved. In Burgundy, since we used so little butter (it was relatively expensive), we always saved the fat of the pork, chicken or goose, each in different crocks for later use.

I do not often cook in those saturated fats today, of course, but as I look back on it, the practice, born of necessity and culinary intelligence, is one I recall fondly. It was a cooking approach derived from the desire to waste nothing, but along the way we learned that these fats imparted flavor, often sublime, to the foods cooked in them. We used lard derived from pig fat to make the quintessential peasant dish, *choucroute garnie,* the renowned sauerkraut with ham and sausage (see recipe page 208), and we always mixed lard with butter to prepare the dough for a tart, whereas others might have used only butter. But it was not so much the savings in money that counted for us as it was the taste, the richness and subtlety of the combination, that we had grown to admire.

One of my mother's favorite tricks was to render pork fat until only the crackling was left and mix in that crackling with her bread dough, the result being a familiar French bread with crunchy surprises all the way through; it was marvelous, almost like finding almonds embedded in chocolate.

Today, I bake the same sort of bread with crumbled bacon because the smoky meat in the bread is spectacular, even more flavorful. But in my mother's day it would have seemed excessive to employ prized bacon in that fashion. It is partly this farmhouse reliance on rendered fats, I think, that gave rise to the notion in the expensive restaurants, the temples of French haute cuisine, that butter should be the fat of choice for them, that butter represented refinement.

As EXCITING and festive as these pork-preparing days might have been, there was nothing like hunting to quicken the beat of my heart. From the first Sunday in September through March there was hunting of one kind or another. In the fall it was hare and birds. In December came the big game, the deer, wild boars and roebuck. Now, in my seventies, I still hunt when the weather turns cool, but the experience today can't begin to match the exhilaration a boy on the way to becoming a man felt on each of those Sundays.

The possibilities for hunting, like those for fishing, were myriad, in the nearby fields full of rabbits and in the woods. The least sporting (perhaps that is how you will view it, anyway) was the rabbit shoot. We would determine the route of a burrow, the rabbits' tunnel refuge, and place a pet ferret in the hole at one end. The ferret would chase the rabbits until—and this would startle me every time—you could hear the rabbits racing ahead of the ferret underground. Then suddenly the rabbits would burst out of the tunnel at what seemed like two hundred miles an hour, and the hunters would start to shoot. It was not easy. Rabbits often escaped. We also hunted hare, a bigger animal, which does not burrow, but is also a mainstay of the Burgundian *cuisine bourgeoise.* One of my jobs was to beat the bushes with a stick to frighten a

hare into a clearing. I did not actually shoot a rifle until I was sixteen, but as early as age four or five I was charged with running to pick up rabbits and bring them back to my father. I was a human retriever. We always had dogs, too, fine hunting dogs. One of them was usually a Brittany spaniel

After hunting, the Franey family poses with a hare. My father is holding one of several in a line of our hunting dogs named Kiki. To the left is a family employee.

named Kiki. As each Kiki would move on to the final reward, he or she would be replaced by another spaniel named Kiki. My latest, a smart and sensitive animal, died only recently.

The dogs played one of their largest roles in the boar hunt. To hunt boars my father would leave behind the local fields with their rabbits and partridge and head for a hunting area about thirty-five miles away. The land was owned by a family friend, Paul Gérard. In the morning the dogs would be assigned the job of picking up the scent. When they located the boar, all the hunters who had forgathered at the local bistro near the village of Villier Le Haut would head off with their rifles. I did not join this activity until quite late in my youth because it was so dangerous. An infuriated boar actually once gored one of my uncles.

The hunting was always part of a broader event having to do with socializing and eating. My father would call this bistro—it was always

My father with some dogs   the same one—a week ahead. The owner, as it happened, was also the game warden. He and his wife
would prepare something of great robustness for the
hunting party, say, rabbit stew, or game, including
wild boar (*sanglier*).

WHILE some of the men were out hunting, others would stay behind
and play cards at the bistro. They were the ones who brought additional
food for the day. There might be a wine maker at the card table, or a
baker. A butcher might be there to help cut up a boar if one was brought
back. The meals at the bistro were always sumptuous, but so were the
ones we might have back home after a successful day of hunting. The
boar needed tenderizing, as do so many of the game animals; it would
have to be hung before cooking.

During that period its own enzymes would, in effect, begin the cooking process by breaking down the tissue. Four or five days would
accomplish what we wanted, but the weather could be our enemy; if it
suddenly turned warm, temperatures rising into the 40s or 50s, the
boar might spoil in the relative heat, so care was absolutely necessary.
A tough boar was better than a rotten one. After the boar had been
properly hung, it would be marinated in wine, herbs, carrots and leeks,
the acidity being needed to further tenderize the meat.

Once, when I was sixteen and home from work in Paris, I joined the group at this same bistro. By that time I knew a thing or two about cooking and was inclined to boast about my prowess. The cook announced that he would serve wild boar stew, made especially for me, he said. I was ravenous (as usual) and plunged my fork into it. It tasted quite lean, too lean, to tell you the truth, but I thought nothing of it. My father asked, too solicitously (but again I thought nothing of it), "How do you like the *sanglier,* Pierre?" I told him that I liked it fine. Then he told me it was actually badger. I must have looked as abashed as any teenager has ever looked while in the process of mortification. People laughed. The truth is, I never even knew you could eat badger, thinking those animals were good only for the bristles of brushes. I was sick to my stomach, more embarrassed and sickened by my display of ignorance than by anything more directly linked to the eating of badger. Of course, the Burgundian sense of humor being what it is, I never did live this one down. That damned mock *sanglier!*

So MUCH of my early life was rustic, close to the earth, and narrowly focused that you might wonder how I ever did get a taste of the world beyond. Well, I did, every now and then, and it always hit me like a thunderbolt. One of the biggest revelations came on a 1931 trip to a colonial exposition, a kind of world's fair limited to the French colonies. It was held outside Paris at the Bois de Vincennes.

I was already ten years old, but until that day I had never tasted ice cream. It was summertime and the whole family—Jacques, Hugues, Michel and I, my mother, father and grandmother—drove to the great park with its racetrack and ball fields. People were picnicking everywhere on the rolling lawns. Kites filled the sky. There were exhibits from places as strange to me as Cambodia and French Africa. But they were no stranger than the custard carried in the little carts. The carts, with their red-and-white painted wheels and their colorful umbrellas, carried blocks of dry ice, along with ice cream: vanilla and chocolate, much like the ice cream we all know now. But at the time I had never in my life eaten anything that was actually ice-cold. So when I was handed a soft cone topped with ice cream, I bit into it—too avidly, of course— froze my mouth and throat, went into a kind of spasm and spat it out.

Always the intrepid eater, I went at it again, slowly now, with great caution. I licked it, got the knack and fell in love with it. Decades later, when I worked as a vice president at Howard Johnson's, I would pride myself on being able to taste everything in the ice cream, including the

overrun, as the percentage of air is called. But here, at the age of ten,
licking with great circumspection, I tasted only the smooth, rich chocolate, and that was enough.

It wasn't that there was anything really new about ice cream. It had
been around in one form or another since 1660, more as a sorbet at
first, and was brought to France by one Francisco Procopio, a Sicilian.
Eggs were introduced later to create the sublime custard called French
ice cream, which quickly replaced cheese on many tables at dessert
time. But after the eighteenth century the recipe hardly changed. Of
course, it never reached St. Vinnemer, or any village like it, because of
the absence of adequate refrigeration; freezers did not arrive in our
town until after World War II. My own affection for ice cream now runs
extraordinarily deep, and I use the basic custard as a kind of painter's
palate on which to place all manner of flavors and colors. If you have
never tasted ice cream with a touch of Ricard (the French anise-flavored
liqueur), for instance, I assure you that you are missing something quite
wonderful (see recipe page 244).

A YEAR or so after my first encounter with ice cream, I had another
one of these experiences that would gently move me even further in the
direction of cooking than my early proclivities and desires had already
suggested. My uncle Francis Ducroux, a wine merchant who owned his
own vineyard near Avignon, had been invited by a wine-maker friend
to go snail gathering in Chablis, and he brought me along. Later we had
lunch at the Hôtel Bergeran, with its traditional, country-style dining
room—white beams and checkered tablecloths—which enjoyed a good
reputation in the region. When the glitterati of the time—the Duke of
Windsor, Maurice Chevalier, Charles Boyer—journeyed to Chablis,
they would stay at this fine hotel.

Monsieur Bergeran, the chef and owner, came to our table, his white
toque regally perched on his head. My father told him that I wanted to
be a chef one day. Bergeran led me into the kitchen, the first big one I
had ever seen. There were ten to fifteen cooks and a huge charcoal stove.
Copper pans gleamed overhead. An apprentice in blue with a little hat,
befitting his junior position, was sandpapering the steel trim of the
stove, placing a tight, swirling design on it as he did. I admired him
greatly. Bergeran invited me to apprentice there one day. I never did,
but the idea, the goal, now had a name: I would be a chef's apprentice
as soon as I was old enough to work.

3

Paris: From the Bottom Up

PARIS SHIMMERED in the daylight and beckoned in the night. It was fast and perplexing. But it was not entirely strange to me. By the time I arrived to work there in 1934, I had already visited on a few occasions with my family. My older cousins, Jean Ducroux, who had a job with Shell Oil, and Maurice Marquis, had briefed me ahead of time. They warned me about the dangers of thieves and prostitutes (the women used to ply their trade openly at the Gare Montparnasse, a train station not far from where I would be living). I was always a quiet boy with a tendency toward shyness, and it did not take much to frighten me. The huge City of Lights might have been more than I could handle were it not for Jean and Maurice. I knew I could count on them. They had lived for a while with Mademoiselle Guignier, too, and now had rooms just a block away.

The day I arrived, wearing short pants, of course—my mother still thought of me as a child—Maurice was appalled: "We've got to get you long pants, Pierre, this is Paris." And he did what he could to jostle me out of my shyness. "Stand up straight, Pierre, look people in the eye. You're not a Burgundian peasant." Maurice and Jean were my only friends in the early days. They took me swimming at one of the city's many municipal pools, and they took me to see my first tennis match, at the Bois de Boulogne. We walked to the Latin Quarter to drink coffee among the students. We went to movies, and once they took me to a nightclub.

Mademoiselle Guignier's apartment occupied two floors of an eight-story apartment house at 246 Boulevard Raspail. Boulevard Raspail is a broad, largely residential street with many trees, so it was quiet, especially at night. On the first floor were the living room, office, dining room, kitchen and five bedrooms. The rooms for the maids employed by the residents of the building were on the top floor. As it happened, Mademoiselle Guignier's maid occupied one of the bedrooms in the apartment, and that left her eighth-floor room for me, adjacent to a gaggle of young women. Mademoiselle Guignier had been single all her life, but her apartment was always full of activity because of her generous penchant for putting up penniless students and relatives. While I was there the other rooms were occupied entirely by medical students.

This was a thrilling time to be in Paris. It is true that the economic woes that had crushed the United States had affected France as well, but the glory was still there, visible everywhere. In the 1920s, just a few years before I arrived, France had reached cultural heights that it might never reach again. I was in walking distance of areas of Paris that will always live in the iconography of the West. At the intersection of Raspail and Boulevard du Montparnasse were four legendary cafés, Dôme, Rotonde, Le Sélect and La Coupole, each with its own particular clientele, hot spots for conversation, moneylending, contact making and loafing. The Dôme once came in for criticism from Ernest Hemingway, who wrote that the people there were "nearly all loafers expending the energy that an artist puts into his creative work in talking about what they are going to do. . . ." Picasso's atelier was not far away, on Raspail itself.

Nearby, too, in Montparnasse, Man Ray had only lately been photographing the exquisite American, Lee Miller. When I stepped into the streets each morning, these were the very streets of Fernand Léger, Joan Miró, Malcolm Cowley and Berenice Abbott. But I would be fooling you, and myself, if I were to tell you that I was aware of much of that at the time.

Moreover, I was part of a French system that would effectively close off my formal education right then and there. Once you chose to apprentice in one trade or another, the next several years were devoted exclusively to learning the job at hand. By choosing to be an apprentice cook, however, I had not deprived myself entirely of art and glamour. Restaurants, after all, were a solid part of French cultural life. The refinement of restaurant cooking was one of France's highest arts, rivaled nowhere in the world, with the possible exception of China. The restaurant had actually been invented in Paris in 1765 by a man named Boulanger, when he began serving soups that he called restorers, or *restaurants.* Before long the restaurants had established themselves in the social life and the folklore of the people. They had become the centers of tradition and of great invention, as dishes were refined and new ones created.

Although the apprentice system that now took me up and directed my life was hard and unwavering, it is often credited with creating the pool of skilled cooks who made possible the continued development of French cuisine. In the years following World War II, A. J. Liebling, the *New Yorker* correspondent and gourmand, found himself lamenting that the "Failure in rudimentary things is typical of large restaurants now in France. . . . The reason is the happy improvement in the human condition; it is harder every year to recruit boys of superior, or even of subnormal, intelligence for the long, hard, dirty apprenticeship, at nominal pay—or none, in the early years—that makes a cook."

But there I was, in Paris while the system was still strong; I was eager to work and felt fortunate for the chance. I was on my way to becoming Liebling's sort of cook: a young boy from a food-revering background handed over to a subculture of cooks and restaurateurs to be completely imbued with their values and sensibilities, to learn every one of the requisite skills through on-the-job tutelage and endless practice.

In a way, indoctrination into this system was like entering the army—one started with the most rudimentary chores (they would have been demoralizing and insulting if one weren't so young) and then gradually moved on to the more advanced. In the beginning I was entrusted with a vegetable peeler and a trussing needle. The needle may seem like an odd first implement, but its use teaches a young cook a great deal about what this culinary experience is all about: it is often tedious, but the care one must devote to doing things right—always, always trussing a chicken whether it is to be poached or roasted—is the price a cook pays on the road to true accomplishment. (Trussing is so often ignored today that I can only conclude that home cooks and professionals alike do not understand its purpose: it is not just to contain stuffing; it ensures that the heat will evenly permeate the chicken, that browning will be even as well and that the chicken will retain its shape.)

The years of apprenticeship would take me through basic preparation techniques from vegetable peeling to butchering, cooking soups and sauces, seafood and meat—but never baking. It is a strange fact, perhaps, but the *pâtisserie*, the baking section of the kitchen, has always been regarded as if it were the headquarters of a different trade altogether, and as a result, although I bake a great deal today, I do not consider myself a true baker.

At each stage—whether it was sauce making or sautéing or shaping vegetables—an apprentice like me was expected to spend at least six months in training, moving from station to station. The cooking schools today have largely replaced this traditional system, and, while they are efficient, nothing can match the kind of total immersion I experienced. Today you see youthful chefs bursting out of cooking school (in two years, sometimes, and often much less, with time off in the summer and on the holidays), having trained a few weeks at this and that, and immediately taking on important responsibilities somewhere, perhaps even as executive chefs.

Many of these young people are not equipped to produce food that is more than an echo of the dishes prepared through the old system. Others are truly gifted, but I have seen many of them burn out so quickly that it is a tragedy; it is as if they got up to speed too fast and never developed the endurance or the depth of experience that would help them survive the hard times, the draining work.

As for me, I did know a few things before going to work for Monsieur Thenin. I had my marvelous Burgundian childhood behind me, after all. I knew how to make a tart and to bottle fruit preserves. I could make a roux for a white sauce. I knew the patience and care required in browning meat for a stew and then coating it with flour that must be carefully browned, too.

Even so, I was ignorant of so much. I had never seen a live lobster before (although cooked lobsters sometimes made their way to St. Vinnemer, causing us all to believe that lobsters lived their lives in bright-red shells). I had heard of pâté de foie gras but never eaten it. I had never tasted anything so exotic as a curry. I had no idea of the dizzying range of French cooking, and one of my earliest purchases had to be Escoffier's *Guide Culinaire*.

Escoffier's masterpiece, written in 1902, was my bible as I began cooking, as it is even today. It is a book that greatly simplified the classic French cuisine, developed by the likes of Carême, at the same time that it codified it, so that if a cook wanted to know the accepted time-honored approach to, say, a lobster thermidor, there it was in plain language.

I had to buy a set of knives early on, too, and learn to chop and slice.

My mother never had more than a couple of sharp knives; now I needed several of them, ranging from a little paring knife to a heavy chef's knife. Efficient chopping is the hallmark of a good cook, the ability to hold an eight- or ten-inch chef's knife with one hand on the handle and the other on the blade and rock the knife rapidly (rather than lifting it off the work surface) to chop parsley or dice celery in seconds.

One of the most beautiful aspects of living on Raspail was the nearness of a spectacular market at Denfert-Rochereau, just a short walk away. It was not as big as Les Halles, but very impressive nonetheless, a whirring array of butchers and fishmongers and vegetable stalls. Belon oysters, swordfish, langoustines—so many marvelous things. I would go there with Mademoiselle Guignier's cook, who taught me how to shop. She was particularly insistent on checking the gills of every fish we bought; only bright red would do—any paleness or, worse still, grayness would result in the fish's being rejected for another. She soon allowed me to help in the kitchen at the apartment on my days off. People who seemed to be of considerable celebrity—doctors, painters, intellectuals—were always being entertained at Mademoiselle Guignier's.

I remember clearly the day in the kitchen I actually prepared, from beginning to end, a trout in aspic, even to the point of cutting the little floral decorations for the aspic out of hard-boiled eggs, with fresh tarragon serving as the petals. The fancy people in the dining room seemed to like it well enough; they ate it all, in any event. None of them ever said a word to me, of course; we were of different worlds. But life at Mademoiselle Guignier's suited me fine, at least in the beginning.

One drawback, however, was that, while I was there, I was situated badly for work at Thenin. I was on the Left Bank of the Seine, and the restaurant was on the Right, too far to make a bicycle practical. So at eight o'clock each morning of my six-day workweek I had to take the Métro at Raspail, change once at Trocadéro and travel to the Place de la République station. The trip took half an hour. I wasn't supposed to begin work officially until nine-thirty, but I was always early. It was more than a matter of being punctual; I lived in fear of being late to work.

Waverley Root, the brilliant food writer, once remarked that there were thirteen thousand restaurants in Paris, of which ten thousand were good. Thenin, I suppose, was OK. It had few pretensions, and a congenial-enough atmosphere. On the ground floor, there were small, round, marble-top tables, where people dined casually. Upstairs, the tables had cloths on them, and the dining was a bit more formal, although I have no idea of who the clientele might have been. My whole experience of Thenin was behind the kitchen door. I never saw the diners, never knew what they were saying or whether they were enjoying themselves.

It was a hectic kitchen. The staff of six cooks was too small for the usual neat breakdown of chores, and they tended to do whatever had to be done. There was no pastry chef. This was not the sort of kitchen, I soon learned, where people were worried about career advancement. Most of the cooks here weren't going anywhere. The fish chef, I remember in particular, was a rough, florid-faced fellow in his thirties. He drank quite a bit and had no compunctions about verbally abusing apprentices. One of the words most frequently issuing from his mouth was "*stupide.*" The woman whose job it was to peel the vegetables was a good sort. (Although apprentices would peel vegetables early on and move to another job, this was also a dead-end job in many restaurants, usually relegated to a woman.) She was from Brittany, a place as harsh as my Burgundy was lush. She was big bosomed, lighthearted and a bit randy (these were days in Paris when women took their sexual liberation seriously). As a suffering fourteen-year-old I found I could share a joke with her occasionally. In fact I can say honestly that all of the staff took to me eventually. I was not a wise guy. I worked hard. We would play cards between meals, and that helped bring us together as a team.

The clarification of stock for consommé (see recipe page 145) was basic work I would do in these early days. The cold stock would be poured into a pot that might be three or four feet high. A mixture of egg whites bound to carrot trimmings, leek greens, crushed eggshells, perhaps some meat or chopped bone, and herbs and spices would be placed in the pot. I had nothing to do with creating the stock or that clarifying mixture. Even preparing the egg-white concoction was thought to be an important chore, a process that would ultimately impart essential flavoring to the stock, and it was deemed too advanced for me. No, what I did was stir with a huge galvanized steel paddle, its size and weight causing it to resemble a shovel more than any usual piece of kitchen equipment.

The egg-white mixture was supposed to draw all of the impurities in the stock to it. Then the pristine consommé could be poured out through a spigot on the bottom of the pot while the impurities floated on top. But as the pot slowly warmed, if any of the mixture was allowed to rest on the bottom, it would burn and contaminate the liquid. So I stirred for fifteen minutes without stop, scraping the bottom. Once the mixture had completely risen, it formed a floating lid. Now for the next three hours or so as the stock simmered and reduced, I had to remember to baste this lid periodically with a little of the stock so that it wouldn't dry up and disintegrate.

The work was boring and tiring, but what I felt, mostly, was apprehension. Consommé, after all, is one of the glories of French cooking, demonstrating that even in a dish seemingly so humble there is artistry and perfection. A consommé cannot have the slightest hint of cloudiness; it must be rich in flavor, even though it is so light in its appearance. A splendid consommé, perhaps garnished with diced vegetables, serves as the opening act for the rest of the meal—imagine how sorry it would seem if the kitchen failed here. A consommé can also be greatly reduced and transformed into aspic, perhaps for a poached egg (again, see how the humblest foods can be elevated, now as the classic *oeuf en gelée*, perhaps with a sliced truffle embedded in the aspic).

And it was I, after all, who was entrusted with the finishing part of the process, relatively undemanding in terms of skill but risky. Others had already put extensive labor into producing a stock, and if I fouled up here I would be guilty of ruining twenty or thirty gallons of what for us was liquid gold. Terrifying to think about, even now. So I worked very diligently, more so than necessary it turned out. But, then, I was scared.

It was also up to me—Petit, as they called me, using a familiar term of endearment for young children—to tend the charcoal stove, fueling it and scouring it with burlap bags and then brushing it with melted fat to shine and protect it. I had to sandpaper the steel trim, carefully, to place a precise swirling pattern on it.

I also had to sieve fish for *mousse de poisson* (see recipe page 160) and quenelles, a gossamer-light creation of pureed fish and cream, often molded into small ovals and then poached. To get the fish smooth, in the days before the food processor liberated us all, somebody had to push the fish through two different sieves, first the coarse one and then the fine, a chore that could take two or three hours. A similar procedure was required in pureeing soups or vegetables. (With a food processor, today's cook can accomplish feats at home that were prevalent only in restaurants then; the penalty we pay is in excess, of course, with too many foods pureed too often.)

My first lessons in garnishing dishes came here, too. With my paring knife I would shape peeled potatoes into one or another of the classic forms: the garlic-clove-shaped *pomme de terre en cocotte* to be neatly arrayed around a roast, or the kidney-shaped *pomme de terre en gousse d'ail* to be strewn loosely around a veal chop.

Before I left Thenin, I also managed to learn to fillet fish and prepare some of the easier desserts, like the basic custards baked in their individual tin molds. (It was then that I learned about the protective qualities of water at a simmer; we baked the custard in the traditional fashion, in a water bath called a bain-marie, and even I, green as I was, could not foul it up.) But at Thenin I never learned to butcher meat in preparation for roasting it. The meat was too expensive, and this little restaurant could not take the chance that I might damage a piece of it. After I had pleaded often, the chef told me, "If you want to learn to prepare a short loin, Petit, I will teach you, but you will have to buy it yourself." I never did.

In any event, I was soon to leave Thenin. After six or eight months, Monsieur Thenin came to the conclusion that I needed to move faster and learn more. He felt that his place could never offer me enough, so he arranged for me to transfer to a restaurant called the Drouant, on Place Gaillon near the Opéra. This was an act of generosity for which I will always be grateful to him. It was at the Drouant that my career took flight.

I WAS READY for the Restaurant Drouant—or at least I thought so. It was as different from Thenin as that place was from my mother's kitchen. Drouant had a staff of more than 100, organized in the rigid hierarchy typical of great restaurants. It was suffused with elegance and tradition, housed in a massive seven-story building, possessing great dignity. Shutters, wrought-iron balconies and a row of dormers gave it a sense of formality on the outside. Inside, there were three dining rooms that served 300 diners a day, the most formal of the rooms— starched white linen, a wrought-iron balustrade—to the right of the entrance. A shellfish bistro section on the ground floor was signaled by etched-glass wall panels with a fish motif.

The Drouant never received more than two stars from Michelin (out of a possible three, that rarely bestowed treasure), but there are those who will tell you that Michelin had underrated it and that it should have received a full three. Waverley Root in his *Paris Dining Guide*

called it "one of the great classic restaurants of Paris." He had eaten there, he said, for forty years: "It can produce perfectly any dish in the standard haute cuisine repertoire and doesn't try to do tricks with it."

The staff of the Pavillon Royale, a Drouant family restaurant where I sometimes worked as a summertime fill-in

In my years it was certainly one of the most famous restaurants in Paris. It had been founded in 1880 as a simple bistro by Charles Drouant and was popular with the likes of Rodin, Renoir and Pissarro. Beginning in 1914, it was the elegant setting for the announcement of the annual literary prize awarded by the Goncourt Academy. In the 1920s, Drouant transformed his bistro into a luxury establishment specializing in seafood and fine wines. By the time I arrived, his son, Jean, was the proprietor and also ran four other establishments of some reputation (one of the others, the Pavillon Royale, flourishes to this day, as does the Drouant, which only recently garnered 17 points of a possible 20 from the Gault Millau restaurant guide).

The Drouant that welcomed me in 1935 specialized in seafood: lobster *américaine,* bouillabaisse, coquilles St. Jacques, poached turbot, fluke au gratin and so on. Roasts were quite popular, but the Drouant could do anything, really. The restaurant had a full complement of stations, each with its own pecking order: a station head (the *chef de par-*

tie) and his subordinates called commis, each of them with their rank (first commis, second commis . . .). The *chef de cuisine* was the overall administrator; under him were two sous-chefs and under them were the various *chefs de parties* with their specialties—sauce, roasts, fish, vegetables, pastry and the garde-manger, or cold section, a pantry and butchering area where most of the chopping and cutting were done.

I knew the Drouant meant business from the first moment I stepped into the kitchen, when I saw that the potato shaping I had learned at Thenin wasn't going to be good enough here: in the garde-manger I saw there were little carved potatoes, not only perfectly shaped to garnish a roast, but each with seven facets! Someone—an apprentice, of course—spent hours with those potatoes, treating them like diamonds, shaping them and then slicing seven—not six or eight—facets on each one. This was a demanding establishment, and I could see it in the organized bustle of the kitchen, too.

The chef, Jules Petit, would shout the orders: one lobster thermidor, one sole Drouant, one roast chicken. Waiters would rush in, demanding, "Where's my lobster?" There was no time to talk. Efficiency was the rule.

One fellow was sautéing the trout meunière while another was preparing a lobster *américaine* (see recipe page 161). Another was sautéing the sole Drouant. Four or five people were at each station. It was hot and they were moving fast. At first, it was hard for me to discern the individual roles, the whole effort was so well orchestrated. Moving through this finely choreographed production was a nervous man, a thin fellow of authoritarian bent named Emile Domas. He was an accomplished sous-chef, about forty years old, with a reputation well beyond the walls of the Drouant. He was a frightening figure who would move from section to section, wearing his knives on his waist like guns in a holster, and whose face was often red from too much drink. Domas would oversee the sauce, fish, roast and vegetable cooks. When he found the pace of work too slow, he would rap the commis on the backside with a wooden spatula and shout, "La cadence! La cadence!" If a particular group was performing poorly, Domas would position himself with them for hours until he figured out what—or who—had gone wrong.

The least efficient aspect of the kitchen was the way the stations were divided up among the building's floors: the hot stations and fish department were on the second floor, the dishwashers on the third, the sauce station and garde-manger above that, and the pastry department on the top floor.

I don't believe I ever walked those stairs—I always ran. The place would not tolerate anybody who took his time. And, at least when I first arrived, I had to prove that I was up to the honor of working in so magnificent a restaurant. Despite my apprenticeship at Thenin, I started at Drouant as the lowest commis at the lowest station, the vegetable department, for four hundred francs a month—not much, but four hundred francs more than I had made at Thenin. My apprenticeship at Drouant would last three years. I was at that stage of adolescence when I could actually sense myself growing older, bigger, more mature.

This business of maturing could not happen fast enough, of course. Although I was old enough to play cards with the other cooks, or bicycle over to Versailles to join them on a soccer field, I was still small enough to be called Mignon (the same term one uses for that little steak, filet mignon) by some, including Monsieur Domas, and still perfectly capable of finding myself in mortifying circumstances.

Once a group of the older fellows decided it was time to make a man of me, which, to them, meant curing me of my virginity. They took me to a house of ill repute on the Rue de Lappe (actually, in Paris in those days, attendance at one or another of those houses was so accepted that their repute wasn't all that bad). The older men tried to hide me as we entered, surrounding me like guards leading a dignitary into hostile territory. I peeked out through the crowd into a living room whose walls were lined with seated women who were tantalizing, it is true, but also profoundly shocking. They were dressed, but in see-through, brightly colored gowns, the colors breathtakingly daring in a time when every woman I knew dressed conservatively, drably. Parts of the anatomy—I remember belly buttons—were completely uncovered. At this point in my life, I had never seen a naked female, and those who sat before me now were by far the closest I had yet come to that experience.

I was tremendously curious but wound tight with fear. It was illegal for me to be there; a boy had to be eighteen before the law allowed it. It was thus necessary for me to do some acting. The men around me told me to smoke to look older, which I tried, and I wore a Stetson. Still I was not persuasive. The whole show lasted less than five minutes. The madame—dirty blond, matronly with a large bust—singled me out at once; she declared, to my tremendous embarrassment, "This is not a nursery!" And I was sent on my way.

This ridiculous, fruitless spectacle caused me to return home to Mademoiselle Guignier's after the place was locked up for the night. I had to ring to wake the concierge's wife, who let me in. She, of course, told a housekeeper that I had been out awfully late. The housekeeper, of course, told the sainted Mademoiselle Guignier, who interrogated me the next day. This was the beginning of the end of my stay there; ultimately I felt I needed to be on my own. Before long I was living in a hotel room at Rue St. Roch, which made much more sense, anyway, since it was so close to Drouant, which had become virtually my whole life.

MANY of my most enduring memories of the work at Drouant have to do with eggs. As it happened, the vegetable station, my first assignment, was where the eggs were prepared. And, as anybody who means to be serious about cooking will come to realize sooner or later, the egg is as variable and useful a food as was ever created on earth. In Escoffier, under "Oeufs," you can go from *oeufs Alexandra* (poached eggs in aspic placed in a tartlet over lobster mousse) and move through a couple hundred recipes until you get to the exquisite *oeufs de vanneau à la royale,* a soft-boiled plover's egg smothered in mushroom puree and topped with truffles. This sort of obsessive drive and skill, which impel chefs to continuously build new creations with the familiar ingredients, makes French cooking so exciting to me; it is the way painters must feel working with a limited number of colors but infinite possibilities.

Oddly, perhaps, we French rarely ate eggs for breakfast (a croissant, jam and coffee with milk—boiled in those days before pasteurization was common—seemed to serve us well enough). But the egg was a ubiquitous element in our cuisine, and still is, even as cholesterol concerns have sullied its reputation. We employed it as a hidden ingredient—to prepare sublime mashed potatoes called *pommes Mont-d'Or,* for instance, in which the yolk enriches the potato puree, or to breathe air into an orange sorbet with whipped egg white. Although the egg can be prepared hundreds of ways, it is fragile, before, during and after cooking.

As we poached eggs at the Drouant, for instance, every bit of the craft was brought into play. First water was poured into a saucepan, along with a little vinegar (to help contract the egg white into a tighter shape), then the eggs were broken, one at a time, and placed in the simmering water. The idea was to cook only a few at a time, for fear of cooling the water too much by the addition of too many eggs. You had to pay attention to where each egg was so that you could move them around the pot, in and out of the hot spots in the simmering water. Then by touch (a sense that every good chef hones), you determined when the egg yolk was done, but only slightly done.

Using a perforated skimmer you lifted each egg out, plunging it into cold water to stop the cooking. (This technique is one that is used in many cooking tasks in which the heat must be removed immediately—for instance, I do exactly the same thing with asparagus to be served cold with a vinaigrette sauce; cook it briefly and then immerse it in ice water to keep the crunchiness.)

When the poached egg was cool, it was cradled in one hand while you gently trimmed the white, so that it was perfect in shape, without messy strings dangling from it. Now it would sit and wait until its turn came. Would it be prepared as a cold dish, encased in aspic? Or would it be reheated—a risky business, with just the slightest carelessness leading to a hardened yolk and disgrace for the cook—to be joined with hollandaise sauce, ham and truffles and bear the name eggs Benedict? Would it be served on a bed of spinach with the Gruyère-cheese sauce called Mornay, as eggs Florentine?

And there was that vast cornucopia of omelettes, so variable and subtle. In fact it was an omelette that changed my life for as long as I was to be at Drouant. The tyrant Domas came to the vegetable station and said (I was still fighting this image problem), "Mignon, today you are going to make omelettes." If he hadn't felt the need to stand over me as the first order came in, everything would have been wonderful, I'm sure of it. I was told to prepare a simple *omelette aux fines herbes*—three eggs, chervil, parsley, tarragon, chives—the very first omelette I was assigned to prepare for paying guests, after a considerable amount of practicing on others (see recipe page 238). I knew what I was doing. I chopped the herbs rapidly, broke and mixed the eggs with the herbs, poured the mixture into the heated pan.

Under Domas's stern observation, I was nervous; my hands were shaking, which up to the point of placing the mixture into the pan was no great liability. But now came the critical part of the procedure. The secret of lightness in an omelette comes from the layering of the egg. As each thin layer of egg solidifies, a new one must be formed beneath it. One method for doing this is to manipulate the pan by constantly jerking it toward you so that the eggs' action is almost like that of waves crashing on the beach and rolling back as undertow. This is a fine art—too much agitation for too long and the omelette will not have the requisite smooth texture.

This one didn't. It was wrinkled. The skinny dictator Domas seethed with scorn. "That's no *omelette aux fines herbes,* that's an *omelette grand-mère!*" he said in an allusion to the wrinkles. He whacked the side of my head with his spatula. I took that malformed omelette and hurled it at his face; it struck its target, and pieces of egg, as if in slow motion, gradually broke away, slipping down the front of his body. I spun around and fled up the stairs, three flights. All I could think was that he was going to kill me. I was changing into my street clothes when Domas reached me. "What are you doing?" he said. I told him I was sorry I had lost my temper and that I was certain he was going to fire me. No, he thought that my anger was a normal reaction, a man's reaction. "I'm not going to call you Mignon anymore," he said. "From now on you are Mon Gendre," his son-in-law, which was his way of saying he thought of me as family and also expressing the hope that I might marry his daughter one day.

I did in fact meet her—she was a brunette of modest looks who worked at a movie house—but we never hit it off. Domas took it well, however, and for as long as I knew him he called me Mon Gendre anyway. We became intimates, of sorts. He would trust me, for instance, with the delivery of gifts to his mistress. Often these were gifts of food; once I brought her a chicken.

My biggest single catastrophe at the Drouant came on a day I was sent to the pastry floor to fetch a crate of eggs. I ran up there, as I always did, taking several steps at a time, grabbed the crate and came bounding back down the stairs. Unfortunately the weight of the box threw me off balance: I tripped and tumbled heavily down to a landing. My muscular, chunky body withstood the fall just fine, but not one of the thirty dozen eggs did. Three hundred and sixty egg yolks had burst, many of them oozing over me. Miserable, I looked up to see the regal chef, Jules Petit, glaring down at the mess that included me.

He was forgiving. He seemed to feel that the energy I displayed was going to take me somewhere eventually. And I sincerely believed that the skills I learned at Drouant would last me forever. Nowadays, I am often asked why I succeeded where others failed in this rigorous system. Certainly, more than a few of the men around me were merely going through the motions and were not on the road to becoming chefs of any particular note.

Two reasons for my growth, I think, were that I was lucky enough to have a few chefs of tremendous skill to teach me (Domas may have been a fearsome drunk, but he knew how to cook) and that I refused to be shortsighted. I was at Drouant to learn everything I could and never left to take a break or go home for a nap if something important was transpiring in the kitchen.

Two examples come to mind of instances when I remained there even though I was free to leave. I remember the cases clearly because they both involved dishes that I felt I had to master if I was ever going to be anybody. One was called a turbot soufflé, and to prepare it the chef had to be in command of several major skills and had to have already acquired a respect for meticulousness that would lead to perfection. First the turbot, a flatfish like a fluke or a flounder, is cleaned and filleted in such a way as to remove the bones but otherwise leave it whole. To do that you make an incision just below the head, cut all the way down the length of the fish with your knife and carefully fold the flaps of the belly away from the center, then you take a pair of kitchen scissors and cut the backbone away, leaving the flesh as nearly intact as possible.

The next step is to fill the fish with the soufflé—ground fish, egg yolks and beaten whites—and close the turbot flaps over the stuffing, placing the fish seam down on a tray to bake it in white wine. If no errors are made anywhere along the line from cleaning to filling and baking, the fish will perform one of the most remarkable feats in the culinary world: as the soufflé expands, it will reinflate the turbot, and the fish will appear whole again, except that now it is a creation of art, a *trompe-l'oeil* of sweet white flesh and fish custard.

Another dish whose preparation was so necessary to my development that I distinctly recall I remained in the kitchen just to observe, even though there was no need for me to be there, was the famous *sole normande*. Its preparation was also extremely elaborate, and yet no chef of the time could ever call himself educated if he failed to do it well. Here the primary glory was a symphony of garnishing so complicated that I do not believe many chefs attempt it today. The sole is sautéed briefly with onions, then poached in cider and Calvados (both the juice and the brandy are apple derivatives, and thus Normandy, the kingdom of apples and cream, is referred to in the title of the dish). The sole is removed and placed in a round, deep dish and garnished with poached oysters, shelled mussels cooked in white wine and the mushrooms from the baking tray. Now come the crucial stages: crème fraîche (the slightly soured cream used widely in France) is added to the liquid still in the pot; the mixture is forced through a sieve and blended with butter. That sauce is used to coat the fish. But wait, there is more: whole crayfish are added after they have been cooked in a fish bouillon.

The amount of work involved in this dish is enormous, and the list of ingredients is long indeed. But the secret here, as I learned through-out my years as an apprentice and never forgot in all the cooking years later, is to achieve a dish in which no one ingredient overwhelms the others but rather they all work together. It is the dish itself, as an entire creation (in this case a complex blend of seafood flavors, textures and forms), that commands our attention and appreciation. When I see many young chefs today, I do not believe they understand this way of thinking—they mix fruit with anything, whether it blends or not; they spice dishes so heavily that they are overwhelming and the other ingre-dients can no longer play a role.

Obviously, hard work—along with some natural aptitude and inter-est—will pay off in any line of endeavor. But to become a fine chef, one also has to be willing to accept diligence as one of the highest values of all. Just to take one example—again a skill that I do not believe many cooks possess these days—all apprentices in my time had to learn to seam a leg of veal. This is because the calf's leg is one of the most vexa-tious pieces of meat available, containing seams of muscle, some tender, some tough. Very carefully, with an exquisitely sharp knife, one has to separate the tough seams of meat from the tender ones (it is not diffi-cult through look and feel to tell one sort from the other; it does take diligence to separate them cleanly). The tough meat goes for stews and the like, while the tender is cut into thin slices for paillard (see recipe page 214), *escalope de veau*, or, as the Italians put it, veal scaloppine.

This hands-on understanding of veal, or any other meat, had to be followed by an educated sense of what happens when heat is applied to it. The key to cooking most protein is that you either cook it short or long: in other words, if it is tough, the cook's aim is to allow the heat eventually to break down the protein so that it becomes soft, and this requires long cooking at low heat. But meat that is already tender needs to be cooked very quickly, perhaps only seared at high heat to seal in the juices. Between short and long cooking is an intermediate stage, a sort of limbo, where the protein tightens but has not yet begun to soften.

In those days, when I roasted or broiled meat, I mostly tested for doneness of the more tender cuts by feel, pushing a finger into the meat. If I sank a thumb into the meat and the imprint remained, the meat was still essentially raw. As soon as I saw some springiness, I knew the meat was at the point of being rare (if it felt hard, then I had been negligent and had reached that limbo stage, essentially having desecrated a tender cut of meat). Nowadays, I often use a thermometer because the quick-read instruments are so precise and fast, but one thing I always try to remember is to use the same hole for the thermometer each time I sink it in; otherwise too much juice will be lost and the meat will look terrible besides.

Today, there are good butchers who can discriminate between tender and tough raw meat by eye, and there are good cooks who can handle either with great aplomb. But we, as apprentices, had to learn to do both tasks well. It built confidence and instilled in us a sense that we could do almost anything, from the most tedious to the sublime.

NEAR the end of my apprenticeship, just as my life seemed to be solidifying and my confidence growing, my family was struck by tragedy. Back home, my brother Jacques was preparing to take over my father's business, learning the trade (Father had branched out into plumbing now, with the advent of piped water in the region). Word had reached my father that one of his workmen, René Michaud, a blacksmith, had to return quickly to his own village fifteen or so miles away because his mother was fatally ill. Jacques offered to drive him in the big Citroën. Jacques was a good, fast driver, but this time he took a bend in the road too fast and hit a tree. He died at once. My mother wore black or gray the rest of her life and never seemed to allow herself to be happy again. I think Jacques's death somehow made her even more protective of me, and as I grew older and advanced in life, she worried more than ever. Nevertheless, I was ready to be on my own now.

When I was nearly eighteen I had done my stint in each of the departments, and so my apprenticeship came to an end. Now I could wear white instead of blue, and my toque would be tall and not the stump of a hat that boys wore. I was a full-fledged cook and would spend most of the next two years at the sauce and the fish stations, working my way up to premier commis *poissonnier,* or the main fish chef's right-hand man.

Again, diligence paid off: besides knowing how to choose a fish that was fresh by the sight of its red gills, I was by now also expert in determining if a fish cooked whole was perfectly done, the most critical judgment of all. The technique is to remove the dorsal fin along the spine with your fingers—if it comes out offering just slight resistance, and has no blood on it, then the fish has reached that magnificent moment of perfection. If it is still bloody, it needs more cooking, just a little more—but if it emerges offering no resistance at all, then hang your head in shame, for this fish is overdone. If I overcooked a fish at that stage of my life, I think "shame" would be too gentle a word, actually; "horror" would be more like it. Chef Petit expressed admiration for my intensity, and he was proud of the work he and his men had done in bringing me along, and he continued to favor me often with praise because he knew I was someone he could rely on.

The staff's lunchtime was one of the most stratified aspects of kitchen life, with the *chef de cuisine* (Jules Petit) eating alone, then the heads of each station, the *chefs de parties,* all eating together at their own special table, and then came the rest of the cooks, followed by the noncooking staff. The food was better the closer to the top you were. The cooks took turns preparing the food, but only the most experienced sauce cooks did the work for Chef Petit. The luncheon dishes did more than just feed him well; they were also his opportunity to test new creations.

I cooked for the chef often during this time and learned a great deal, from him and from the *chef saucier*. It was in my sauce education, of course, that I learned many of the techniques that I employ to this day. The most important, I believe, was the ability to create a superb, fast sauce through the deglazing method. Here, the trick is to remove the meat or whatever it might be from a hot pan and dissolve the solids that are left behind, adhering to the pan, with wine or stock or vinegar, infusing the liquid with the true essence of the food it will rejoin as a sauce (incidentally, a real drawback of today's nonstick pans is that solids do not adhere). Often one enriches the sauce, merely through reduction, allowing the heat to expel some of the liquid as steam so that, if it is wine, for instance, the flavor will intensify.

Many times, then, one wants to thicken this sauce. Cream, arrowroot, cornstarch or flour will do that, of course, but so will just a touch of butter (as little as a tablespoon) swirled in off the heat so that it melts without actually cooking (if it begins to boil, the butter will impart a greasy texture to the sauce).

I remember cooking a veal kidney with a wonderful sauce, cognac based and enriched with mustard. Making the sauce was not a problem so much as treating that delicate kidney perfectly before I made the sauce. The *chef saucier* warned me not to sear the kidney too much; it had to be rare. And once removed from the pan, the kidney had to be allowed to release some of its liquid, which would be discarded, because the juices could be too strongly flavored. On the whole, this was not easy cooking; it took the know-how of a professional to pull it off to perfection, and I was having a marvelous time, gleeful when a dish like that kidney turned out exactly as it should. I was far beyond the basics now, well into the nuances; I was definitely in my element.

Increasingly secure in my skills, I began to be more aware of my surroundings. I was curious about the clientele of the Drouant. The cooks were not allowed in the dining rooms, but occasionally we could get a look through the kitchen doors or—and I don't know if this secret has ever been revealed—peer through tiny peepholes cut into the kitchen walls. And so I knew whenever the great Curnonsky arrived. Curnonsky was the Russian-sounding pseudonym (derived from "why not" in Latin, *cur non,* with a "sky" added) for Maurice Edmund Sailland. Curnonsky, Prince Cur as he came to be called, was a Frenchman who, until his death in 1956, was a food journalist of considerable renown. He was a huge man, and you couldn't miss him when he arrived. He would order the finest wines we had in a cellar full of them and usually one of our best dishes, perhaps the fillet of sole Drouant. This sole was a gorgeous thing: three pieces of fish in a white wine sauce made pink by the addition of sauce from lobster *américaine,* garnished with tiny shrimp and mussels and fluted, glazed mushrooms.

If the regular arrival of Prince Cur was a one-man event, the most important group event we regularly handled was the annual awarding of the Goncourt Academy's literary prize. In a private dining room, twenty or so of the most impressive, formally dressed Frenchmen would gather. For the most part they were graying, heavyset men, and they dined as well as any Parisian could. Lunch might begin with caviar and Belon oysters. The main course might be a *baron d'agneau,* of *pré-salé* lamb. (*Pré-salé* refers to the delicate lamb raised in salt marshes, and *baron* is the style in which the two legs and saddle are roasted and served as a single joint.) We would roast it with a dusting of bread crumbs, shallots and garlic and then serve it with a light gravy (see recipe page 209).

At the fish station, I was often a key player in the preparation of one of the most magnificent dishes we ever served this august crowd, that turbot soufflé I had studied so assiduously. Dessert was always elegant: one I remember was a sweet soufflé into which we had crumbled hazel-nut praline and then served it on a crepe with an almond sauce Grand Marnier, the orange-flavored liqueur that has become a staple in so much French cooking (the Grand Marnier soufflé being the grandest example). At the Drouant we loved putting on this sort of lavish per-formance, but I suppose it is lucky for the Goncourt jury that they came by only once a year.

Aboard the Normandie, *1939*

4

France Is Fading

THESE WERE tense years in Paris and throughout France. The gaiety of the miraculous 1920s—a period of postwar insouciance and frenetic creativity—gradually gave way through the early 1930s until France had become a nation beset by political and labor strife. By the end of the decade, of course, war would very nearly suffocate us; the breath of our prior happiness would be thin, almost gone. There were many omens of the terrible times ahead, but no one knew what to make of them. In 1934, Fascists arose in France, attempting to gain power (foreshadowing the days of Nazi domination and Vichy rule in the 1940s), and there was political violence. In St. Vinnemer, my father, a Socialist mayor, lived with a constant sense of physical threat. Our house was marked as the residence of Socialists. One night someone released the brake of a car parked on a hill overlooking the house, and it came careening through our garden, crashing to a stop at the well. We never knew who did it.

In Paris, labor was fed up with suffering, aggravated by inflation. We French, so renowned for our good times, were actually an extremely hardworking people, too hardworking, many thought. Suddenly, the idea of regular vacations, one week for a year's work, struck everyone as a tremendously important goal. So did higher wages. I did not suffer, living alone, having parents who could help me out whenever I needed it, but others were raising families on salaries that guaranteed nothing more than the most meager sustenance. The hotel and restaurant workers went on strike in 1936. At the Drouant, Louis Petit (ironically, he was the brother of the executive chef, Jules Petit) was the leader of the walkout. We all went, fists thrust high, marching from the Place de la Nation to the Place de la République. I have never been a particularly political person, but I am always thrilled by the chance to act, and this march was an exhilarating moment. I wanted to be one of the guys, not to be left behind.

We were all together—bellmen, waiters and cooks. I threw myself into this strike and must have managed to emanate the essence of labor outrage, because the next day my picture was in the Socialist newspaper *Populaire*. My father saw it and was proud of his rebellious son, but this glow did not last long. Soon my anxious mother talked to him, after which, irritated and angry, he talked to me: "Are you crazy, Pierre? You're so young. You must stay away from these things." He ordered me home for a few weeks. By the time I returned to Paris, the strike was over, and labor had won a fine victory. No one in authority at Drouant, so far as I could tell, resented my participation in the strike or my brief sabbatical. Everything was back to routine.

Except that, by 1938, the sense of impending war was always on our minds. With Hitler growing stronger and more militant every day, the French government began the call-up of twenty-year-olds. I had two years left before I would have to go, but others at the Drouant had to leave for the army at once. It was, as you might imagine, the talk of the kitchen.

If I am not a very political person, I am even less of a ruminative one. Yet it was impossible not to worry. My father had been a prisoner of war in World War I, captured in Belgium and shipped to Germany, where he worked as a blacksmith for his captors. He grew sick during the war, and, though his health would eventually return, the emotional scars never disappeared. He was obsessed with the Germans, talked about them all the time. He never trusted Germany. To his credit, though, he tried to be fair. "Pierre," he would tell me, "there are good Germans as well as bad Germans; just keep in mind that the French are not always so very good either and there are many bad people among us, too." It was the kind of thinking that helped me not to hate, even as Paris became more fearful every day.

Across from the Drouant was a bistro where the young men from the kitchen would go to play cards and drink coffee. There were ten tables, and you could spot us there almost any day, smoking, razzing each other in the jocular manner of young men everywhere. There in 1938 and 1939 we talked constantly about war. Paris itself was now so tense that the lights were dimmed at night for fear of a surprise bomb strike from Germany.

Bomb shelters were constructed. In the event of an attack, those of us at the Drouant were supposed to run into a maze of tunnels just below the streets. Still Paris managed to keep up some semblance of gaiety. In 1938 there was even something called the Lunatic Ball, at which a Milton Berle sort of comic named Pierre Dac entertained. It was part of an effort, at times nearly manic, to push the Germans out of mind. As for me, I was eighteen and my hormones had other things to whisper about.

Although I now lived in the city purported to be the most romantic on earth, I had never actually been in love. Romantic love takes a bit of dedication. You have to commit time to it, and I felt I had too little to spare, what with the long hours at the restaurant and regular trips home to Burgundy to see my family for a day or two. But I did manage to commit a certain amount of time to playing cards in that bistro across the street, where a slender, shy, redheaded girl about my age wiped the tables and swept the floors. She and I would flirt, share a joke, occasionally take a walk. I thought about her a great deal, and on the first of May, when young men collect flowers for their girls, it was she I had in mind.

A group of us took our bikes to the Bois de Boulogne to collect lilies of the valley. The day was clear and alive; I collected a prodigious bunch of flowers and tied them to my back with a cord. On the return trip, over the cobblestone streets, the bike bounced and lurched, and the cord broke. The flowers tumbled from my back, still in a bunch, and the stems were mangled by the spokes of the bike. I had nothing to present to my little redhead and never told her about it. This May Day was just about a year before I would be departing Paris for the greatest adventure of my life.

The day I learned I would be leaving, Jules Petit called over to me that he wanted to meet after lunch. He was in his office, the kind of cubicle where the managers of American supermarkets work, elevated a bit, glass on three sides, no ceiling. He ate in solitude at his desk, set with silverware and plates, so that it was surprisingly elegant. I was sitting at the table for the cooks assigned to the sauce station, that is, in the privileged spot right next to his office. "Petit," he called, using one of the diminutives I'd hoped I had outgrown (never mind that it is pronounced exactly the same as his last name; no one ever confused us, I assure you). "I have something special to tell you."

I thought I was getting promoted, maybe transferred. I was now the second commis in the sauce department, a reasonably impressive thing to be when you realize there were six commis and this was the most prestigious of the stations. I was certain that something major was about to happen to me because the chef spoke to me so rarely. In our stratified life, the officers only spoke to the enlisted men when they had to, and the fellows on the lower rungs (like me) never spoke to the top men unless spoken to first. One didn't just shout, "Bonjour, Monsieur Petit," in the kind of easy camaraderie so common today. By the time lunch was over—as I recall, it may have been a cassoulet with confit of goose, and I had a terrible time trying to finish it and maintain a calm exterior—the whole place was abuzz with the news that something was about to happen to little Pierre.

I climbed the couple of stairs to his office and said, "OK, Monsieur Petit, I'm here." In a very orderly, decorous way he told me that the French government would be running a big restaurant at the top of its exhibit at the World's Fair in New York. (Ah, this had something to do with the fair, an event that had occupied the thoughts of my provincial young mind almost not at all.)

"Monsieur Drouant has been selected by the government to get a team together," he said. "They've already chosen the *chef de cuisine* from the Hôtel de Paris in Monte Carlo, Marius Isnard, and two sous-chefs, a Monsieur Roueault from La Coupole in Montparnasse and a Monsieur Nioux from Paris-Plage at Le Touquet in Normandy." The supervision of the dining room would go to a dapper man named Henri Soulé, an assistant maître d' at Café de Paris, also owned by Drouant and of high reputation. Although he was not even a full maître d', Soulé was already something of a legend for his efficiency and his imperiousness. But the fact that he spoke English must have played as large a role as his skills in getting him the assignment.

Petit told me that the *chefs de parties,* the chefs for each of the main departments, were coming from all over France. He told me that two of the commis to serve at these stations would be drawn from this very place, the Drouant. I was to be one of them, designated the premier commis at the fish station, and my friend Jules Jeannin, a year older than I was and a heavy-drinking, amiable guy, would be the other commis, working at the garde-manger, the station that served as the pantry and also the butchery headquarters.

I nearly leaped over the office's glass partitions, or so I remember my ecstasy; more likely, I revealed almost nothing, smiled and thanked

Petit in a courtly fashion and made my way back to the other cooks, where I commenced to gloat. Bragging, it turned out, was a bad idea. There was immediate jealousy, even though I don't believe I had ever made an actual enemy on the whole staff up until then.

Resentment, I learned, was particularly sharp among the commis at the fish station. But the truth was I had earned this trip. Petit had backed me; in fact it was he who had told Drouant about me. The dictator Domas had supported me for the job, too, even if I never would marry his daughter. Now the main obstacle was my parents. The government would not allow me to leave without their written authorization. I called them, and permission seemed easy enough—at first. My mother and father saw this as recognition of my skill, and they were pleased.

But war was close. France was preparing to mobilize. Was it wise to cross the Atlantic in a huge ship—the great and symbolic *Normandie,* no less—at a time so full of a sense of impending danger? Many people had canceled plans to go to America aboard her. My mother, proud though she may have been at my selection, tried to talk me out of going. "I've already lost one son," she said. My father felt otherwise. "Pierre's a man now," he said, "if he wants to do this thing, let him," and his argument won the day.

I may have been a man, but I was a man earning all of 950 francs a month with half of that going for my room at the Hôtel St. Roch; I was a man who had no money and therefore not nearly the wardrobe for a grand crossing to New York. So my parents agreed to buy me *pantalons de golfe,* those long knickers that men wore to play golf and go touring, and a plaid suit for the times when more formality was in order.

This was in March 1939, and with departure for New York just a month away, I needed a passport quickly. My father, pulling his weight as a mayor, went directly to Auxerre, the capital of our department in Burgundy, and managed to get the papers processed in what I remember as record time. Soon I was ready not just for a summer in New York City, but for the amazing voyage on the *Normandie,* the biggest transatlantic ship by far when it was commissioned in 1935. Off and on during the few years of its brief existence—a life that would be cut short by war and negligence—it held the speed record, too, capable of making the voyage in just under four days, when seven days had only recently been the norm.

The ship was the great pride of the French, and although it would end its days pathetically, right now its majesty was greater than that of its rival, HMS *Queen Mary,* more chic, so Parisian. It represented France, a nation that felt robust before the humbling days of war. On one voyage, the records show this mammoth ship consumed 590,798 tons of oil, while her passengers drank 572,519 bottles of table wine and champagne.

The restaurants—and this stunned everyone I worked with at Drouant—might serve as many as 1,500 people a day! That was accomplished with no loss of quality thanks to the labor of 120 cooks. These were not second-tier cooks but some of the best the country had ever trained. Many of us—myself included—had aspired to work on the great ship one day. At the Drouant I was always being asked if, during the crossing, I would get to meet the chef, see the kitchens. Of course I would.

My parents met me in Paris, where I and a large part of our World's Fair contingent gathered to take the special train that ran directly to the *Normandie*'s pier in Le Havre, right up to the side of the ship. From my mother and father there was the conventional parental palaver: be careful in New York, be a good boy, don't get involved with any bad women. My mother, dressed in black as usual, was reasonably cheerful and did not cry, although I have since learned that she wept once I had departed. I was wearing my sporting knickers, a matching jacket and cap and a black armband in memory of my brother Jacques.

The hubbub at the train station verged on chaos, and when I saw a young brunette—I'll call her Marie—struggling with her bags, I pushed my way through the tumult to help her. She was grateful, laughing. We talked a little. She would be in first class. I would be in third. But maybe we would see each other on the ship.

When the special train pulled up to the *Normandie* in the gray port, I was impressed beyond measure—the ship was more than one thousand feet long. Some sense of foreboding might have befallen me if I weren't simply an eighteen-year-old too thrilled to be scared. Within sight of the *Normandie*, the dignified ship *Paris*, loaded with art for the World's Fair, had recently been set ablaze by (many suspected) arsonists and would never sail again (nor would the art ever make it to New York). The *Paris* had rolled over, and her masts blocked the way of the *Normandie*; for our journey to begin, part of the *Paris* had to be cut away.

On board the *Normandie,* I immediately had the sort of experience that might have depressed someone else. I and the other cooks of similar station in life had to make our way down to the third-class cabins (Soulé and Isnard were in first class, of course). Now, this was a ship made for first-class travel, and anything less was almost an afterthought. If the first-class suites were as luxurious as anything in the finest hotels of Paris—with their picture windows and curtains and rugs from the greatest looms of France—the third-class rooms were smaller even than on some other ships. Mine was six stories below, a tiny enclosure with two double bunks, and I was to share it with my friend Jules, also Gaston Esnault, a baker who had worked on the ship in the past but was now headed for duty at the fair, and a man named Bérichon, the premier commis *entre metier* (in charge of sweet dishes served between courses), from a restaurant in Paris.

Even assigned to that little cell, I was not downhearted. First of all, I knew my place. I had always traveled third class. I was still something of a rube from Burgundy, no matter how much I might have come along in the past four years. And now I was on the *Normandie!* A little lower and I would have been in the Atlantic itself, but so what? My life was beginning. As it turned out there would be more room in the cabin than we had at first imagined, because Gaston was never there. His experience on the ship was such that he could find more favorable quarters elsewhere—exactly where or how, I'm not sure. In any event I was never entirely comfortable in first class even when I did manage to experience it.

The formal way to get into those rarefied areas was to take the tour, which I did, along with just about everybody else on board on the first day at sea. We saw the eighty-two-foot-long indoor swimming pool adorned by a frieze executed by Sèvres. We walked through a banquet room made all the more opulent by a bas-relief in gilt stone of figures representing Norman peasants and assorted deities engaged in various agricultural pursuits, picking fruit, tending the geese (it was as if my own childhood and its people had been mythologized).

In the kitchen, I saw cooks literally shoveling the caviar out of four-pound containers, and there were ceramic terrines of foie gras in such number as I had never seen before. I saw electric stoves for the first time, and, instead of the copper pots I knew, there were huge stainless-steel ones.

On the walk through the ship I ran into Marie again. To put it more candidly, I had searched everywhere for her and then drifted over to her side as casually as I could. She was so lovely, just about my age, the daughter of a man working for the French government in Washington. I imagined he was a diplomat but never knew for sure. She was attending a university there. I had a little more time now to tell her who I was, a cook taking the trip of his life to work at the World's Fair. I think she was impressed, although I don't know. If a commis in France was regarded as some considerable distance from high society, a cook in America was even further away. Cooking, even by the best chefs, was not especially well appreciated in America in 1939. Dining well was not a widely held experience, as I was soon to learn. But Marie was a French girl transplanted to America and receptive enough to my occupation. So I bragged, but pleasantly enough, I guess, because we agreed to meet again, later, in the first-class bar. I was in heaven.

Getting to the fancy saloon was no easy chore. I needed Gaston to help me: through the huge kitchen and down forbidden corridors until we arrived at our destination undetected. In our suits, Gaston and I managed to fit in well enough. I met Marie (Gaston slipped away), and we stood around awkwardly, listening to stuffy classical music among mostly older people, some of them in formal dress. It was a big and beautiful place, certainly, but I felt as trapped and as vulnerable as a breast of chicken in aspic. I took Marie by the hand and led her back through those alien corridors and through the kitchen to the tourist-class bar, where life was possible, where people were actually enjoying themselves. No fancy ballroom dancing here but rather Bal Musette. A chanteuse sang "La Vie en Rose." An accordion breathed the love songs of France. We danced until 2:00 a.m. and then walked to the top lounging area of the ship, where we kissed.

The next day a storm came up. Most storms could not trouble the *Normandie*. When you see old photos of the *Normandie* in choppy seas, she is stable, cutting her way at high speed through the whitecaps. Not so this time. The storm was terrible, and the great ship rolled so forcefully that I thought it might sink (and wouldn't have cared at that point either; I was so sick).

Retching and wretched in the tiny cabin, I had managed to engage the compassion of Jules, who told me to climb to the highest level and get some fresh air. I did, and as the ship rolled from this side to that, a wave—the single wave that I will never forget as long as I live—came crashing completely over the ship, drenching my miserable self. As I was to learn years after, during this storm, which had taken on something of the proportions of legend, there were people aboard still having a great time. In the first-class salons, the champagne flowed and sloshed, and entertainers carried on. A juggler managed to juggle under these tortured conditions, while those immune to mal de mer laughed the hours away.

The ship survived the trauma in relatively good shape, and so, amazingly enough, did I. Wobbly, but all right, I went off in search of Marie, who had been in her cabin the entire time, sick, too. We reserved a couple of deck chairs and spent much of the next two days talking, although as I remember it I seemed to do most of the talking, about food and cooking, which was all I knew. As romances go, this was no big deal. Strictly a shipboard meeting of two people of different classes. On ship, as everyone knows, society has a way of loosening its grip a bit.

In America, Marie and I would never meet again. She was supposed to visit me at the fair, but if she came—and just about everybody did—she never looked me up. I have always imagined that her parents could tolerate this friendship on a boat but could never have accepted it in America, where a cook was just a cook, and a liaison with one would have certainly been mortifying.

*World's Fair cooks, Flushing
Meadow, 1939*

5

Innocents in New York

THROUGHOUT THE TRIP, when I wasn't wandering off with Marie or retching, I was gorging myself on wonderful food. Even those of us relegated to the tourist-class dining room had nothing to complain about. You could eat all day long, and it wasn't the sort of mass-produced, overcooked and leaden fare that was often served in big hotel resorts. No, even the common folks on this ship were served elegantly. Dinner started with an appetizer, or several: hors d'oeuvres, tomato salad, pâté, mackerel in white wine sauce. Then came the fish course, sautéed sole, perhaps, or trout. Then there was a meat course, which included poultry, and one dish I remember particularly well was a roast breast of guinea hen. All this was followed by salad and cheese, lots of great cheese from France, and then tarts and puddings. As if three huge meals weren't enough, the ship offered some dining in between just to make sure you would make it to the next excessive meal: consommé and fresh fruit at 10:00 a.m., always tea at 4:00 p.m., and then a huge buffet at midnight. Also, my friends and I, who had soon become buddies with the kitchen staff, were constantly pilfering the caviar. Eating like this can endanger your health, but fortunately the ship was fast, and the journey short.

The *Normandie* was so reliant on French foods that it had to carry enough of many staples for a round-trip: enough wine and cheese, fish, frogs' legs and even flour. Gaston, my friend the baker, contended that the fresh-baked bread required not only French flour but also French water. The chauvinism was not all encompassing, however, and the ship did pick up some supplies in New York, including beef and veal. Some commodities were carried on the ship to New York without ever being officially registered.

The French crew was big on smuggling Pernod and Ricard, the anise-flavored liqueur that, like a good Burgundy, can remind you of France wherever you are. (Also, on any typical trip, there were people stowed away; it was the commonest sort of practice, and getting into New York as a stowaway was never a real problem.)

Every day the World's Fair contingent gathered in the tourist dining room for a briefing of about an hour. All the tables were pulled together in rows. In the very first row always sat the *chefs de parties*. Then in groups behind them were the rest of us, assigned to sit with those who would be working with us later. Note taking was expected.

We saw a movie on New York City and were warned to be careful if we chose to visit Harlem. On no account should we visit it alone or at night or for the purpose of finding women. (This rule was broken not two months after we arrived by at least one of our number, a waiter who supposedly knew the ways of the city, whose body was found after he had been hurled from a rooftop on 125th Street.) We were also lectured by the men who were going to be our bosses at the fair. Soulé strode into the room with confidence and stagy elegance, like any man who has more or less invented himself. At the briefing he delivered—it was the first time I had seen him on the trip—he was perfect and one of a kind. He was dressed immaculately, in striped pants, a double-breasted blazer, polka-dot tie. I don't know why I remember this so clearly, but it must have something to do with how deeply this man could impress people. There was a folded white handkerchief in his pocket, and he wore a prominent gold tiepin.

He was formal and pleasant, but not friendly. I already knew he was not supposed to be an amiable man, and nothing about his presentation conveyed warmth. He introduced those of us on the kitchen staff to the people who would be directly under his supervision as the maître d'. These were the captains who would be his main assistants in the dining room. He described the kind of service we would be providing at the fair. There would be, for instance, carving of all roasts at the table, just as it was done in the best French restaurants, just as it was done at Drouant. Soulé said he was pleased to meet us and looked forward to working with us. But I knew I had better watch my step around this guy.

Marius Isnard was the *chef de cuisine*, the man in charge of the kitchen, and when his turn to brief us came, he was practically a buddy compared with Soulé. You had to observe the niceties with him, of course, but he was capable of a joke and an occasional laugh. His briefing brought little news to me, since it was mostly intended to tell us about the jobs we would each be doing in the kitchen, and I knew the requirements of the fish station very well.

It was during the trip, too, that I met the man who would be my immediate superior, the *chef de partie poissonnier,* Cassius Fabius. He was a man of some reputation who had been lured out of semiretirement to join us. His sense of himself could be seen in his dress: he was a goateed man who usually looked like he was on his way to the racetrack, always carrying a silver-knobbed cane, always wearing an ascot. At the fair, Fabius would turn out to be something less than the hardest worker I had ever met. He took it on himself to finish a sauce with some butter or cognac, give things a taste, and that was about it. But he wasn't quite the fop he seemed to be, either.

As the ship entered the port of New York, all of us experienced the sort of transcendent feelings that immigrants have always talked about, that effervescent elation bubbling inside that gradually seems to take over your whole body, no matter how calm you want to be. With the Kodak my mother had given me, I took pictures of my friends on the deck as we glided into the maw of the immense city. At the Ambrose lightship, we picked up a pilot to guide the *Normandie* the rest of the way.

Moran tugs, painted with the big "M" of the company, joined us and nudged us onward. I could see the bridges spanning the East River—the Brooklyn, the Manhattan, the Williamsburg—one after another like elaborate stone-and-steel joints tying Brooklyn to Manhattan. Cars rushed steadily along the elevated highway that sealed off the great towers of Manhattan from the Hudson. And the *Normandie* pulled into Pier 88. It was a mild April morning; the temperature was in the 50s and the sun was shining.

None of us could know that we had taken the *Normandie* on what was very nearly its last voyage. After another crossing in August, with the war on in earnest, it would be taken out of passenger service to be converted into a troop carrier. But it would never see service of any kind after that. Slow-moving bureaucracy and the disuse caused by red tape and conflicting national claims would ultimately render the vessel a firetrap.

And when fire finally did deliver the coup de grâce, and the *Normandie* filled with water, the mutilated hulk rolled over on its side right there at Pier 88. That was in 1942, and a reporter for the New York

The house in Flushing, New York, where I and other French cooks at the World's Fair roomed

Journal-American wrote: "You just can't believe it, confronted by the bleak facade of the pier, the mottled bulk of the once-mighty Normandie. This is the end, you say to yourself."

I have since talked to people who went out of their way to see it, driving down from Westchester, say, just for this bizarre view. As pathetic sights go, this was certainly the largest you could imagine, like a beached whale—no, a hundred beached whales, lying in a row. When I was able to come back to see it, still there years later, I wept.

But for now, on my arrival in New York in the brilliant spring of 1939, there was nothing grander on earth, as it tied up beneath the elevated West Side Highway. Our group marched down the gangplank more or less together. Members of the press were there; our arrival was part of the growing hoopla over the approaching fair. The pier was crowded with people, and as we got our bags through customs, we tried to stick together. The idea was that the World's Fair group was to head for the Vatel Club on Forty-eighth Street between Eighth and Ninth avenues. The Vatel then was a hotel for French chefs, an employment agency and social club, too.

Most of us walked (Soulé and Isnard took taxis). I'm glad I did walk because it gave me the chance to see that even though I was far from France, from my Burgundy, I had not entirely left home. Much of the West Side, near the French Line, had a Gallic air about it. After we walked past the industrial buildings between Tenth and Eleventh avenues, our procession moved past row houses and tenements that housed, in large measure, Frenchmen, many of whom had jumped ship at one time or another and now worked in New York. "Bonjour!" they called out to us from laundry-strewn fire escapes. Some strode up to us on the street to shake our hands.

At the same time, the reality of New York was stunningly apparent. As we lugged our belongings across broad Ninth Avenue and glanced to the right, the Empire State Building peered down at us from the clouds. And the avenue itself! So many cars. Dazzling yellow cabs cruised past, not the dull black variety of Paris. Although the day was lovely, it seemed terribly humid, more humid than anything I could remember in Paris. I must say, too, that immediately I felt the place was not only more noisy and boisterous than Paris, but dirtier. Yet the harsh and the unfamiliar aspects of this city seemed only to accent its greatness, the vinegar in the oil, heightening my experience of the place.

By the time we got to the Vatel we had walked past any number of French bistros and bars and learned about others as well. The Champlain, for instance, which survived until only recently, was a regular hangout for the French who lived in the neighborhood. So was Du Midi. These were places where Frenchmen could go for venison stew or tripe, places where garlic and parsley were used lavishly. To the American palate it was still all so foreign. People here would carry on about garlic—the smell of it seemed so troubling to many of them—as if it weren't one of the most magnificent products of the earth. Anyway, that kind of food philistinism was going to change soon, and Americans, some of them, would eventually move into the vanguard of cuisine, joining the French, the Italians and the Chinese, as unlikely a prospect as that might have seemed in 1939.

I arrived at the Vatel exhausted from the walk, just a few blocks, but very long ones. Immediately, I was introduced to a Mrs. Mathis, an Alsatian American who had agreed, as did many others, to put up members of our group in New York. She was a tiny, open sort of woman with a tall young daughter who, although it was of no significance to me at the time, worked in the advertising department of the *New York Times*. Along with three others who had traveled with me on the *Normandie* I was now about to take another, equally exotic, trip into Queens, aboard the Flushing Line subway.

There was so much new to absorb in that urban expedition that I think I missed most of it. What I remember is that we rode the fantastically loud, screeching El train to Junction Boulevard. There, in a big handsome house across the street from the Long Island Railroad tracks, we would reside, two to a room, just a couple of train stations from the fair itself.

In many ways, my arrival here in Queens was the end of a long, sheltered childhood. The fair still lay ahead of me, but so did war, and so did the boom in cooking that would transform American taste. Little did I realize that I would get the chance to participate in that, even help lead it. In the months and years to come, I would go home often but, as it turned out, never for more than a year, usually just as a visitor. I did not foresee any of that as I dropped my bags in one of Mrs. Mathis's rooms. I was a young Frenchman, working in Queens, New York, for the summer. Still far from war, in a country apparently trying hard to stay at peace, New York City then was a marvelous block party. I was deeply relieved to be away from the fears of Paris.

In New York there seemed to be so much genuine happiness and so much energy spent on having a good time. *Wuthering Heights* was the feature at the Rivoli. Mickey Rooney had opened in *The Hardys Ride High* at the Capitol. On Broadway, Tallulah Bankhead was playing in *The Little Foxes*. Joe DiMaggio was on the rise and Lou Gehrig was on the wane (on the very day I arrived, the papers reported that Gehrig had decided to sit out a game after playing in 2,130 straight; he felt weary and didn't know why). Mayor Fiorello La Guardia was everywhere, making pronouncements on international affairs as well as those closer to home. Of course, at the time, I was aware only of the hubbub, the glitter. I knew that this bustling, harrowing, hustling city was the center of a great many things, but as to just what they were, well, I wasn't so sure. I spoke no English and knew little about American sports or politics. During one of the briefings on the *Normandie* someone in our group had asked what baseball was, and the answer, delivered with considerable savoir faire, was that it was "football with a baton." Ah, well, there was a lot to learn about this place and what people did in it.

Initially, it wasn't too difficult. I was among Frenchmen, after all. On our second day in New York, Jules and I traveled back into Manhattan—a cinch, even for foreigners. The new express line to Queens had recently been completed for the sake of the fair in Flushing Meadow: the train raced along, from Junction Boulevard to Roosevelt Avenue to Queens Plaza and into Manhattan. We went to the Champlain for lunch. It was owned by a man named Larre, whose grandson runs a restaurant of that name in New York even today. Larre was a short, jovial fellow, happy to see us. We weren't just cooks, you know, we were World's Fair cooks, celebrities. The strange idea that we might be so admired struck me at once. People pointed us out; others nodded from across the room and smiled. At the Champlain we had sardines and *saucisson* and beets—very good sardines, as I remember.

After lunch, one of our group who knew New York—Joseph Esnault—took us to a burlesque show. Despite that French "que" at the end of the word, this was nothing like what we knew in Paris. There, girls would dance nude, of course, and there were shows that included sex acts. But here what you saw was a kind of ritualistic performance in which a woman revealed herself with painful deliberateness, one article of clothing at a time. It was diabolical, certainly, but I think I was having the time of my life. In the evening we went to dinner at the Monte Carlo, a nightclub catering to Frenchmen, with the familiar accordion to soothe us into our new life.

It was May 3 and the World's Fair had already officially opened, though many of the pavilions and exhibits were yet to debut. The Restaurant Français at the French Pavilion would be the first part of the French exhibit to open to the public, but even that would not open for several more days.

ANYONE who has ever tried to cook well knows that about 50 percent of the job is in focus, the willingness to concentrate. It is impossible for most of us to cook well while talking to someone on the phone or watching the TV news. This seems to me to be true no matter how advanced you are. I recall the time not too long ago—I had already been cooking for more than four decades—when I had a visitor to my kitchen, a young woman I had chatted with at a party who wanted a glimpse of me at work. She arrived just as I was preparing a cheesecake. She glowed with pleasure as she watched my hands manipulate the ingredients. I am ordinarily not much of a show-off, but this time something in me had snapped. I glowed back. And, of course, while basking in her admiration I managed to dump something close to an extra tablespoon of vanilla into the cake. It was ruined beyond repair, and my glow extinguished like an ember of charcoal caught in the rain. You have to be able to concentrate, or the butter will burn, or the veal will go dry, or some ingredient will be forgotten; so much in cooking happens fast.

The kitchen at the fair was designed, like all great kitchens, to allow each cook to focus on the work at hand with a minimum of distractions. My own job at the fish station required the manipulation of ten black steel sauté pans at the same time on a flat range top, pulling one toward me to brown the butter for a trout meunière as I thrust another away with its cargo of battered frogs' legs. As I worked on a fillet of *sole à la russe*—sole in a cream sauce with very thinly sliced onions, carrots and leeks, which is what earns it the *à la russe* in its name—the vegetables were all prepared and waiting. This early preparation of those ingredients that need to be chopped and sliced or otherwise labored over—fluting the mushrooms, shaping the carrots—is called the *mise en place* and is something that every cook ought to get used to doing. It is the only way to be free to do the actual cooking when the time comes. I would start chopping, slicing, fluting and peeling at 8:30 a.m., getting ready for lunch, which was served from noon to 2:30, and would even have much of the *mise en place* accomplished in the morning for the evening seatings at 6:30 and 8:30. This was possible because, although the menus appeared to change completely from one meal to the next, actually the evening meals were merely variations on the lunch. For example, if we offered salmon poached in the daytime it might be broiled in the evening. (This sort of efficiency extended to the plats du jour, which were largely prepared in advance of the meals and were ordered by perhaps 50 percent of the 350 or so people at each seating, thus freeing us to cook to order everything else on the menu.)

As I cooked, there was a continual rhythmic movement all around me. When a pan had done its job I would drop it to the floor, where the *plongeur,* the washer, would come running by to pick it up, scurrying like one of those kids who dash onto the court during a tennis match to recover loose balls. The *plongeur* would replace each pan with a new one, placing the fresh pan above me on a hot shelf over the stove, so that it would be preheated as I reached for it to do the next job. No wasted

energy, no wasted time. Meanwhile, the air was punctuated by the *chef de partie* singing out the orders: "I need four *merlan*" would be the call.

The kitchen staff at the Pavillon de France restaurant, 1939

Then so quickly that I would never lose my stride by searching for anything or worrying about it, four breaded whiting (the *merlan*), elegantly butterflied with the heads still on for appearance's sake, would be trotted out from the garde-manger's station and brought to me at once for sautéing.

When I think back on this work, my mind often turns to the frogs' legs. It seems to me that we must have cooked millions of them, literally. Frogs' legs were very popular in America at the time, and we French were stereotyped by our own appreciation for them, hence the pejorative name for us. Where do you see frogs' legs these days? Louisianans still prepare them, but they are about the only people who do in America, which is a great pity. Frogs' legs are lean, and they are tender, as long as you don't overcook them. They allow for a great many different sorts of preparation, and at the Restaurant Français we offered a fair range of possibilities: *grenouilles murat,* for instance, frogs' legs sautéed in butter with cubed potatoes, artichokes and truffles; Provençale style, with tomatoes, garlic and parsley (see recipe page 184); in a red wine sauce rich with mushrooms and onions; poached, served in a cream sauce with white wine and shallots.

The kitchen at the fair was very well laid out, not on several floors as at Drouant, but on one level. It was hot, though, so that we were always

The French Pavilion

exhausted. Summer in New York can be torture, so humid, with no air stirring. Sometimes, during my afternoon break, I would slip into the movie theater of the French Pavilion, which was showing off France and its wares, and fall asleep (once I did this just as Ravel's "Bolero" began and awoke in near panic as it reached its booming conclusion; to this day "Bolero" sets off panicky explosions in my brain).

Often, when the work became unbearable or simply when there was a lull, we cooks would step out onto the roof of the restaurant, and from it we could view the whole fair. Finally our eyes could focus on something other than those pans, and the panorama was awesome.

The French Pavilion was wonderfully situated on the Lagoon of Nations, and all around us were the magnificent exhibit halls of Great Britain, Belgium, the United States, the USSR. Every night, when darkness fell around nine o'clock or so, this lagoon was the site of a spectacular display of fireworks and music. Thus, our second seating, at eight-thirty, was extremely popular. The customers would take their tables, order, and, when the fireworks began, the lights would dim in the restaurant so that its big picture windows could be completely taken over by the brilliance outside. Service would stop. We would even stop cooking and sometimes go to the roof. No matter how tired I was, the spectacle was unfailingly invigorating.

The fair always had that power for me and everyone I knew. On my first encounter with it, I remember taking the train the short ride from Junction Boulevard to Flushing Meadow. The fair was already in full swing as Jules and I arrived to help set up the French kitchen, and as we stepped off the train onto an elevated walkway, the fairgrounds stretched out before us. (Not long before, the site had been the Corona Dumps. The offical guidebook described the dumps as "1,216½ acres of primeval bog, spongy marshland, and the accumulated debris and ashes of many years.") Its aspirations were signaled by the Trylon, a seven-hundred-foot-high obelisk adjoining a hollow globe called the Perisphere, standing eighteen stories high. Together they were supposed to suggest a luminous world and its soaring spirit. At the time, there seemed to be no overstatement in it.

As we walked from the train with hundreds, maybe thousands, of others, the cleanliness of the place was dazzling. People dressed up for this visit, as if it were the event of their lives; you saw little boys with new haircuts wearing suits and ties, girls in party dresses, whole families huddled around their guidebooks, pointing this way and that in giddy anticipation.

Greyhound buses carried some visitors from the amusement center to the commercial exhibitions, such as GM's "Highways and Horizons" exhibit or to Borden's mechanical milking display, where cows on an "electrically operated rotolactor"—a revolving platform—were washed, dried and milked by machine. (The food displays, as you might have guessed, always drew me with the greatest force. I spent many hours watching those cows, a rural boy like me getting a glimpse of the future; at the Heinz exhibit, I avidly collected pickle pins to take home to friends.)

Courtesy and gentility were the rule of the day. Mocking it a bit, Meyer Berger reported in the *New York Times:* "Overemphasis on politeness was a mistake, too. The gondola-type observation cars, for example, played a bar from 'East Side, West Side,' to warn pedestrians out of their way. Unaccustomed to such gentle treatment from New York drivers, the walkers just grinned and blocked the right of way."

On my first day at the fair, I spotted a wallet full of money. Although I did not understand American currency yet, this seemed to be quite a lot. I remember ten-dollar bills, twenties, fifties in it. I believe I always would have done the right thing on finding this kind of money, but here when I walked all that cash over to one of the smartly uniformed policemen it was with a sense of being in the proper spirit of goodness and altruism (I just hope the cop shared that spirit; I never gave him my name and never checked to see that he found the owner). Jules and I knew almost no English, but we did know that "beer" was *bière*, and to slake a thirst we stopped at a vendor who seemed to be selling tall, frosted glasses of dark beer—root beer, it was called. I took a swig and could barely swallow this sweet miserable liquid—soda pop, but how was I to know?

When we reached the restaurant, Jules and I set right to work with the others, preparing the kitchen for the first big affair, which would be on May 8. It would be in the pavilion's elegant replica of a room at Versailles, with fine silver and glassware and crystal chandeliers. Our first guests included the ambassador from France, the mayor of New York City and, if memory serves, the governor of New York, too. But before we could pull off anything so elaborate as this meal, there were problems that had to be worked out.

The natural gas in New York was different from what we knew in France, and we had to adjust our burners. The electric ovens brought from France needed adjustments in their wiring so they would get hot enough. The *chefs de parties* were furious that these technical things had not been solved before we arrived. The butter in America was not bad but contained more moisture than we were used to, and we had to adjust our cooking style slightly to let the moisture evaporate. The cream was not heavy enough to suit us, but we would make do.

On the other side of the balance, the beef here was terrific, and the veal and lamb were fine. In fact, we saw immediately that we would have to make very few compromises in our menu or style (a silly concession, as I look back on it, was the first-course grapefruit, which would have been very strange in France, but we heard that Americans could barely start a meal without it). For the most part, we realized the United States was about to get its indoctrination to French food, and it would be authentic, for sure.

It is true that the rich in New York and the United States knew something about French food already (Thomas Jefferson, after all, had employed three French chefs). They could eat at the Colony or other fine restaurants in the city and had the means to travel in France. They

could go to the great hotels, such as the Waldorf in Manhattan, where the chefs were French, or wander into the French area of the city in the West Forties. But we were about to serve more than a thousand Americans a day from all over the land, California to Maine, as they poured into the fairgrounds from buses, trains, cars and boats.

In the dining room of the Fair's restaurant: I'm on the left. I was the assistant fish cook. Standing with me are (from the left) the sous chef, the assistant sauce cook and the assistant vegetable cook.

We were extremely confident. Marius Isnard, the *chef de cuisine,* was calm. The sous-chefs and the *chefs de parties* at each station were in their element. As were we all. When you learn to work in a French restaurant, you submit to a militaristic organization. Even with a team of 150 workers, most of whom had not worked together before, the assignments were so well defined that we knew precisely what to do and how to behave.

On May 9 we opened to the public, and it was a great success, reported fully in the *Times* the next day: "Guests occupied every chair in the five semi-circular tiers of the handsome glass-walled retreat that overlooks the Lagoon of Nations. . . . Every gesture of the staff, from the august Jean Drouant, director of the establishment, down to the most unobtrusive waiter, signaled the pride of the employees in what was instantly signed, sealed and delivered to the Fair-going public as a retreat for epicures." I quote the paper because the truth is I got to see almost none of all that, toiling at the fish station, thrusting my pots this way and that. Occasionally, I got the chance to peek through the kitchen door, though, and it surely was a well-dressed, beautiful crowd that

night, awestruck when the fireworks show interrupted dinner, and
seemingly as appreciative of the food as any diners one could imagine.

The first-night menu was:

Double consommé de viveur
Paillettes dorées
Homard Pavillon de France (see recipe page 162)
Riz pilau
Noisettes de pré-salé ambassadrice
Chapon fin à la gelée d'estragon
Coeur de laitue princesse
Fraise sati
Frivolités parisiennes
Café

The chicken consommé, of course, was marvelously clear, having
been labored over for many hours, and it was served with cheese sticks.
The lobster Pavillon was really a lobster *américaine* to which we added
cream and gave it a new name. We took morsels of the lamb from the
saddle and served them with potato balls and stuffed artichokes. The
cold capon was encased in a tarragon aspic. Asparagus vinaigrette was
positioned on lettuce. Then came the strawberries and ice cream and
petits fours. Wine flowed all night long, a Sauternes, a red and then
champagne with dessert. Soulé had arranged for a toothpick holder to
be placed at each table, but toothpicks in such surroundings seemed
unfamiliar to our guests, and they were taken home as souvenirs.

The prices at the restaurant will seem quaintly low as I describe them
to you now, at least for so ambitious a kitchen. Actually they were moderate even for the times, lower than many of the prices in New York
hotels, for instance. The most expensive wine was the champagne at
$6.50 a bottle. The appetizers were mostly a dollar or less. Soup was
usually sixty to eighty cents. Salmon—*darne de saumon, sauce riche,* to
take one example—was $1.60. I know there were many complaints
about the high prices for food at the fair, but if those complaints were
addressed at us, I never heard them.

At first, we worked seven days a week, but soon it was only six.
Finally, there was time to relax. I took the bus to Far Rockaway for a
swim with some of the other men—by now I had a number of friends
other than my housemates—and managed to get the first sunburn of

my life. On another day, I met a sixteen-year-old girl near my rooming house. She smiled, I smiled, we went for walks together, but since she spoke no French and I had so little English, we communicated very poorly, with eyes and giggling and the like. I took her to the local candy store once, and she introduced me to ice-cream sodas in the form of the classic black and white, a treat.

Life away from the fair had Gallic flavor to it, as the mishap that befell the chef Marius Isnard will testify. Every married Frenchman, so far as I could tell, had a mistress somewhere if he was able to arrange for one. Isnard's was a good-looking married woman in her middle years who lived in a third-floor apartment not far from the fair. Her husband was a traveling man and often away, but this time he traveled home in the middle of the night unexpectedly. The mistress heard him, pushed Isnard out the window onto the fire escape and threw his clothes after him. We had no fire escapes in France, and Isnard, a dignified, big man, must have been very unfamiliar with this mode of egress and very ungainly out there. He made his way down the ladder half-naked, swung from the last rung and dropped to the ground. He broke his ankle and could not get up, until, as luck would have it, a friend who lived nearby spotted him crumpled there and assisted him to the hospital. Isnard never told us about this incident himself. But it created quite a commotion. First the boss was out for a while, and then he hobbled quite badly.

By September—as the fair neared its closing for the 1939 season, with our restaurant alone having served 136,261 customers—France, after so much worry and so much denial, had finally gone to war. A kind of sadness settled in: not only were we run-down, worn-out, in need of a rest, but I was ready to go home. The *Normandie* was already out of commission, scheduled to become a troop ship, and it would have been suicide now to try to cross the ocean on anything that looked French, given the way the Germans were patrolling the waters.

I booked passage on the Dutch ship *Statendam* of the Holland-America Line, a great ship even if it wasn't the *Normandie,* departing from Fifth Street in Hoboken, New Jersey, on October 6. There were similarities to the *Normandie* voyage, but they were mostly superficial. I met a girl again, a German returning to a nation that was now the enemy of mine, but, remember, my father had always warned me not to hate all Germans. Anyway, it was hard to hate this one. We talked, made out; we danced. But we were rather grim. As we docked in England on the way to Rotterdam, an armed seaplane flew overhead, swastikas painted on its sides, machine guns jutting from its wings. It was so sleek, and it roared with such great power. I recall how the girl and I looked up at it as we held hands, our grip tightening and moist with fear. We parted, permanently, in Rotterdam.

Holland, at least, was bright and alive. By the time I reached Belgium on the way to Paris, I had journeyed into darkness. In Brussels, in the evening, the lights were out everywhere; the shades were all drawn. I arrived in Paris at midnight, stayed at a friend's home for the night, visited the Drouant in the morning and then headed for Burgundy to see my parents. I was carrying those Heinz pickle pins and a newfangled vegetable peeler (one that had a blade that swiveled) as gifts. I had just been gone a few months, but I felt so much older. An incredible summer in America was behind me. Now a war was ahead of me.

In Le Pavillon

6

War

THIS, OF COURSE, was not to be the last time I saw Paris, as the song has it, or the last time I saw Burgundy. I would always be a Frenchman and travel home often. But these few months when I returned between the summers of the fairs of 1939 and 1940 were in fact a kind of shrouded valley between two wonderful peaks in my life, my youth in France and my stunningly different life as an adult in America. Had I only known how fine the days would be later—for all of us—I might have been less depressed. But these were terrible times in Paris and in the countryside, we were not yet physically damaged by the conflict, but our spirits were so low. Most of the young men were off to man the doomed Maginot Line, which was supposed to keep the Germans off our soil. (I was not scheduled to be drafted for another few months.) In the villages, it was mostly the older folks who had to carry on.

In St. Vinnemer my father was busy enough. In his official capacity he went about on a recruitment mission of his own, trying to find older people and women to work in the shops and elsewhere, people willing to fill in for the younger men who had gone off. But everything about him conveyed war worry. Hadn't he been in World War I, captured, interned and sickened, body and soul?

I tried to cheer people up a bit, but I can't remember anything working very well. My grandfather still resented me for stealing that damned pear in the bottle all those years before. My mother was distraught over the possibility that the war might take me. She had, after all, already lost Jacques.

Back at the Drouant in Paris the staff was depleted. Many of the cooks were off to war, sort of, cooking for generals mostly. They needed me in the restaurant that winter. I can't say I was miserable about heading back to Paris and leaving St. Vinnemer to its quiet sadness. At the restaurant, as a matter of fact, things were not all that bad for me. I was promoted, now premier commis at the fish station, just as I had been in New York. My salary went from nine hundred francs to one thousand per month. The man I worked for at the fish station was named Bourguignon, an amiable fat fellow who used to urge his cooks on by nudging them with his belly. He was a good cook himself, this Bourguignon, and I liked him a great deal.

My own chores now involved more responsibility than they did before, more skill. I wasn't sautéing the sole but doing more complicated things than before. In the morning I would begin the preparation for some of the great sauces of French tradition, a champagne sauce (see recipe page 226) or a *sauce vin blanc*. It was in the morning that I might make my reduction of wine and shallots and mushrooms and then add the fish velouté (fish broth, flour and butter). Without machines to come to one's aid, the sauce would be poured through a strong cheesecloth stretched over a kettle, and then to extract all of the flavor from the solids left behind, the cloth that had just strained most of the sauce would be rolled into a tight rope. Two people would grab opposite ends and twist, wringing the cloth dry over the kettle. (To this day, on a smaller scale, I still use this method for some quite different tasks. If I am pureeing vegetables—cauliflower, for instance—and want to be sure the puree is not too watery, I extract the water by rolling the cauliflower into a cheesecloth and twisting it.)

There was not as much work for us to do. Restaurant business, as you might imagine, was down everywhere. But the Drouant was a better place to dine than most, if you wanted to avoid that Death Valley feeling at some of the big dining rooms around the city. Because the Drouant had a collection of small rooms, it was possible to simply close off some and leave diners with the sense that the place was busy and they were not alone in their effort to continue a pursuit of the good life, what remained of it.

That charade would end soon for me. By January, I knew I would be going back to the fair for sure—or almost for sure; there was some question in our minds about whether it would open at all, as war in Europe would necessarily take away much of the luster. As it turned out, even the Drouant chef, the great Jules Petit, was going to get his chance to go along this time. He had obtained an official favor from the government that would allow him to leave Paris during the war and serve his country in New York. I cannot get too smug about this, since I was deferred from the draft to go, too. He and I talked a little about the experience, only a little, in that he still occupied such a position of respect that I was constrained from having any real conversation with him. I told him how hard we all worked at the fair and revealed what I could about the Americans, who, I must say, were still mostly unknown to me.

Petit was hoping to go to the fair as the executive chef, replacing Isnard, but he was in for a disappointment. The job he would get instead was that of a roving *chef de partie,* who would fill in for the others when they were off for one reason or another. He hadn't actually worked as a cook for so long that I think he was rusty. He wasn't all that spectacular as a cook once we did get to the fair, but I'll give him the benefit of the doubt.

We had to be ingenious to cross the Atlantic this time, in April 1940. There was no French Line now, so we took an American ship, the *Washington,* from a port in Genoa. Just as we made it out into the Atlantic, Italy decided to make war on France, bombing Burgundy. I would learn later, much later, that Tonnere was hit and people had died in a church. St. Vinnemer was never struck by a bomb and would simply live out the war in the ignominy of German occupation.

WHAT A DIFFERENCE a year made. When our group arrived in New York the novelty was gone, of course, and the war had done its damage to the American psyche. We had our French friends still. My buddy Jules, in fact, had never left, working at a restaurant on the West Side until he could get the chance to rejoin us at the fair. But the fair itself was a weary thing that summer. We continued to introduce Americans to French cuisine, Americans who had never had the chance to try it before, but the crowds were gone. The ships from abroad were not arriving; America itself was nervous, and the fair's billing as the World of Tomorrow seemed, to anyone who bothered to think about it, a cruel mockery in a time when tomorrow seemed so much in doubt.

When the fair drew to its tired close, I didn't know what to do. France, depending on the region, was either occupied outright or under the rule of the Vichy government. It may be a rationalization for staying away from the war as long as I could, but all this confusion left me completely ambivalent, a man of action with no decent plan. No gov-

ernment, officially, knew where I was. The French certainly had lost
track of me, even the consulate in Washington no longer had records
about me that were meaningful.

Then, in September, President Roosevelt signed into law an immi-
gration bill that would give any of us who wanted to stay the right to a
permanent visa. We just had to reenter the country according to some
appropriate ritual. So a group of us, including Soulé and Drouant, took
the train to Buffalo, New York, crossed over into Canada (accompanied
by a lawyer who would help us through this rigmarole) and then walked
back across the "peace bridge" into the United States. We each declared,
truthfully, that we had arranged employment in the United States. The
visas were ours. Drouant had already made plans to open a restaurant
in New York with Petit as his chef (Isnard was among those who chose
to go back to France) and Soulé as the maître d'. I was still a small fry,
really, not part of the planning committee, although I was scheduled to
join the new restaurant later, and needed a real job for the time being.
The Waldorf-Astoria agreed to employ me for the short term.

The Waldorf in those days was the king of the mountain, the greatest
New York hotel, with a restaurant even I couldn't believe, so large that
my first job, which was in a kitchen designated exclusively for the
preparation of banquets, was to slice two thousand lemons for the trout
meunière. This was going to be some strange experience for me. The
Waldorf was capable of serving—and often did—truly marvelous
French dishes, despite the staggering volume. But this restaurant also
put fruit—strawberries and grapefruit—in its salads. It struck me as so
strange and unappealing (California was a long way from making its
sensibilities popular in its own style of cooking, but even now I don't
exactly love that grapefruit in my salads). It wasn't long before I was
moved from the buffet section to the room-service kitchen, a separate
place where American breakfasts were prepared.

It turned out, to my amazement, that Americans were not satisfied
with a bit of jam and a roll on an ordinary morning, with maybe a croissant on special occasions. No, they ate all of these warmed-over grains:
oatmeal by the ton, and something called Wheatena. I had never seen
things like this before, and it would take me a while to stomach the idea,
much less the breakfast.

Even now, when I have come to enjoy so much that is in the American taste, I don't eat that gooey stuff for breakfast, although I can toler-

ate it well enough when I observe others who do. There was no instant oatmeal then—this substance had to cook for an hour and twenty minutes—and among my jobs was the tending of these great vats of the cereal, each in a bain-marie.

Overall charge of the room-service department at the Waldorf was given to a man from Dijon named Auguste Chardenet. We barely ever spoke, although we were destined to become much closer outside the Waldorf under circumstances I will relate before long. (It is funny to me now that whenever the old Waldorf cooks, the big shots, hold their reunions, I am always invited, my lowly station forgotten.)

You arrived at the Waldorf, worked for eight hours and then left for the day; none of this split-shift business, which managed to ruin the whole day. And the day off was regular and unchanging. So it was possible to escape from the oatmeal with predictability. What I and a few friends—including my old roommate Joseph Esnault, the baker—often did was take the train out to Hartsdale in Westchester County, where a friend ran an unlicensed inn (Prohibition was long gone, but, officially, this was still a speakeasy, where the liquor flowed illegally). The place was run by a former bootlegger named Alphonse Tordo, who had another establishment in Manhattan, too, no better licensed than this one. (Tordo's legacy is a Hartsdale restaurant that exists to this day bearing his name.) His wife, Margot, was the cook in Hartsdale.

There, we Frenchmen would play *pétanque,* the kind of lawn bowling that originated in Marseilles. When I wasn't playing the game or drinking wine and learning what news I could gather from my compatriots about the war back home, I was cooking. Here, miles and miles from the oatmeal vats, Margot allowed me the great joy of preparing *tripes à la mode de Caen,* rabbit *à la moutarde* and one kind of pâté or another. It kept my hand in and my mind alive.

And the gathering in the dining room was endlessly fascinating to me, America at its most raffish, all these colorful people showing up all the time once word got out about this illegal French place. Actors would come with their girlfriends, as would members of the Mafia. Some days it seemed like sex—or at least the promise of it—flowed like wine. Life wasn't that bad, actually.

But it changed abruptly on October 15, 1941, with the opening, finally, of Le Pavillon, at 5 East Fifty-fifth Street (where La Côte Basque is today). There were twenty of us, all from the fair. There was no exec-

utive chef initially but a tripartite rule in the kitchen with Cyrille
Christophe, Jean Douat and Emile Delorne each equally in charge of
the kitchen. I was put in overall charge of the fish station.

Soulé brought along some mementos from the fair, bottles of wonderful wine—he is credited with introducing the fabulous Bordeaux
Château Pétrus to the United States—and a collection of copper pots.
But these souvenirs do not even begin to signal how much Soulé really
was carrying. Just as he had brought France to Flushing, now he was
bringing the fair, almost intact, to Fifty-fifth Street. He brought members of the same staff, and he intended to serve virtually the same menu
in a place named to evoke the French Pavilion at the fair. Since this
restaurant could not be identical to the one in Flushing in looks, Soulé
designed it to closely resemble the plush Café de Paris, where he had
been employed in Paris. Nearly everything would be classic, from the
crystal glasses manufactured by Baccarat (so thin that the glass would
actually bend when you put pressure on it) to the red banquettes, the
flowers and the mirrors.

If the fair had a democratizing effect—exposing thousands of Americans to French haute cuisine for the first time—Le Pavillon would be
as elite as any great Paris establishment. It is true that New York already
had its French bistros on the West Side, but they were largely the haven
of the French in New York. The bistros, which had existed in the West
Forties since at least the turn of the century, were mostly the products
of Frenchmen who had come over to America on French luxury
ships—as cooks or waiters—and decided to stay. They opened their little establishments as exact replicas of the bistros they knew back home
and served what is now so familiar in America as "bistro food," a blend
of home-style cooking with restaurant expertise. In accordance with
French custom, a typical meal would start with a tray of hors d'oeuvres,
such as salads and pâtés, sardines and sausages, and then move on
through the soup—onion soup (see recipe page 147) was perhaps the
most popular—fish, meat and dessert. There might be accordion music
and dancing on the weekends.

These were very plain, wholesome places that reminded me precisely
of home. For one thing, French was spoken by all the service people and
even at the tables, since the bistros were a magnet for French tourists as
well as French residents in New York. Over the years, even though the
restaurants were often handed down from one generation to another,
most changed to accommodate fancier notions of what French food

should be and expectations about the French atmosphere: gone were the paper place mats, replaced by tablecloths—and the accordion music disappeared, too.

In any event, when I had arrived in 1939, there were not many Americans who knew anything about French food, much less haute cuisine. Soulé seemed to understand that once you gave Americans a chance to see what French food was really about, the word would spread and the craving would grow to make his new establishment the most alluring restaurant New York had ever seen.

It wasn't all Soulé's doing. Originally, the restaurant was Drouant's idea. It was he who arranged for French businessmen (and, some say, Joseph Kennedy) to bankroll the establishment. It was he and Soulé who picked out the spot—a defunct restaurant sitting empty and poised for another try—an ideal location on East Fifty-fifth Street, just off Fifth Avenue and across the street from the St. Regis Hotel, familiar surroundings for the wealthiest visitors to the city.

Drouant, at the last minute, decided that he missed France and his family too much and decided to return, leaving Soulé to embark on the enterprise on his own, with the help of the rest of us, the old World's Fair crew. And we soon created a sensation with Le Pavillon, with virtually none of the kind of public relations that is part of the promotional hoopla today. But opening night, a private gala did demonstrate Soulé's public relations acumen: he invited some of the richest, best-known people in New York—from the Vanderbilts to the Cabots, the Rockefellers to the Kennedys—and did not charge them a dime.

My adrenaline was pumping as the show got underway. But I was not intimidated or frightened. Psychologically, it was all very easy for me. I was assigned to the fish station, which I knew well, and there was no reason to fear a run-in with the overbearing Monsieur Soulé, who was always kind to me, if not to the others. (I think the reason I got along so well with some authority figures and not others was that if I greatly respected someone for his accomplishments and skill, then I was willing to put up with a great deal and earn his respect in return.) I was by now, although barely twenty years old, experienced in the way only a French cook from the old apprentice system could be. I had labored at every station in the restaurant kitchen, taking on the tough, muscular work like butchering as well as the artistry of sauce making. In actuality, I had mastered all the techniques and the rules of one particular kind of cuisine. If you had asked me about Chinese or Italian food I would have been lost (spaghetti, even, was still an alien food to me). Yet I could make a beurre blanc—the classic white butter sauce—blind-folded, sautéing the shallots, adding some acid such as wine or vinegar to infuse the shallots with richness of flavor and then whisking in the butter bit by bit until I had transformed these simple ingredients into a frothy, transcendental sauce. What might strike someone else as an elaborate undertaking—remember how daunting I once found that turbot stuffed with fish mousse?—I now saw as nearly routine. (This command of traditional French cuisine would liberate me in later years to modify and create, because I understood, the way a painter does, what had worked for centuries and could imagine how, in a very disci-plined way, to diverge from those classics.)

I was so at home in a traditional French kitchen that even on Le Pavillon's opening night, with all those chauffeur-driven customers arriving in their tuxedos and gowns, I can't recall any jitters. And my job was rather demanding right at the beginning. As I remember it, one of the dishes I prepared was a mousse of sole, one half with lobster sauce, the other half with champagne sauce, truffles in the center. I dec-orated the top of the mousse with a design, a musical staff, drawn in *glace de viande* (a reduction of stock that has had so much of its mois-ture removed that it is denser than a demiglace and actually rubbery. It generally was used to enrich a sauce, but it made a good drawing medium, too).

There were huge amounts of caviar, smoked salmon, a roasted fillet of beef in truffle sauce. The guests drank champagne, as well as the wine of the Château Pétrus. The guests, since they were handpicked by Soulé, were already familiar with the kind of performance we could put on. There were no concessions to "American taste": we were preparing dishes in the best way we knew how. The menu was in French, of course, and most of our educated and wealthy customers could work their way through it, with at least some comprehension, but if they did not understand a particular term, I am certain they would hide the fact for fear of seeming gauche. (Thank goodness, this sense of intimida-tion, real or imagined, is long gone.)

Soon the greatest celebrities in America showed up at our doorstep, the same sorts of people who had come to the opening for free, except now they were paying. They came with enormous reverence, as if arriv-ing at a temple. To be considered royalty in this setting one could be merely notably rich—or celebrated in other ways. There was genuine royalty (the Duchess of Windsor was a favorite). All through the war Charles Boyer was a regular. So was J. Edgar Hoover. Cole Porter used to have lunch at Le Pavillon all the time, except when he took ill. Then Soulé would send a whole chicken in the pot, beautifully presented, over to Porter's apartment at the Waldorf, where it would be carved by the songwriter's butler. If you needed an introduction to some or all of these people, all you had to do was tell the renowned organizer of socialites, Elsa Maxwell, and she would throw a party at Le Pavillon. They would all attend.

The more at home the celebrities could make themselves—the more familiar and routine they could make their visit to Pavillon—the more it proved that they were the great people they imagined themselves to be. Soulé capitalized on the celebrity trade, that is, he used them as bait to attract the other customers required to sustain so lavish an enterprise. He understood that, much more than was the case in France, Americans wished to view one another. So he arranged for the American nobility to be seated in a section toward the front, known, fittingly, as the *royale.* The rest of the dining room was rated in direct relationship to how well the customers could see the *royale,* feel close to it, as if they were almost a part of it. The section of the dining room that was next in desirability had no particular name—I always called it the regular part—and then there was an area off to the side called the *nouvelle salle* that offered virtually no view of the *royale.*

Soulé was unyielding in his assignment of seating. Once a grande dame to whom he took an immediate dislike arrived and, after being seated, requested another table. Soulé refused.

"That's your table," he said, indicating where she already sat.

"But I don't like this table," she insisted.

Soulé asked, in the most superior tone he could bring to bear, "Tell me, good woman, did you come to eat at Le Pavillon, or did you come to argue with Soulé?" He was impossible. He decided who was royalty for the *royale,* and that was that.

I did not get to see a whole lot of this, at least not before the war. My station was still not high enough to allow me easy access to the dining room. But the waiters were notorious gabbers, and they would come back to report on the doings in the dining room, often with considerable glee. We had a regular patron, for instance, Dr. Voronoff, who had gained worldwide fame for his technique of transplanting monkey glands into human beings to increase their virility. This monkey business was extraordinarily lucrative, and he dined at Le Pavillon regularly for years. The waiters got a great kick out of Voronoff; they said he looked like a monkey himself, with his exceptionally long fingers and slouching walk. They would laugh at him in the kitchen and imitate his walk for those of us who couldn't witness it ourselves.

If the upper crust was indispensable as an attraction for all the regular folks who also patronized the restaurant, they were paid back amply in ways other than preferred seating. For instance, the "royalty" was never expected to feel in any way limited by the menu for the day. All they had to do was order ahead. Whatever they desired would be obtained and cooked.

A typical special order might begin with beluga caviar, move on to a light consommé with truffles, a lobster soufflé, a roast fillet of beef smothered in truffles (see recipe page 200), with side dishes of *pommes anna* and braised lettuce with beets, assorted cheeses and an ice-cream bombe with fruit sauce. The meal was often accompanied by champagne to start and then a variety of wines. Those special orders were presented to the kitchen on pink slips that would line the walls for days before the customers arrived. This method of ordering got to be so popular that, as the years went on, I believe as many as one-third of our meals were ordered ahead.

There was another amenity for the favored few. Every day Soulé would arrange for certain specials (today, everyone does this, but it is a greatly watered-down version of the tradition that Soulé exercised so regally). The dishes might include a *côte d'agneau champvallon* (see recipe page 211), for instance, or a chicken *beauséjour* (see recipe page 190). Only Soulé could dispense the ten portions that were designated to be sold as his own specials. He would approach a favored customer and say, in his formal, assured way: "Countess, I have something very special for you."

Many times people would not even inquire as to what it was. They would just say "Fine." Other times they would ask for a description— and then they would take it. Almost no one ever refused Soulé. The remarkable thing was the great simplicity of these dishes, but, of course, they were prepared with enormous care, as was everything at Le Pavillon. A seemingly mundane breast of veal with tarragon sauce would be braised slowly for a long time, so that the fat melted away and the tendons became gelatinous and delicious. (In fact veal, in those days, was always cooked longer than it is in many restaurants today; I have never gotten used to the uncooked taste of rare veal.)

Soulé himself was highly appreciated by the customers and often feared by the staff. Now, when we revere authority less, we might laugh at his penguin-shaped body and his precious mannerisms. But then, no one did. He was surely a difficult man, yet a good deal of that difficulty was the product of his authoritarian approach to his work. He believed in rules. He believed in "never." Soulé never went into the kitchen during the hours when the service was in progress. His domain was the dining room. The chef ran the kitchen, although the chef was answerable to Soulé. If Soulé had a problem, he would summon the chef and wait for him at the top of the stairs to the kitchen, where he would berate him.

Soulé also believed in "always." He always wore a blue suit with a gray tie at lunch and always wore a tuxedo at dinner. His portly presence in the dining room was without question superior to that of any of the other people on the staff. He felt free to assign himself any job that seemed appropriate at the time: often you might see him standing at the elegant, Cristofle-designed carving cart, masterfully dividing up a striped bass at lunch, or he might even take an order, if you happened to be a really big deal. At all times, he paid attention to the work of his maître d'hôtel, Martin Décré, and would mumble directions to him: "Maître d' Martin, please place so and so at table such and such." He was in complete control of the dining room. If one of the captains had already begun to serve a particular table of dignitaries, Soulé would think nothing of literally thrusting the man aside, with a perfunctory announcement that he was taking over. There was no room for a captain to let his pride get in the way.

Soulé would always begin his work with a fanfare, raising both of his arms above his head and vibrating them the way a minstrel singer might, the ostensible intention being to get the sleeves of his tux down a bit and out of the way. But the most notable result was that as the tux sleeves slid, they revealed his magnificent gold cuff links. Oh, mishaps were possible, of course. Once he was carving a couple of pheasants and managed to knock both of them onto the floor. Imperiously and unperturbed, he told the waiter he was in need of two new pheasants. As certainly you will guess, it was the two old pheasants that emerged from the kitchen a few minutes later, brushed off and gussied up.

Some demanding people manage to alienate everyone around them. Soulé did not, even if there was no great love for him. But at least his rules were always clear, the dining room organized with breathtaking precision. Beneath Soulé's gaze, there toiled one captain for each three or four tables, and two waiters for each of those sections. The captain would take the orders and serve. One waiter would hover about the table, replacing water or rolls or whatever. Another was the runner who would hurry back and forth to the kitchen, not only to get the food but also to orchestrate the meal. It was the runner who might tell the cooks that the fillet of sole would be needed in two or three minutes so that we knew exactly how to allocate our time.

This was all highly skilled work. Back then, in the early 1940s, there were people like my friend Gaston Large, a waiter and proud to be one. In fact, Gaston told me often that he never wanted to be a captain. He felt born to be what he was, and he was, in fact, the best waiter I ever knew. If he, rather than the captain, was called on to carve, he would do it with tremendous grace. If he was asked to recommend a wine (we had no actual wine steward because Soulé disdained the uncertainties over tipping that adding a wine steward always brought), Gaston was also expert. He knew better than anybody exactly when the kitchen had to get that calf's liver cooking so it would arrive at the table on time; the kitchen could rely on his urgings.

Soulé's dining room was a model of precision and provided a daily tutorial in how a lavish establishment must serve its clientele. When I look back on it, I realize Le Pavillon was running a culinary university, training French cooks and dining room staff for service throughout America. Le Pavillon's influence would be so great that in 1954 the French government awarded Soulé the *chevalier de la Légion d'honneur,* the only French restaurateur in America ever to have received that recognition.

In uniform

7

Yes or No: The Army

AT TWENTY, having spent much of the past two years in North America, I still could not speak more than a few words of English. It was largely my own fault; I simply never made an effort to spend time with English-speaking people when I had free time away from work; and at work—whether it was at the Waldorf or at Le Pavillon— everyone in the kitchen spoke French. At least, however, I could read English reasonably well (the written language has always been easier for me than the spoken). In any case, there were so many foreigners in America who spoke English poorly or not at all—Italians, Asians, Germans—that I never felt particularly troubled by the shortcoming. I knew I could get along, even on the day I reported for induction into the U.S. Army at the examination center in Grand Central Station (in those days the train station had a separate area for expositions and the like, and it was here that the doctors peered and pawed to determine our health). Hundreds were there when I showed up, and when orders were barked I just did what everybody else did. I was resilient and willing enough. Strip naked? Fine. Bend over. What? Then I saw all these naked men bending over, and I got the message.

I found myself at the induction center, preparing to join the U.S. Army, not entirely by choice. The United States had forced me to make up my mind on just what I intended to do in this war. As an alien working legally in the United States, I had been sent a questionnaire inquiring whether I wished to join the U.S. Army. I could answer yes or no, but I decided to return the document without any answer at all. I truly did not know what I wanted to do, although I knew that the liberation of France, with Paris now occupied by the Germans and the nefarious Vichy government installed in unoccupied France, was on my mind all the time. True, de Gaulle had gone to England to form a resistance, but I was not especially enamored of de Gaulle in that he had always represented the right wing to me, and I had been raised in a Socialist family.

The sense of paralysis I felt about what the correct, the most effective, action to take might be was heightened by my deep concern for my family. I had not heard from them in many months, and since all communications between France and the United States had been virtually cut off, I could not reach them.

As it turned out, the American government would not accept my noncommital answer and asked again: yes or no. Well, I thought, at least the Americans seem to know what they are doing, and through this army, perhaps, I can participate somehow in the freeing of my own country. I answered yes. I understood very little about war or armies or what my role might be, but a kind of tranquillity settled over me now I had given my life over to the American military, and that was that. My behavior was more mechanical than fearful; I would simply allow events to take their course—as long as I got the chance to be in on the liberation of France.

There was no send-off back in New York; many others were leaving just as I was, and Le Pavillon was stoically going about the business of making do with the older staff until we returned. At Upton, it was the usual hurry-up-and-wait routine. Weeks went by, and I still had no idea about my future. Nothing was happening, and finally I did grow concerned. The one friend I made, a Swiss who had been a waiter at the fair, kept reassuring me, "Don't worry—when they decide, they'll call you." Meanwhile, others (without my knowledge) were making plans for me: Soulé had been making recommendations; rich patrons at the restaurant had been talking to the brass.

The waiting ended when I was summoned to the Pentagon in Washington. After finding my way through the endless corridors, I wound up in the office of a French-speaking officer. He said he had been told about my qualifications and mentioned a job offer that he thought would delight me. "General MacArthur in the Pacific needs a personal cook," he said. "We would like to send you."

The befuddled look on my face must have hinted that I had no idea who MacArthur was. Nor did I have any desire to go to the Orient, the opposite direction from France, my family and the liberation that was my only goal now. I thanked the officer for the offer, but declined it. "I know my rights," I said, "I'm not an American citizen yet." American law said that noncitizens could not be shipped abroad without their assent.

Legal technicalities held little sway with this fellow, however. He was simply incredulous when I held my ground. He kept me in Washington for two days and continued working on me, to no avail. From that moment on, I believe, the military had it in for me. I was promptly dispatched to cooks' and bakers' school at Fort McClellan, Alabama, to learn the inelegant task of chow preparation, as if I were a novice.

What that meant essentially was that I had to learn to hold my knife sharpener with a slightly different grip, that I had to accept the practice of mixing water and flour to enhance a sauce instead of cooking the flour with butter in a roux (this library-paste mixture the army insisted on using struck me as bizarre). I had to do what the staff sergeant, who liked to call me Frenchie and Frog, told me to do—and not show him up. But I did unavoidably embarrass him a few times (I carved faster than he did, even when I didn't want to), and he clearly resented me for it. I was happy even under such circumstances—glad to be in the infantry, glad to be preparing to serve on the American side, and especially thrilled to be awarded U.S. citizenship. I had joined thousands of other foreigners who were sworn in as citizens on the spot there in Alabama. But I was very lonely, too. You have to get the appropriate picture of Fort McClellan: there were seventy-five thousand men in the hot middle of nowhere—and no women.

At the time I happened to be infatuated with someone back in New York—Philome Ajas was her delightful name. She was very striking and more than ten years older than I. She had been running a shop in the city for some time and had taken it upon herself to look after me. At Fort McClellan, I determined that I needed some looking after. I called her and told her I was lonely. When she agreed to come to Alabama to see me, I was giddy. Immediately, I applied for a three-day pass, which seemed assured, and reserved a hotel room in Montgomery. It was the day before she arrived—she was already en route—when the hotshot staff sergeant came over to me while I was sharpening a knife in my own style. I liked to grip the sharpening steel with my thumb and fist wrapped around the handle rather than with my thumb placed on top of the handle, as the army prescribed. My method, I felt, allowed a firmer grip; the army's approach was supposed to be safer in that it kept your thumb out of the way in case the blade slipped. This thumb placement of mine was a transgression and occasioned a brief speech from the sergeant: "Now I know you've applied for a three-day pass," he said, "but I'm going to see to it that you don't get it—not because you are a Frenchman, but because you are a stubborn Frenchman."

I delivered a little speech of my own: "You can go to hell," I said, my frustration with this jerk finally getting the best of me, "you and the whole goddamned American army." Rebellion was in my heart. Without a pass, I met Philome at the train anyway and took her down to the Gulf of Mexico, to Mobile instead of Montgomery, where we stayed for a week, taking in the nightlife, going to the beach: definitively AWOL. The MPs were probably looking for me, but I had a lot of competition out there in the world of AWOLs. When I returned to camp, the MPs hauled me before the company commander, who must have sympathized with me at least a bit. I was never court-martialed or officially punished. Instead, in a shocking turn of events, my 060 designation, my cook status, was taken away.

"Fella," he said, "you have just flunked out of cook school and you're about to become a rifleman" (a machine gunner to be more precise). This was not as intimidating a sentence as it might have been for someone else; I had been around firearms most of my life; I was a good hunter, a good shot. I was promptly shipped off to England, where I joined an infantry division. In Britain and everywhere else I went afterward, I would always find myself cooking anyway as soon as the guys discovered that I had some skill in that area. I would do simple things to dress up K rations, garnishing them with chopped shallots, for instance, or mixing in fresh garlic. It was fun, really.

MAYBE I had fouled things up in the past—turning down the MacArthur job—but it had all worked out brilliantly. In my army career I did get the chance to join in the taking of Normandy, to come home.

One evening toward the end of the war, my division bivouacked just three miles from the village. I went to my commanding officer that evening and said, "Sir, my family lives just over that hill and I haven't seen them in five years. I must go see them." The commander resisted; Nazis still occupied much of the surrounding countryside, he said, and heading off now would be foolhardy. I could not accept that sort of answer; I was so near home, so concerned about my family for all this time, and I just could not be stopped now. I put it to him another way: "I haven't seen my family in five years; I'm going to see them with or

The flag my mother waved as St. Vinnemer was liberated. It now hangs in the den of my home in East Hampton, New York.

without permission." He relented and I was given permission to take his jeep, and his driver, too—"Don't let me see you do it," the officer said, "just take it."

I wanted to drive alone, but the driver would have none of that. I don't know, maybe he didn't trust me. Maybe he wanted to see France. Whatever, the two of us set off in the direction of St. Vinnemer, driving through areas only recently evacuated by the Germans. Excited citizens waved and called their friends. The Americans had arrived! Word preceded us as we drove on. Some of the villages were in bad shape, buildings destroyed; other villages were untouched. St. Vinnemer, as we moved slowly through the fields at the outskirts and then into the village, was obviously in excellent shape. We drove toward the old chestnut tree in the center of town. As the jeep came to a stop, I stood up—like Patton—and there were my parents. My father, the mayor (looking awfully gaunt), my mother, and my younger brother, Hugues, were waiting for the Americans they had heard were coming. My mother was waving a U.S. flag that she, like many Frenchwomen, had made herself. I don't know exactly when they realized who one of these liberators was. I was grinning beneath my crew cut. Suddenly my mother started to weep, and all hell broke loose. "It's Pierre," the people shouted. "Pierre!"

During my two-day return to St. Vinnemer, I visited relatives and ate simple, wholesome food—my family, always close to the soil, was even more so now, eating almost exclusively what they grew or raised. As warming as the food and the affection were, the talk turned to some of the most unhappy news I had received throughout the war. Now, sitting in my family home, with one family member or another taking turns in relating the horrors, I was to understand why my father, only in his early fifties, looked so frail.

This war, like the first world war, had treated him very badly. In his official capacity, this courageous mayor of St. Vinnemer had spent the early years of the war helping Jews escape to Spain, providing them with false, yet "official," papers that would help them travel from one village to another. The participation in the underground railroad continued until the police—Frenchmen loyal to the vanquishing Germans—came after him in the night. He tried to hide in the dark, but the police said they would take my mother and Hugue if he did not surrender. He did and was jailed in Paris, where they tortured him to get the names of others working with him. They shocked him with electricity and twice pretended to take him out to be shot, only to tell him they had changed their minds. So far as I know, he never yielded.

Now, with Paris liberated, and with it my father, he had come home. But he had lost a great deal of weight and contracted tuberculosis, which he refused to nurse. He was a stubborn man: instead of taking it easy he insisted on performing his mayoral duties, even carrying his official paperwork by motorcycle (he no longer had a car) to Auxerre, the capital of our regional department.

My visit ended too quickly. It was so very hard to leave my family now (my father, in fact, died two months later). But I had to head back to the division and join it as we marched through Belgium and Holland, the Germans fleeing before us. Just as we were saying farewell, my mother ran into her bedroom and came out with a going-away gift. She gave her homemade American flag, the one she was waving as I arrived, to the driver and thanked him for bringing back her son alive and freeing the village from the Germans.

Years later, my career as a chef and columnist well established, I received a phone call from a man in Michigan. He said he was curious because his hometown newspaper carried a cooking column by a Pierre Franey. He wanted to know if by any chance I was the same Pierre who was in the army in France. When I said yes, he replied, "Well, I have something for you." To my great joy, this man was the jeep driver who had brought me to my family thirty-five years before. He mailed a bundle to me. I opened it carefully. It was my mother's American flag. He had treasured it all those years, but now he wanted me to have it. I display it today, proudly, in my home. I pray that my children and grandchildren will hang it proudly, too, one day.

* * *

DURING the same period in France another of my escapades was recorded for the world. In Holland, at Venlo, I was going about one of the chores that regularly fell to me: everywhere we went there were wholly abandoned areas with vegetables growing or livestock roaming, and it was my job to scavenge for fresh food. It would be, to say the least, a welcome addition to those K rations and the C rations that would otherwise be our meals, and I must say my comrades in arms greatly appreciated a good roasted chicken, cooked in the oven of a wood-burning stove in some uninhabited farmhouse. It created a party, really, boisterous and full of camaraderie. In Venlo, I came upon a baby pig and decided to carry it back to the boys for a bit of a feast. There was a rickety baby carriage in the street, so I placed the pig in the carriage and pushed it back to our camp. Along the way, a *Stars and Stripes* photographer spotted me and snapped a shot that made the paper. It was a bit foolish, but funny, and I liked it, although I don't have the picture today.

Our victorious division was shipped back to the States, where we were told that, even though the bomb had already been dropped on Japan, we were still to be sent to Okinawa. It seemed unfair after all the time we had already spent in the field. And what took place then was a little-known mutiny in the military. The whole division refused to go to Okinawa. A general was sent from Washington to placate us, but he was shouted down. And the division was quietly, ruthlessly broken up. I found myself at a separation center in Indiana, where I waited for several weeks for a discharge—an honorable one, the military taking great pains not to let the world know about the defiance of orders among everyone in my group.

At the separation center, I was cooking again, even though I was not supposed to. I had run into another waiter from the World's Fair who knew of my talents and enlisted me to help with the big Saturday dinners at the officers' club. This turned out to be a full-time job, what with all the traveling around I had to do to find the sort of food the officers wanted—fillet of beef, rack of lamb, salmon, wine, fruit. When I was finally discharged, the officer checking me out of the army knew me as the soldier who worked on the Saturday dinners. He discharged me as an 060, cook.

With Henri Soulé

8

Soulé and Me

WHEN I RETURNED to New York after the war, I did everything I could to pretend it had never happened. It had been three years since I left, but the same furnished room I had lived in before was still available at 27 West Seventy-fifth Street, just off Central Park and not a bad walk to Le Pavillon on Fifty-fifth. So I had my old room, as well as my old walk to work, back. It was comforting.

At the restaurant I was welcomed warmly but also as if nothing had really transpired: I was immediately restored to my job as fish cook, and it seemed as though the kitchen staff had not changed at all (other young men were back, too, now). What had changed, and profoundly so, was that I felt immeasurably more certain of myself as a man, a grown-up. Oddly, although I had learned next to nothing about cooking in those previous three years, I felt more secure than ever in my work and less inclined to accept orders for their own sake.

This confidence would play an important role in the future of Le Pavillon and in my own career. It would help liberate me in the way I worked with others. I would be better prepared to lead instead of follow, more ready to experiment in my cooking. In the kitchen I returned to, I found a chef, Christophe, behaving like a dinosaur, begging for extinction. Even though the kitchen was still magnificent, we no longer had the kind of dining room help that we needed. In the old days if a waiter was a waiter for life, he might like it that way. He knew his craft. Now a waiter was just as likely to remain a waiter only until he got his next acting job. So the cooks had to do more with the food before it left the kitchen and not rely on fancy carving and serving at the table—an age-old performance art. Instead of a whole salmon in aspic, delicately portioned out at the table, a restaurant was more likely to send out, already plated, a picture-pretty cold salmon steak in a light vinaigrette, brightened by a sprinkling of fresh herbs. The new need for color to embellish these paintings in food caused the emergence of vegetable purees that had never amounted to much before. And to add a little excitement, cooks were starting to experiment with sauces; they might even divide two over a single dish.

It was so daring, it seemed at the time, to spoon out red wine sauce on one side of the plate and white wine sauce on the other (when searching for a design on the plate always arrange the components symmetrically; it never fails). Instead of sending a whole chicken breast out to the table, now it would be sliced and the slices arranged in a circle; the chicken could then be sauced and a waiter would merely carry it to the patron and set it down on the table. It was so easy for those waiters awaiting their next audition.

Not only would Christophe refuse to recognize the need for change, he had the habit of getting cranky on the issue, too, especially when he drank. This ordinarily sweet-tempered man evidently saw himself under attack. I believe he was under the impression that he was the only one being forced to change. Even in the most tranquil of times he never voyaged out of Le Pavillon to see what other restaurants were doing.

Christophe's whole life—like that of many a French chef before him—was the kitchen. He was isolated. So how was he to understand that elite kitchens were changing everywhere? And his kitchen was changing, too, while Christophe was drinking. He resisted the idea, for instance, of sending individual portions out to the table, but the circumstances forced him to do it. This might have been easier on him if he had ever talked to the customers; then he would have realized that even in the *royale* the new service was now what they wanted. They appreciated smaller portions—yes, even in the 1940s, before nouvelle cuisine and all the nutritional bullying we have been subjected to—and they were impressed by artistic presentation.

So Christophe would carry on in his rigid way, drinking and shouting at the waiters and other cooks. He would call them *monte-charge,* French for "dumbwaiter." He might as well have called them "my slave." He became a difficult man to work with, a hard man for Soulé to direct. Fortunately, I didn't have to put up with him much. Early on, I was made the night chef, meaning, among other things, that I was in charge of the cleanup at closing time. It wasn't too glamorous, but at least I had my own crew of dishwashers and floor sweepers to supervise. I also was in charge of the buffet part of the daily luncheon service. A couple of years passed in which Christophe and I kept our distance.

The buffet table was an island of independence. I could experiment as I liked, and one of my most successful creations was a cold crabmeat omelette. It grew out of a dish I had seen in France on what by now—a year or so after the war—was the start of my regular trips back in the summertime to see what the cooks there were up to. I had noticed somewhere that a chef had made several cold, flat omelettes and then stacked them, with some filling in between. Then the stack was cut into wedges like a birthday cake. I didn't do that, but the notion of serving cold omelettes appealed to me. I started filling individual omelettes with a chunk-crabmeat mayonnaise. It was a great success and also the kind of innovation that led Soulé to feel closer to me, as he recognized my desire to continue growing and to be someone who would help Le Pavillon move forward, too.

If he could no longer talk to Christophe, Soulé found that he at least had me, and I was not afraid of change at Le Pavillon. Christophe was never fired; he just faded. In the early 1950s his health, his drinking and his declining spirit all did him in. He retired. I wasn't told at once that I was taking over, but it simply happened that way. Whenever Christophe had been away previously, for a holiday or whatever, I was expected to step in. Now I did so permanently, as executive chef of the most renowned restaurant in America. I know that this is hard for people to accept, but I have such a practiced, well-honed sense of insouciance that comes into play at critical times in my life that taking over didn't faze me. Like so many things in life, this promotion grew out of such a natural evolution that, when it happened, it was almost as if there had been no real change. I just took over. I did, however, immediately modify many of our practices, especially improving communication between the kitchen and dining room.

Soulé and I, along with the maître d', Martin Décré, would meet regularly to discuss our plans for the day or for the week. There had never been anything resembling discussions before: Soulé would command, and, when he didn't, the kitchen would go its own way. Now every day at 12:15, I would tell Soulé what to expect: nice pike from Prince, the fishmonger at the Fulton Fish Market, or that I liked the calf's liver from Tingaud, the butcher down the street.

I might call Tingaud several times a day, as my needs changed, just as I would be ordering continually from the fruit vendor Ferraro on West

Fifty-fifth Street. Seen from my vantage point, a couple of these crosstown blocks in Manhattan amounted to a whole countryside full of supplies, a cornucopia in Midtown. One ritual Soulé and I enjoyed engaging in together was meeting the caviar merchant. At Le Pavillon, it was nothing for us to go through twenty pounds of beluga a week. We were such big customers for the caviar man that he would arrive with ten to twenty four-pound tins, open each with great deliberation, and we would taste from them one by one, selecting a few and rejecting others, which would be sold to someone else. Soulé himself ate caviar in prodigious quantities nearly every day with his champagne. He knew the good merchandise.

Soulé also knew how to pick a fight, and just when we were going so strong, he was, in his stubborn, self-destructive fashion, preparing to get into the argument of his life. It had more to do with real estate than food, but the effect on Le Pavillon would ultimately be irreversible.

The building that housed Le Pavillon changed hands several times, one of those changes turning out to be fateful. The Cohen brothers, who ran Columbia Pictures, also owned our building in the mid-1950s, which meant that we saw an even greater number of movie stars coming. But one of the Cohens demanded that Soulé start respecting the Cohen ownership of the building and begin allowing him to sit in the *royale* instead of all the way in the back. Soulé refused. As he related his tribulations to me, he said, "These are not beautiful people." I believe what he meant was that they were Jewish, and he concluded that they would not fit in with the likes of the Duchess of Windsor and Joseph Kennedy.

Soulé, by almost any definition, was an anti-Semite. In fact, the upper echelons of all New York in those days were blatantly anti-Semitic, no matter how great the contributions of the city's Jewish citizens; even the *New York Times* matrimonial pages managed not to report on the weddings of many prominent Jews, presumably because they were not among the beautiful people.

The Cohens, however, were not easily beaten on this issue. They warned Soulé that if he denied them a better table they would raise the rent. He still refused. They raised the rent from a nominal eighteen thousand dollars a year to a truly astonishing forty thousand dollars. Now Soulé had his back up, all right. He wouldn't pay and declared that he would close the restaurant, which he did, soon opening a new Pavil-

lon in the Ritz Towers building on Fifty-seventh Street, a few steps off Fifth Avenue.

In Central Park, on a break from Le Pavillon

The ambience was totally different, less inviting. Patrons had to climb a few steps to get into the din-ing room, a small inconvenience it would seem, but the women in heels and those more advanced in years never did like those steps. And, although there was still a section called the *royale*, where celebrities were seated, it was not situated so that members of the rest of society would find themselves passing through it on the way to a more plebeian section. Some of the fun was gone, and the restaurant also lost some of its intimacy. As for the rich, well, they were inconvenienced now: their limousines were not permitted to wait on such a main thoroughfare. Business fell off.

Meanwhile, Soulé announced to me: "Pierre, I have good news for you. We're opening a new restaurant back on Fifty-fifth Street." It was not just on Fifty-fifth Street; it was in the very same spot where the great original Pavillon had thrived. There, he opened La Côte Basque, paying the Cohens their forty thousand dollars to do it. It seemed to me that, incredibly, he believed he was the winner in all this. He had registered his displeasure by removing Le Pavillon from the premises, hadn't he? And he must have felt that was an extremely potent punishment to inflict on the landlord. On the other hand, he was an excellent busi-nessman, and he knew that the old Fifty-fifth Street address was per-haps the best in New York. Why waste it? Oh, well, Soulé was a strange

The château owned by the family of Auguste Chardenet at Maxilly sur Saone, near Dijon

and perverse man. The decor at La Côte Basque was changed to include landscape murals that depicted Soulé's home in southwestern France, his days in Biarritz. But otherwise it was pretty much like the old Pavillon (and if you visit it even today—my friend Jean-Jacques Rachou is the wonderful chef there now—it will give you an excellent idea of what the original restaurant was like). For my part, this two-restaurant operation was an exhausting proposition: I found myself racing from one restaurant to the other, in charge now of both kitchens.

RUNNING the two kitchens was a wearing routine. If I had not fully appreciated before how much life a cook must give up to work these crazy hours, now I certainly did. It was undeniably hard on me and extremely difficult for my wife, who had by now already become one of the pillars of my life. Betty and I had met in 1947 when I was on the first of my regular summer pilgrimages to France—dropping in on the great chefs like Fernand Point at La Pyramide in Vienne and Alexandre Dumaine at Côte d'Or in Saulieu.

Her name was Betty Chardenet, a French-American. She was adorable, auburn-haired and, then as now, very shapely. I was setting off for Cherbourg by train to meet up with the ocean liner that would transport me back to America, and so were she and her family. They had spent the summer at the family château in Burgundy near Dijon, a

Betty and I at our wedding,
June 6, 1948

place that had once been lost to the family but then was repurchased when her father did well in the stock market in the 1920s.

Auguste Chardenet, the room-service manager at the Waldorf, was once my boss, in the days when I was making vats of cereal for the hotel's guests. Then he had little time for me, no more than a greeting or two passing between us. Now, at the railroad station before boarding the train to Cherbourg, I ran into Betty's cousin, an acquaintance from New York, and she introduced me to Betty. When I was brought to meet her father, the grand Auguste, it was as if we were old friends. He was so pleased to see me. The reason, I slowly deduced later, was Betty's engagement to an American back in New York, which did not make her parents happy. And so here I was, a young, available Frenchman cruising into view. If this sense of welcome needed any underlining, it came when Betty and I went to a movie and found ourselves sharing a few timid intimacies as the lights came up. Just a couple of rows behind us I spotted Mr. and Mrs. Chardenet, grinning. They approved, all right.

By the time we got back to New York, I felt comfortable enough to ask her out, even knowing she was engaged. It wasn't long, a matter of

*Our first home, in Valley
Stream, Long Island*

days or weeks, before she told me the engagement had been broken. And it wasn't long after that before I asked her to marry me, although we didn't actually do so until several months later, June 6, 1948, when our first house—in Valley Stream, Long Island—was completed.

The wedding at Betty's parents' home in Lynbrook, near Valley Stream, had about it the aura of royal families joining forces, in this case the Waldorf and Le Pavillon. Auguste Chardenet brought all sorts of foods, from smoked salmon to cakes. At Le Pavillon, I cooked in preparation for my own wedding (it has always been one of my life's blessings that the same activities I do for a living I also find so pleasurable). In particular, I remember the roast fillet of beef with truffles. But there were also braised endives, puree of celery root, cheeses such as Brie, Roquefort and *époisse* and salads and caviar. There was chocolate and strawberry mousse.

All the wines were from Burgundy. And like Burgundy, my Betty would be a stabilizing influence for me in the decades to come. She was with me while my relationship with Le Pavillon grew and also while a friendship, with the journalist Craig Claiborne, carried me in a direction I had never imagined. And she was with me when first one and then the other faded.

She made sure that my relationship with my children would flourish, no matter how busy I might be at Le Pavillon. Our daughters, Claudia and Diane, were born in the early 1950s, when Le Pavillon was in its glory. I could not see much of them early on, working such long hours six days a week. But Betty used to drive into the city with them during the two hours I had free in the afternoon, just so I could be with them,

*Betty and I with our daugh-
ters, Diane and Claudia*

just so they could be sure they had a father. It was a strain, but it
worked, and my family enriched my life immeasurably.

In 1958, someone else arrived in my life and changed it forever, too.
Craig Claiborne, thirty-seven years old, had been hired by the *New York
Times*. A reporter who learned cooking at the school for cuisine of the
Swiss Hotelkeepers Association in Lausanne, Switzerland, Craig
seemed to many who met him to be almost the perfect Southerner,
droll and smart, shy and haughty, by turns. He was the sort of young
man who was capable of standing on the margin of a gathering and
yet quietly dominating it at the same time. He was troubled by self-
doubt but that anxiety was rarely seen by anybody who didn't know
him well. In his quiet, almost-retiring way, he was to become an inspiration to journalists, home cooks and to people eating out. He would
compile a recipe book, *The New York Times Cookbook,* that would
become one of the best-selling of all time. He developed a restaurant-
reviewing style—elegant and authoritative—that would position him
to take on the sort of role that used to be reserved for theater and book
critics. He could, literally, make a restaurant overnight, so reliable and
important did people deem his reviews.

This courtly young man, smiling shyly and eager to learn, came to
interview Soulé and ended up writing a piece that said a great deal
about me, published in the *Times* on April 13, 1959.

After that, Le Pavillon became Craig's postgraduate cooking school.
He started coming by to visit about once a week just to watch us cook.
Before Craig could become pivotal in my life, I had to leave Le Pavillon
and Soulé, something I did in a celebrated case, covered by Craig for the

Times. It was March 3, 1960, and the *Times*'s headline at the top of page 31 said: "Le Pavillon Shut in a Gallic Pique." The pique was mine. Another headline, running over the pictures of Soulé and me next to the article said, "Restaurant Men Simmer, and Menu Goes to Pot."

The paper was having a lot of fun with us. But as casual as I tried to seem about this, it was one of the grimmest, most gut-wrenching events of my life. I had worked for and with Soulé for more than twenty years, and now our relationship was shattering.

In that year, 1960, the restaurant business was in a lull throughout the city, and Soulé was squeezing Le Pavillon for every economy in staff that he could find. Soulé had asked me to reduce the amount of time the kitchen staff worked. He wanted them to work thirty-five hours each, the union minimum, instead of forty. I know it sounds relatively unimportant, but I had already cut down considerably in the costs of running the restaurant and felt that Soulé's proposed additional cuts would finally reach bone. I did not want to alienate the staff further— they needed their overtime, and we were already losing too many good people. Also, whether I was right or wrong, I felt one more cut was going to do us in with regard to the quality of service we could provide.

I said to Soulé, "This time you have cut me, too." That was on February 16. And I walked out. Others followed me, and two weeks later he had to close the restaurant temporarily. "From the beginning," he told Craig, "Pierre, or Pierrot, as I called him, was like my son." Be that as it may, I did not intend to return and never did. Soulé reopened, and the restaurant, I concede, did well enough—until Soulé's death in 1966 of a heart attack in the men's room at La Côte Basque. (Craig, in a formal appreciation in the *Times*, called him "the Michelangelo, the Mozart and the Leonardo of the French restaurant in America.")

I never spoke with Soulé after we broke up, which caused me great pain. After all, two men who had spent much of their professional lives together should have come to an accommodation no matter what. But that just was not in his character. I vividly remember walking along Fifth Avenue shortly before he died. At a distance I saw the stocky, determined-looking Soulé marching in my direction.

"Mr. Soulé!" I shouted as he approached. I know he heard me, but he kept his eyes fixed on the sidewalk. "Mr. Soulé!" I called again. No response. Now he had me furious. I walked alongside him for a block,

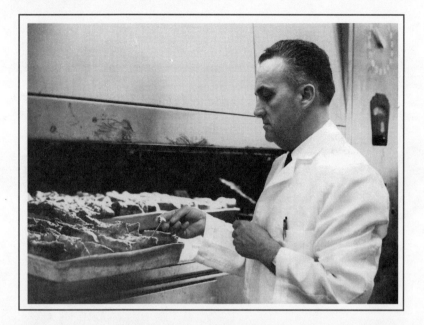

demanding, "Mr. Soulé, look at me! Look at me! It's Pierre!" He did not. It was one more loss of a stubborn friend (I am thinking of my difficult grandfather now) whom I could never recover.

Cooking in a test kitchen at Howard Johnson's

On the rebound from Le Pavillon, I took a job as a vice president of Howard Johnson's. Howard Johnson, Sr., had gotten to know me at Le Pavillon and had even tried, unsuccessfully, to bring the feud between Soulé and me to an amicable end. So he said, "Come to work for us—do nothing for six months but look around; if you're not happy, leave." It was a fabulous invitation, especially given my state of mind at the time. The hours were nine to five, with weekends off! It meant I would get the chance to learn to ski with my daughters and be close to my son, Jacques, as he grew.

I traveled around America, really getting to know it as a HoJo emissary, while inspecting and upgrading many of the operations. I know that many people now, especially at this time when the restaurant chef seems to have such a glamorous life, will see this work as, somehow, a comedown, a mortification after those vibrant years at Le Pavillon. But for me it was not; for me, it was a chance to live a normal life and at the same time take on challenges of scale that few cooks can ever imagine.

Howard Johnson, Sr., wanted me to revamp everything—test all the

With Craig Claiborne, cooking together on the set of a television show

recipes, change the ones that I didn't like—and in test kitchens around the country that is exactly what I and a handpicked group of cooks that came with me from Le Pavillon did. We decided not to change the ice cream because it was too good and too popular, and we left alone the clam chowder, another favorite, but everything else was under assault. It was a French-cooking approach to be sure; one of my most trusted aides was Jacques Pépin, the now-renowned chef and cookbook author, who worked with me at Le Pavillon and then, for ten years, at Howard Johnson's. He was in charge of the test kitchen in Queens Village, New York. At the request of Howard Johnson, Sr., I lured Albert Kumin, the great pastry chef who would later serve the White House, away from the Four Seasons.

This stellar crew would take on projects like the revamping of the restaurant chain's chicken potpie. The key to everything we did was to try to bring true cooking to great scale. We discarded the condensed bouillon and the precooked chicken that the chain had been ordering from elsewhere and started from scratch, cooking two thousand pounds of chicken a day, preparing our own stock with real vegetables, thickening it with real butter-and-flour roux (no margarine anymore), just as if we were at Le Pavillon but had been told thousands of people were arriving for lunch. The only thing is that now we had to freeze these dishes and send them off around the country.

It was my job to travel from restaurant to restaurant to be sure the work done in the main kitchens around the United States was not being wasted through shoddy treatment. The idea was not to cook the dishes in great batches and let them sit around, as had been the practice, but rather to thaw them out under refrigeration and finish the assembly of the dish as needed.

To assemble the chicken potpie, for example, one of the major commissaries around the country would send the cooked, frozen fillings, in precise portions, to each restaurant. The ingredients would have to be thawed and kept under refrigeration until needed, when they would be put in a saucepan, brought to a rolling boil and poured into the crust (Albert Kumin's dough, which would be baked ahead of time at each restaurant). All of this was intended, of course, to execute my plan to approximate closely real cooking, even in the commissary-supplied, portion-controlled world of a restaurant chain. I intended to see my instructions on the various procedures followed precisely. My great friend Jean-Jacques Paimblanc was my principal aide in Boston. I know, from what he has told me and others, that I managed to take on a certain fearsome aura during those days. If the restaurants knew, or even suspected, that I was coming to town, they made sure no flaws were showing. All this attention to detail, it turns out, was no more expensive than paying middlemen to provide those precooked ingredients to the chain. Howard Johnson, Sr., told me often how pleased he was—he felt, and I agreed, that we were influencing the American palate all across the country—and he placed no specific restrictions on my time.

So I STILL had plenty of time left over to pal around with Craig. By now, he was using me as a sort of silent partner in his restaurant reviewing. We would go from place to place, making our judgments. We would cook together to prepare the dishes for his weekly food story. And we would cook together to prepare for his glamorous parties. Increasingly, as a matter of routine, Craig would invite somebody remarkable—the fashion designer Pauline Trigère comes to mind— over to his small Manhattan apartment for dinner (and later, after he moved, to his home in East Hampton).

I would cook; he would figure out how to get a newspaper story out of the evening's activities. I did most of this for the fun of it. For all of my working life I had been confined to one kitchen or another. But here I was suddenly getting to see an entirely different world.

Betty and I had acquired a summerhouse at East Hampton some years earlier (during a period when Soulé opened an ill-fated, summer-time-only restaurant, called the Hedges, that had me running back and forth from East Hampton to New York City and left me with an ulcer that I have to coddle to this day). Then we bought a second house there for year-round living, so we could reside on the beach in the summer and inland in the winter. This complete move to East Hampton made it difficult for me to work with Craig at his Manhattan apartment. When we took him to a party on Shelter Island, a similarly beautiful area used by many New Yorkers as a summer retreat, he decided that he wanted to live in just such a place, too. We would be close. We could still work together.

Betty told him she knew of a piece of property in East Hampton that was everything he could desire. That night we ferried back to East Hampton and took Craig to the site. He saw it first at midnight. It's true; it was perfect, lacking only a house. Craig's house was built in just a matter of months. The kitchen was spacious, professional. And it was there that we would create most of our recipes in the late 1960s and early 1970s.

Craig and I never talked about how we would go about doing this recipe business. But we were natural partners. I was orderly and so was he. Our tastes in cooking merged. He might have in mind what to cook, or he would leave it to me. On a given morning I might not even know what we would be cooking that day; I let the day's shopping govern the work we would do with whatever was available.

If I liked the shad I saw, I might pick it up and then decide how to prepare it. Perhaps there would be some good cherry tomatoes in my garden. Maybe I would think of making shad and roe garnished with those tomatoes—the tomatoes briefly sautéed with garlic—and I would call it Provençale, since garlic and tomatoes are among the signatures of Provence.

I would line up my ingredients in Craig's kitchen: the shad, its roe, salt and pepper, milk and flour for dredging, oil and butter for cooking, those tomatoes, some garlic and, of course, the parsley that I can't resist under most circumstances, but wouldn't even try to resist for some-thing I was about to call Provençale. I would start to cook things in the logical way, heating the skillet, cooking the fish, setting it aside while preparing the tomatoes and so on. As I would proceed, Craig would sit at a typewriter set up in the kitchen. I would call out weights and measures: "It's a quarter cup of milk . . . eight tomatoes, no better make it ten."

Whenever I cook, I rely on certain axioms. One is that creating a dish is like writing music in that you want the various elements to blend into one statement, not all trumpets or all drums, but one harmonious expression of your intention. Think about that garlic-and-tomato combination. It became classic because of the way the two merge into one and then together join yet another element, the fish, in that case, to create a third, wholly new flavor. I also believe in tasting and smelling food continuously as I cook. To get the aroma I lean over the pot and wave my hands to brush the bouquet toward me. I swear I can smell the lack of salt. Also, I always taste with my fingers, dipping them into a sauce or other hot liquid. Not that everyone should do it, but for me a taste of food on a metal spoon takes a second to register completely in my mind, whereas from the fingertip it seems to take no actual time.

Part of our job, of course, was to broaden the culinary awareness of Craig's readers, introduce them to dishes they may never have known about before. Tripe has never been an especially popular food in America, but we were undaunted by the revulsion some people might feel toward it and offered a recipe for tripe lyonnaise, for instance, a rather simple and straightforward dish—the "lyonnaise" referring, as it often does, to the use of sautéed onions. All we did here was simmer the tripe for five hours (remember how I said protein needs to cook long or short—tripe is one of the extreme examples, requiring incredibly long tenderization). Once the tripe is fully tender, it is cut into pieces and sautéed briefly with the onions and garlic.

ONE OF those more unfamiliar dishes (to Americans), *tête de veau,* a traditional peasant dish employing most of the meat in and around a calf's head, led to a truly bizarre episode during our time together in East Hampton.

We were at Craig's home overlooking Gardiners Bay. It is in a stunning setting; from his house you can see Orient Point at the end of Long Island's North Fork, and you can see Connecticut, Gardiners Island and the ocean beyond. But I can't tell you I was impressed by the scenery when four calves' heads arrived from Provimi, a provisioner. The heads were not cleaned, and that very difficult, time-consuming chore still had to be done. I, as you might imagine, am not squeamish about these things, but I did not have the patience or time to remove all the fur from the heads. I was furious. I turned to my son, Jacques, who for some years by then had been serving quietly as a helper in our kitchen, and I told him: "Take these things and feed them to the seagulls." I don't know what I meant exactly. Maybe I meant for him to just throw them away. Maybe I meant that he should actually hurl them into the bay. Anyway, he did the latter.

Some days later strollers on a nearby beach stumbled on a calf's head here and a calf's head there. They were frightened and mystified. They told the police. The local paper learned about the heads. Speculation was rife. Were these the gruesome evidence of experiments into hoof-and-mouth disease at the quarantined government installation on nearby Plum Island? Were they the grisly refuse of one of the Russian boats lurking on the horizon? Did some careless ocean freighter deposit them in the sea when the tides were wrong? Had some satanic, animal-sacrificing cult invaded tranquil East Hampton?

The mystery was solved by a retired butcher who lived in town. He knew enough to note the registration numbers on the tagged ears, and he inquired at the U.S. Department of Agriculture. The heads, he learned, had come from Provimi. And Provimi told him they had been sold to us.

Fortunately, we had by now achieved the status of local celebrities and were granted the right to be eccentric. Instead of throwing us into the East Hampton jail for defacing the area, everyone who heard of the episode, generously, took it as funny.

Often, when Craig and I cooked, we were not alone. The practice of drawing guests into the job and turning it into an event had grown into a kind of social institution. Friends from East Hampton and surrounding towns, as well as visitors from elsewhere in the United States and abroad, flocked to Craig's house to join us. I cannot describe here everyone who joined us; it would be like trying to name all the stars in the sky. But a few of them stand out particularly well in my mind.

Diana Kennedy, the reigning expert in Mexican cuisine (she was married to Paul Kennedy, a longtime Mexico City correspondent for the *Times*), visited and brought with her an introduction to her kind of cooking that has stayed with me for years—after all, how would I, given my background, ever have had the chance to make tacos? Diana is a vivacious and amusing woman. Craig always liked to tell the story of how Diana's fruitless search in the United States for epazote, the Mexican herb, came to a remarkable conclusion when, while jogging in Riverside Park in New York City, she found it growing wild at her feet.

Another cook who has had an invaluable influence in broadening the taste and skill of Americans is Marcella Hazan, certainly one of the finest Italian cooks I ever met. In Craig's kitchen she would expound on how one species of sauce, the thicker kind, with bits of meat and vegetables in it, usually required a pasta whose shape (perhaps spirals or holes) would hold the lumpy sauce, whereas thinner sauces, generally speaking, were better suited for thinner pastas, like spaghetti.

When you see a Chinese influence in the cooking Craig and I did then and that I do now, a good deal of the credit goes to another guest, Virginia Lee. She was born in Shanghai but practically set up house at Craig's place for two years, when the two of them collaborated on a fine book of Chinese recipes.

The world's most renowned chefs were there, too, like Jean Troisgros, who, I am certain, had arrived with doubts about the quality of the produce we had available compared with what he might find in France. He went off to a local shop in search of striped bass and found a marvelous specimen, declaring it so after inspecting its gills and eyes with all the care of a specialist in internal medicine. But what he did that was most surprising was to serve salad—greens tossed with herbs, truffles and sautéed chicken—as a first course (this was at a time when Craig was eager to let Americans know that salad first was terribly unsophisticated; well, in this case it wasn't). When Paul Bocuse, another French chef of enormous stature, arrived, he was assisted not only by me but Jacques Pépin as well, and together we prepared a lobster navarin, baked lobster with vegetables (the vegetables were cut in the traditional French style, called *batonnets,* which these days I tend to describe in my recipes as matchstick shaped; the method is time-consuming but especially attractive, I think). All of these recipes were destined for publication after our labors.

My friends from the old days in New York came by regularly. Jean Vergnes, the founding chef of Manhattan's celebrated Le Cirque and a great buddy of long-standing, brought his ebullience to Craig's house. And I met the artist Ed Giobbi, a gifted cook in the Italian country fashion, for the first time through Craig; he, too, would bestow on me a deep friendship that lasts to this day.

Jean and Ed would go on to join in a momentous creation in American cooking: *pasta primavera*. When Jean and his partner at Le Cirque, Sirio Maccioni, decided the restaurant—French though it was—would need to diverge from its expected menu with one pasta dish, they went to Ed for inspiration. Ed told them about something called *pasta primavera*, which was a much less involved dish as he knew it from Italy than the one we are so familiar with now. It was pasta with an uncooked sauce of tomatoes, garlic, basil and parsley. Jean put something close to that on the menu at Le Cirque. But soon he was embellishing it—with pine nuts, vegetables, cheese—the whole thing blooming and proliferating like the springtime it is named for, but all starting with the seed of Ed's dedication to freshness and pure flavor.

We had great fun at Craig's place, and it seemed like it would never end. Beyond the vitality all these chefs brought to these cooking parties, they helped lend verve and newness to the stories Craig would write. And many of the participants gained in reputation as well from being with us, because Craig by now was such a widely known personality himself, virtually anointing cooks with additional greatness in the minds of his readers. It is true, for instance, that Bocuse was one of the reigning princes of French cooking already—but that was in France; now he was becoming famous here, too. And the career of Giobbi, who went on to become a wonderful cookbook writer as well as an artist, was altered profoundly. Through her partnership with Craig, Virginia Lee gained widespread renown.

But for Craig and me, the good times were going to have to wind down. I was getting worn-out. I felt the need to cut back on the seven-day cooking weeks, which is what they had now become. I wanted to spend more time with my family in leisure activities, and to go fishing and hunting. My children needed me more, I felt. So I told Craig I wasn't going to work weekends anymore—the family days in this country—and that I really meant it, although I would still certainly work with him on other days.

This decision diminished much of the entertaining, as I knew it might. But once more in my life, I had that stubborn feeling. I was not going to yield now any more than I would when the army wanted to send me to Asia to be MacArthur's chef, or any more than I would agree to cut the staff beyond what I already had done at Le Pavillon. I wasn't going to yield. I knew what was right.

Craig was angry and felt betrayed. I can understand that. But he did not just turn on me, he turned on Betty, too. He believed, evidently, that she was making me stay home more, as if I couldn't make up my own mind about things like this. One night, at one of those parties, when Craig had been drinking quite a bit, he told her off, crudely.

Talk about Gallic pique. I was piqued now, as piqued as I could be. For the most part, we thereupon went our separate ways, Craig and I, in the late 1970s. It happened gradually but definitely. We still saw each other often, and in fact I think about him all the time, even now. At formal functions—weddings, birthdays, tributes—we would join each other, and be genuinely cordial, honoring the warmth of the past. But sometimes, he would see me sitting on the jitney to Manhattan, say hello in a friendly way and then move down the aisle to sit elsewhere. Just as surely as the doors of Le Pavillon closed for good, our relationship, Craig's and mine, had diminished forever, although we never told each other so.

With Jacques and Betty

9

My Own Column

OF ALL THE WONDERFUL THINGS Craig helped me accomplish in my life I sometimes wonder whether introducing me to Arthur Gelb wasn't among the most important. It was through the association with Arthur that I got my column in the *New York Times.*

Arthur is a hard man to describe. He is very tall, rangy, and he wears his enthusiasm on his sleeve. Back in the mid-1970s, before Craig and I began to split, Gelb was supervising the start-up of the new "Living" section in the *Times.* He was determined to woo Craig back (Craig and I briefly had gone off on our own to publish a food newsletter, a financial fiasco), and Craig told him that he wouldn't come back unless I was hired—not as a kind of silent partner, but as a full-time employee of the paper. It fell to Arthur to figure out just how I would contribute. As it happened, Arthur and his wife, Barbara, often spent time with me in East Hampton; they both like to fish. And after fishing, regardless of our success, it was my habit to cook our dinner based on some last-minute inspiration, maybe flounder in a white butter sauce, or a quick fish chowder (see recipe page 148), or pork chops with capers if we had an unsuccessful day angling.

This, I think, never failed to impress the Gelbs, who, like everybody else, must have expected professional chefs to carry on at great length and make a big to-do over each meal. But at home I want to cook most things fast. And when you have been at this business for as long as I have, you learn the dishes that will cook the fastest with the least fuss. That means eliminating elaborate sauces in favor of the simple deglazed ones I have already described, and leaning heavily on fresh herbs, which can dress up and give nuance to the simplest dish. It also means turning to fish frequently, because seafood, in general, cooks faster than any other protein. The key to simple, fast cooking is magnificent, fresh ingredients whose flavors can virtually stand on their own without a cook's intervention. And, at my house, I do have my garden on one side and the sea on the other (although by saying that I do not mean to diminish the fine produce obtainable elsewhere).

It was Arthur who eventually persuaded me to become a newspaper columnist. He came to my house one day ostensibly to go fishing with me on my boat. Once we were out there on the bay, I quickly figured out that the boat would not be returning to shore until I had agreed to join the staff of the *Times*. Barbara already had an idea for the column's name: "The 60-Minute Gourmet."

I had two objections. One, I was not a writer. Don't worry, Arthur assured me, I would do the cooking and Craig would help with the words, just as I had been helping Craig with the food all these years. I said OK, but the name—"Gourmet"—was too pretentious. Why not simply "The 60-Minute Chef"? Arthur was adamant. "Gourmet" had the right feel to him, and that's what it was going to be.

The first "60-Minute Gourmet" was a shrimp dish; I was playing it safe, since the cooking takes less than five minutes, and the rest would be relatively simple preparation. But I knew it had to be unusual if people were going to notice. So I made something called *crevettes "margarita."* These were still the days when recipes in the *Times* were freighted with their French name first, so we were trapped into the French for "shrimp," followed by a Spanish name for a drink, and under the name was the simpler title: shrimp with tequila (see recipe page 175). "With inventiveness and a little planning," the introduction to this first column said, "there is no reason why a working wife, a bachelor, or a husband who likes to cook cannot prepare an elegant meal in under an hour." Indeed. The *crevettes "margarita"* were practically instantaneous in their preparation.

So we got through one recipe, then another and another, and even when Craig and I split, I kept it up for many years, working with the new young restaurant critic Bryan Miller. Those recipes made it into one and then another book bearing the column's name. An efficient and speedy approach to cooking is now my hallmark, and I have employed it in all the public television shows that I have done, including the series called "Cuisine Rapide," of course, and the later one called "Pierre Franey's Cooking in America." I may have been teaching others to cook with a dedication to streamlining, but the effort has taught me, too, forced me continually to adjust my repertoire.

Over the last twenty years or so I have had the good fortune to produce more than a dozen books with Craig and others, including two compilations of my "60-Minute Gourmet" column. Through the book titles one can see how my, and America's, tastes have evolved since the early 1970s. The 60-Minute books struck a chord for ease and simplicity, while *Craig Claiborne's Gourmet Diet* heralded the health revolution in cooking. Then came my *Low-Calorie Gourmet,* which was in part prompted by letters from *New York Times* readers who wanted to reduce fat and cholesterol in their everyday cooking.

My theory in low-calorie cooking is not to prepare dietetic food but rather to rely on the same principles that guide me when I cook dishes in the traditional fashion—just employing little tricks to cut down on the fat. If I wish to make three-fourths cup of vinaigrette, for example, I whisk together the usual ingredients, mustard, vinegar and oil—but it is diluted with three tablespoons of water. Of course, the axiom is that oil and water do not mix, but here, with the mustard as a binding agent, and good vigorous whisking to create a thick emulsion, this reduced-oil dressing works beautifully.

The "60-Minute Gourmet" meant that the light deglazed sauces would become even more prominent than before, and even lighter. Say you have just sautéed chicken breasts and would like to create a quick sauce for them. What I do is remove the cooked breasts from the pan, pour off all the fat, and add some chicken stock, scraping the pan's bottom to dissolve the flavor-packed particles that cling there. Then I reduce the stock by half or more so it intensifies in flavor, and swirl in a small amount of butter—a teaspoon or two for four portions is sufficient to bind the reduction and add a little flavor. It is critical to remember to add the butter when the pan is off the heat.

I also began to thicken sauces and soups with vegetable purees. I wrote a story in the *Times* in the early 1980s with Bryan about using simple home blenders to emulsify light, low-fat sauces. We would make a ratatouille-like vegetable combination, add a little stock and puree it in a blender. The high-speed blender works far better than a food processor for this, yielding a wonderfully light, almost frothy, sauce for grilled fish. If we needed a little more binding, we added a dab of ricotta cheese, or maybe yogurt.

* * *

ALSO IN THE MID-1970S, in the fall of 1976, one of the most
unbridled, caution-to-the-wind dining experiences of my life occurred.
It began with a fund-raising auction for Channel 13, a public television
station in New York City. One of the prizes, underwritten by American
Express, was dinner anywhere in the world for two, price no object.
Craig, unable to resist such an offer, phoned in a bid for three hundred
dollars to get the action started. To his astonishment, there were no
higher bids. Craig asked me to join him in this gastronomic tomfool-
ery, and we began contemplating where we should go. After considerable research involving up to forty restaurants, mostly in Europe, we
decided to try a small but ambitious bistro on the Right Bank in Paris,
near the Place des Ternes, called Chez Denis.

Craig had received a tip about the restaurant a few months earlier
from our mutual friend Carl Sontheimer, a scientist, inventor and
entrepreneur best known for introducing the Cuisinart food processor
to America. He had told Craig about a terrific meal he had enjoyed at
Chez Denis, and in particular an appetizer called chiffonade of lobster.
The restaurant's near anonymity, at least in this country, appealed to
Craig's journalistic instincts.

A few months after the auction, Craig and I were in Paris and recon-
noitered at Chez Denis, having a sumptuous meal that started with the
chiffonade (it was indeed special, a cold dish combining foie gras,
cognac and a tarragon mayonnaise). Because I speak French, Craig
asked me to call over the proprietor and present our ruse. I told him
that a rich friend in America wanted to throw a birthday party for my
colleague—expense be damned.

The owner, Denis Lahana, was a flamboyant character who rose to
the occasion with élan. He later sent us a letter outlining a thirty-one-
course dinner with "extraordinary" wines, for the 1975 price of 17,600
francs, or roughly $4,000.

"Wonderful," Craig replied. "We'll be there."

On the appointed evening the restaurant was half-empty, except for
a few reporters and a *New York Times* photographer, who took some
predinner photos of Craig, myself and Denis, all with the anticipatory
expressions of boxers about to jump into the ring. The kitchen was
working triple time preparing our feast. Denis had brought in outside
help to make sure everything went smoothly.

"Let the hostilities begin," the puckish chef declared.

More than four hours and four pounds of foie gras later, we rose from the table—wobbly, but like tenacious fighters, proud to have gone the distance. The festivities began with spoonfuls of Iranian beluga caviar and champagne. On the menu were *tartelettes* of quail mousse, a gratin of lobster and truffles, a Provençale pie of red mullet baked with tomato and black olives, roasted partridge in cabbage, baked sliced potatoes with truffles, fillets of wild duck in red wine sauce, foie gras in aspic, a *chaud-froid* of woodcock and much more. Not only was the food extraordinary, but also the wines were memorable (and expensive): 1918 Château Latour, 1928 Château Mouton-Rothschild, 1929 Romanée-Conti, 1961 Château Pétrus, an 1835 Madeira, to name a few. It was a rare exercise in excess. Craig's account of our meal appeared on the front page of the *New York Times*. Readers' reactions were mixed: some reveled in the fantasy; others took us to task for such conspicuous consumption.

NEARLY every day I'm reminded of something I cooked at Le Pavillon or at the fair or at the Drouant in Paris. But almost always when I prepare something today I trim it down, paring it of burdensome effort and time and, in accordance with the changing desires of Americans and French alike, make it lighter, too.

My approach has taken twists and turns that startle even me. When I began *60-Minute Gourmet,* for instance, the main goal was speed and elegance, but I cannot say I was very concerned about calories. One quick dish I chose was *suprêmes de volaille Véronique* (see recipe page 191)—chicken breasts with grapes (the "Véronique" part of a dish's name always refers to grapes). It was a distinctly traditional choice: although you will not find this particular dish in Escoffier's *Guide Culinaire,* you will find *filets de sole Véronique.* And chicken breasts are not so very different from the blander fishes; many approaches to the two are almost interchangeable, in fact. So, using chicken breasts, I cut them in strips for quick cooking, sautéed them in butter briefly, removed them from the skillet, and created a sauce with grapes that included one and a half cups of cream—a heavy dose for just four servings.

These days I am certain I would get criticized for using a cup and a half of cream, and I would avoid it, but I am also now open to devising much broader adaptations from culinary traditions I never knew before, just as so many other Americans, starting from a French foundation, have been doing. It is the nature of creating new recipes that you start not from some void, but from a foundation that you understand well, so that the substitutions, modifications and flourishes will make sense. The resulting dish, although completely different, will—like a domestic kitten and a leopard—still belong to the same species.

A good example of how I now venture far from my friend Escoffier, without completely cutting the cord, can be seen in my Asian dishes. Like so many other American cooks, I have fallen in love with certain Asian flavors that I never knew as a young man—ginger and coriander, among them. So it occurred to me one day, using those chicken breasts again, to prepare them as a kind of Far Eastern meunière. You may remember when I discussed the standard French procedure earlier that I mentioned its most common application is in flouring and sautéing fish fillets, then pouring browned butter over them.

But now instead of sealing in the chicken breasts' moisture with flour, I use sesame seeds, which serve the purpose well but have an assertive flavor of their own as they toast in the sauté pan, with just one tablespoon of vegetable oil and a few slices of ginger to flavor the oil (see recipe page 192). Then I lightly brown some butter as I would have in a meunière (I despise margarine, by the way, and believe the true flavor of butter is still one of the transcendent, irreplaceable elements in much of what we regard as fine cooking, although I use less of it now). I pour the butter over the chicken, along with chopped corian-der, the signature herb of the Far East, instead of the parsley I would ordinarily use. Done! And I dare say few people would associate it with a meunière—unless they had just gone through the steps I had in working my way from Escoffier to the chefs of Japan and Thailand. Truly content people, I believe, are always reaching out to challenge themselves and learn, but they do it within the possible, within the parameters of their capabilities.

Hunting with Maurice Bertrand

Epilogue: Cooking with Friends

MY WIFE CONTENDS that one of the factors that makes our lives so different today from what they were in the old days is that we have more time for friends now. She remembers how, when I was a chef, I used to work six or seven days a week and sleep late on my one day off, if I had one, leaving very little time for socializing. It wasn't so different a little later, when I worked so closely with Craig, days of frantic recipe production and wining and dining aimed expressly at producing good newspaper stories. I think Betty exaggerates a little about the lack of true socializing through all those years, but she does have a point. As I look back over those decades and over the pages of this book, it seems to me that there is a great deal of talk about food and family and not all that much about the friends I have made and managed to keep for forty or fifty years, even through the periods when I was working the hardest.

Some of those old friends—just a few, but some of the very best—showed up at my beach home at East Hampton not long ago, and we spent the day in what for me, and for them, was a typical get-together. We cooked, we carried on, we remembered where we had been and what we had done, and, astonishingly after all these years, we still had things to teach one another. Mostly, it was a calm, lazy day the week after my son, Jacques, married his wife, Trish, on this very spot. For both occasions, the wedding and this informal gathering, the weather was what I dream about when I think of home.

Gardiners Bay was glistening in the sunshine, there was a hint of the great Atlantic beyond, and sleek boats glided past us just a stone's throw from my backyard. On the back deck, sitting in the shade, five of us—

With Jacques Pépin, a good friend since the day he arrived for work at Le Pavillon in 1959; here on a trip together out West

Ed Giobbi, Jean Vergnes, Dick Frampton, Maurice Bertrand and I—were, as usual, talking about food.

At one point, Dick, one of the best fishermen I have ever met—he had contributed a thirty-seven-inch striped bass to the day's larder—leaned forward to unburden himself of a master's lecture on the nature of the beast. As you might guess, I knew a lot about this area already, but it was wonderful hearing Dick talking about it, as if my father were still alive, still giving me pointers, only now it was not about trout or pike but about those magnificent bass. When I listen to conversation like this, a kind of familiar warmth comes over me, and I find myself enthusiastic and engaged, almost as if I were still naive.

Dick had caught the bass that had occasioned this lecture in a spot of water well known to fishermen, a turbulent area that lies beyond Gardiners Island toward Fisher's Island. There the water's depth starts at 120 feet, goes quickly to just 90 feet and then to 17 feet, dropping off again to 70. It is, in fact, the site of a submerged hill. As the tide races over the top (the area is actually called the race), the bass lie in wait on one side of the ridge for the smaller fish, now forced into a much-reduced volume of water, to come over that hill densely packed in schools—and the bass feast.

What Dick does is drop a lure in among those smaller fish and try to fool just one really big bass. It sounds easy. But it's not. The bass stay lower than so many of the other fish, especially the blues. If you fish just a little too high, you are likely, in fact, to end up with nothing but blues and go home thinking there are no striped bass in all the Atlantic. And on a day when the northeast wind is stirring the water up, you might as well forget it altogether. The great striped bass swallow pebbles as ballast to stay out of the turbulence and are too low then, on those northeast days, to be caught even by my friend Dick.

As we were talking, Ed Giobbi remarked that the striped bass really was not a well-known or desirable fish until we French made such a big deal out of it (I do think it is the best eating fish available in America, so sweet and flavorful, yet strong enough to stand up to sauces and all sorts of preparations). And it's funny, we must never have talked about striped bass before, Ed and I, because he was under the impression that it was in fact a French fish—it is not, but it is close.

The best fish in the Mediterranean is the *loup de mer,* also known as bar or sea bass. It is not adorned by the attractive striping seen on its American cousin. But when I came to this country and worked at Le Pavillon I noticed the remarkable similarity in taste and texture between the striped bass and the bar and would serve something we called a bar *rayé,* or striped bar. It was a beautiful thing then as now.

When we had just about talked ourselves out, we started to prepare lunch. Ed had brought some home-canned tuna that he was going to blend with parsley and sliced onions. I was throwing together a traditional pot of steamed mussels to go with some bread I had baked earlier. The wine was a bottle of Ed's own, along with one I had bought, a Chablis from William Fèvres (a family I knew well from my childhood). There was also supposed to be some freshly caught whitebait, tiny minnowlike fish that are incredible just deep-fried and eaten whole. Maurice went off wading in the back, in the shallow, rocky water, with a net, trying to bring in whitebait, but, inexplicably, these little fish that are usually as common as weeds were nowhere to be found (and Maurice does not give up easily).

I met Maurice through my father-in-law in the days when Maurice was a waiter and then a captain at the Waldorf (he soon came to work for me at Le Pavillon). We have been hunting and fishing companions ever since. He is a powerful man. I can remember the fun we had in the postwar days when we used to enjoy bonfires on the beaches of Long Island, and Maurice always had to gather up the biggest piece of wood. One day he came trudging up the beach with a plank more than twenty feet long. It was absurd, but we threw it on the fire anyway. The blaze must have been visible from the moon.

Now Maurice was determined to bring in those whitebait. He was frustrated. I could not get him to come out of the water for lunch. I called his name and called it again. "Maureeeeece! Come in!" But he kept on dragging that net. "Ah, that's Maurice," I muttered to nobody in particular and headed back to the house. He came in, but in his own good time. No whitebait.

If you had dropped by in the early evening of the day I am recalling now, I can't begin to imagine what your first impression might have been. If you were courageous enough to sidle your way into the kitchen, I think it might have seemed hectic, confused. But really it wasn't. I mean we knew what we were doing. Maurice was certainly calm enough, chopping garlic, making the rhythmic knock, knock, knock of the heel of his knife on the chopping board as the blade rocked. I asked him whom the garlic was for. "I don't know," he said, never looking up, "I just do what I'm told." Right.

The garlic, it turns out, was for Jean Vergnes, who was in the kitchen working at the same time. Where Maurice is all focus, Jean likes to break the tension with laughter and song, or something that resembles song. He and Maurice have a bond that goes way back. Jean also started his career in the United States at the old Waldorf, in 1950, but lasted just three weeks—"I'm no production man," he declared as he left the job, referring to the mammoth scale of the work. His reputation (earned through his training and restaurant assignments in France) was such that he was immediately hired as the executive chef at Colony. In those early days Jean and I would take our breaks together, he from his restaurant and I from mine, and sit in Central Park to chat about food and ogle the girls. Jean went on to a splendid career but is mostly retired today. It is one of the joys of my life that he and his wife, Pauline, decided to move in as my next-door neighbors a few years ago.

On this evening at my house, he was preparing something that, for him, is the height of simplicity, a macédoine of vegetables—string beans, carrots, zucchini, cubed potato, some herbs. The trick he uses is to blanch them each individually in boiling water until they reach that perfect point where they are just starting to be tender. That way when he sautés them in butter and garlic he can do it all at once, and they will reach the final stage of al dente doneness at exactly the same time. Jean,

I must say, was accompanying the knock-knock-knock of Maurice's knife with a mock operatic version of something that sounded like "La, la, la." It wasn't all that musical, to tell you the truth.

Ed Giobbi was cooking in this same kitchen at the same time that my other buddies were going about business in their characteristic ways. In the intense East Hampton kitchen, Ed was preparing a pasta in fish stock, and he was, of course, true to himself: he started the stock from scratch, an aromatic liquid made from vegetables and herbs and the head of Dick Frampton's bass.

When the stock had simmered for twenty minutes or so (fish isn't like beef; you don't want to cook it forever; the flavor is extracted quickly and that's that), it was declared done and then was strained. Ed's approach to the pasta, although polished and knowledgeable, is nevertheless perhaps most notable for its pragmatic logic: his technique is to treat the pasta like risotto; he half cooks it in the broth first, then drains it (reserving the hot broth) and adds the pasta and just two or so cups of the broth to a saucepan where a light sauce is already simmering. He stands over it, as he did the other day, stirring and staring, impossible to distract, a short, balding man in blue jeans focusing on a pot of sauce and pasta the way a hunter fixes his stare on the woods, waiting. As the pasta absorbs the liquid in the pot, Ed slowly ladles in more. The trick is to stop feeding the thirsty pasta at the very second it reaches the desired texture.

As for that recently beheaded striped bass, I was determined to treat it as simply as possible, too: some fine olive oil, chopped fresh rosemary, a few sprigs of thyme, salt and pepper and the good auspices of a very hot outdoor grill. (Preheating the grill is absolutely essential if you want to prevent the fish from sticking.) When I dropped the fillets on the fire, the grill was so hot that the oil coating the fish burst into flame as if fuel had been thrown on the coals. And the thyme sprigs clinging to the fish were also alight at once. I closed the lid to keep the thyme-scented smoke from escaping and cooked the fish flesh side down first, briefly, just to achieve a nice bit of charring, but then quickly turned it so the bass's thick skin would prevent the fish from drying out in the intense heat as it continued to cook. The whole procedure took less than ten minutes for fillets that were, on average, two inches thick.

If I make this afternoon at my house sound like it was all food and food talk, that is not quite true. In the late afternoon we had taken a

Playing pétanque *in East*
Hampton with Jean Vergnes

break for *pétanque.* For years we have been playing
it out on the bit of grass that grows in front of Jean's
house. The game involves throwing one small, light
ball to a point a few yards away and then carefully
tossing larger metal ones to get as close as possible
to the little one or, sometimes, to knock away an

opponent's ball. The team with the closest ball earns a point. We played to thirteen, with two opposing teams composed of some of the men and a few of the wives.

Jean was, as usual, aggressive and pinpoint accurate. I didn't do badly, either, striding up and down the length of the playing area, shouting instructions—in French, in English—to my team and, when my turn came, tossing with some accuracy. Mostly. In a moment meant to devastate my opponents I looped one ball high, intending for it to land on top of the well-positioned orbs of the other team. I missed, and the thing bounced soundlessly on the grass, then rolled down the country road.

The afternoon and evening reminded me—as did many like it—of nothing so much as a picnic along a riverside in Burgundy. The cooking outdoors, the brilliant bay and the playfulness of it all with family and friends brought me to realize that my life's course had been set long ago, with a few additions, emendations and other changes—and a great deal more happiness than heartache.

Back then, in the old days along l'Armançon, these *pétanque* games that we now play in front of Jean's house would not have stopped traffic because there wasn't any, of course. But when we play now, the cars pass by—not many, but some—and stop, mostly to observe us for a moment as we play this exotic game and to listen to us carry on as we call out to each other with encouragement and directions. "Bien!" "Bravo!" "Very good!" It is a mélange of voices and accents. Each of us has taken his own idiosyncratic journey to arrive at this spot in America, here where a narrow strip of land points toward the far reaches of the Atlantic.

Recipes

SOUPS

A beef broth is delicious even without clarification, but it is the time-consuming clarification that transforms it into that delicacy called a consommé. I offer here the true old-fashioned approach. Frozen, it will last at least a month.

Beef Consommé

1. Place all the bones in a large pot and cover with water. Bring to a boil and simmer for 3 minutes. Drain and run the bones under cold water. Drain again.

2. Return the bones to the kettle and add the 6 quarts of water. Add the remaining ingredients. Bring to a boil and simmer for about 5 hours, skimming the fat from the top often. Strain the broth; there should be about 3 quarts of liquid. The meat from the bones can be used to make various meat sauces.

3. To clarify the consommé place the egg whites, beef, celery, onions, carrots, leeks, tomatoes and parsley sprigs in a large, clean kettle and beat until the egg whites are frothy and all the ingredients are well blended.

4. Add the strained broth to the mixture and salt to taste. Blend well. Place the kettle on the stove and

3 pounds beef neck bones
3 pounds beef bones with meat, such as shins or short ribs

BROTH
6 quarts water
2 cups coarsely chopped leek greens
4 sprigs parsley
4 celery ribs, cut into 2-inch pieces
2 cups carrots, cut into 2-inch lengths
4 sprigs thyme or 2 teaspoons dried thyme
4 whole cloves
2 cups coarsely chopped onions

CLARIFYING MIXTURE
5 large egg whites
1 pound lean ground beef

½ cup chopped celery
½ cup chopped onions
½ cup chopped carrots
½ cup chopped leek greens,
    carefully washed
½ cup chopped fresh toma-
    toes or ½ cup canned
    crushed tomatoes
6 sprigs parsley
salt to taste

YIELD: ABOUT 10 TO 12 CUPS

bring slowly to a boil. It is very important that you stir this mixture from the bottom until it boils. Scrape the bottom constantly to prevent the egg whites from burning.

5. When the broth starts to boil, stop stirring and let it simmer slowly. To clarify, look for bubbles in a clear spot on top of the consommé. Dip a ladle or spoon into one of these holes and sprinkle the clear liquid over the entire surface. Simmer and repeat this process for about 30 minutes.

6. Line a colander with a clean towel. Carefully strain.

 ## Chicken Broth

5 pounds chicken bones,
    with most of the fat
    removed
2 cups coarsely chopped
    onions
1 cup coarsely chopped
    carrots
1 cup coarsely chopped
    celery
2 garlic cloves, peeled
6 sprigs parsley
2 bay leaves
4 sprigs thyme or 1 tea-
    spoon dried thyme
6 peppercorns
2 whole cloves
4 whole fresh allspice
4 quarts water

YIELD: 10 CUPS

1. Place the bones in a 6-quart stockpot, cover them with water and bring to a boil. Discard the water at once and rinse the bones thoroughly with cold water. Return the bones to the stockpot.

2. Combine the other ingredients along with 4 quarts of water. Bring to a boil.

3. Reduce the broth to a slow simmer. As fat and particles rise to the surface, skim thoroughly, using a ladle for fat and a perforated metal skimmer for the tiny particles. Simmer for 2 hours, skimming every half hour.

4. Strain the broth through a fine sieve into a stainless-steel bowl (this allows rapid cooling).
5. Let the broth reach room temperature before placing it in the refrigerator. When it is cool, remove the fat that solidified on top.

NOTE: This broth can be frozen and kept for about a month.

When I worked as a young cook in France, at Restaurant Drouant and other establishments, we purchased all of our fish whole the same day it was served. Cleaning fish was a never-ending task, and we learned to do it quickly and efficiently. The bones were always used to make fresh fish broth, a fumet, which was the foundation for all kinds of wonderful seafood soup, stews and sauces.

In those years I learned something valuable, the kind of thing you never read in cookbooks. When we made a fish stock with freshly cleaned fish bones, it was immeasurably better than a stock made with bones that had been cleaned hours before and stored. Why? I can't say exactly why, but unquestionably the freshly cleaned bones had a much more concentrated flavor.

Fish Broth

Chop the fish bones to fit in a kettle or large saucepan. Add the remaining ingredients to the kettle and bring to a boil. Simmer for 20 minutes, skimming often. Strain well. This can be tightly covered and refrigerated for several days.

NOTE: Fish broth can also be frozen in ice-cube trays, and the soup cubes then placed in a plastic bag in the freezer.

5 pounds fish bones from
   nonoily fish, with heads
   and gills removed
½ cup coarsely chopped
   onions
1 cup chopped celery
6 sprigs parsley
4 sprigs thyme or 1 teaspoon
   dried thyme
10 whole peppercorns
6 cups cold water
2 cups dry white wine

YIELD: ABOUT 6 CUPS

Onion soup was one of the first bistro dishes to become popular in America and is still in evidence today.

Onion Soup Chablis Style

1. Melt 2 tablespoons of the butter in a saucepan. Add the garlic and the onions. Cook, stirring, over medium-high heat until the onions are golden brown and begin to darken.
2. Sprinkle the onions with flour and stir in the broth and the white wine, using a wire whisk. Add salt and pepper to taste. Bring to a boil and simmer

4 tablespoons unsalted butter
1 tablespoon minced garlic
5 cups chopped white onions
⅓ cup all-purpose flour
5 cups fresh or canned
   chicken broth (see recipe
   page 146)
1 cup dry white wine

salt and freshly ground
white pepper to taste
Grated Gruyère cheese

YIELD: 6 TO 8 SERVINGS

for 20 minutes. Remove the soup from the heat and swirl in the remaining butter by rotating the pan gently. Serve immediately with the Gruyère served on the side.

As a fisherman, I am always looking for new ways to prepare my catch. When cod is plentiful I like to use it in my version of quick fish chowder. I have used cod in bouillabaisse many times, and it works splendidly. This recipe is less time-consuming than bouillabaisse, yet wonderfully flavorful. The recipe calls for a second fish as well. You may use halibut, another firm, lean fish, or red snapper, fluke or any other mild white-fleshed fish.

French Fish Chowder

¾ pound skinless boneless
codfish
¾ pound skinless boneless
halibut or red snapper
3 tablespoons olive oil
½ cup finely chopped onions
1 cup finely chopped celery
1 tablespoon finely chopped
garlic
1 cup diced sweet red or
green pepper
2 teaspoons fresh turmeric
¼ teaspoon saffron stems,
optional
1 cup dry white wine
3 cups canned crushed
tomatoes
1 bay leaf
2 sprigs thyme or 1 teaspoon
dried thyme
¼ teaspoon dried red pepper
flakes
4 cups fish broth (see recipe
page 147) or water
salt and freshly ground
pepper to taste
½ cup orzo

1. Cut the fish into 1-inch cubes.

2. Heat the oil in a large saucepan or kettle, and add the onions, celery, garlic and peppers. Cook, stirring, over medium heat, about 5 minutes. Add the turmeric, saffron if using, wine, tomatoes, bay leaf, thyme, pepper flakes, fish broth or water and salt and pepper. Bring to a boil and simmer for 5 minutes.

3. Add the orzo, stir well and simmer for 7 to 8 minutes, or until the orzo is tender.

4. Add the fish, stir, bring to a boil and simmer for 3 minutes. Remove the bay leaf, sprinkle with basil or Italian parsley and serve with the garlic croutons.

¼ cup chopped fresh basil
or Italian parsley
garlic croutons (see recipe
page 233)

YIELD: 4 TO 6 SERVINGS

Billi Bi is much more than merely one of my favorite soups. When I was incorporated it was under the name Billi Bi; my Boston whaler in East Hampton, Long Island, is called Billi-Bi; *and, who knows, if I had had a second son, he might have carried that soupy designation all his life.*

Billi Bi's origins can be traced to an American, William Bateman Leeds, a celebrated gourmand who was a particular fan of Chef Louis Barthe, who worked both at Maxim's in Paris and Ciro's in Deauville, in Normandy. Leeds was a great fan of mussels, especially those in a particular sauce prepared by Chef Barthe, which Leeds would unceremoniously slurp with a mussel shell. One day the American was having a dinner party and wanted to show off the mussel dish, but in a more dignified fashion. He asked the chef to come up with a similar recipe. The result was a cream of mussel soup that the delighted guests dubbed "Billy B's Soup," which later became "Billi Bi."

Billi Bi

1. Place the mussels in a deep kettle or saucepan. Add the butter, shallots, onions, thyme, bay leaf, parsley sprigs, salt, pepper and wine. Cover and bring to a boil, and simmer for 5 minutes, shaking and tossing the mussels in the kettle to redistribute them. Cook the mussels only until they open.

2. Remove the mussels from the shells and discard the shells. Keep the mussels warm.

3. Strain the cooking liquid through a cheesecloth or a fine strainer. Return the liquid to the kettle.

4. Blend the creams and the yolk well and add them to the mussel liquid. Warm through but make certain the soup does not boil or it may curdle. Add the

2 quarts cleaned mussels
2 tablespoons unsalted butter
4 tablespoons coarsely chopped shallots
4 tablespoons chopped onions
2 sprigs thyme or ½ teaspoon dried thyme
1 bay leaf
4 sprigs parsley
salt and freshly ground white pepper to taste
1 cup dry white wine
2 cups heavy cream
1 cup half-and-half cream
1 large egg yolk

2 teaspoons finely chopped
    fresh parsley, optional
croutons (see recipe page
    233)

mussel meat just to heat through. Sprinkle with
chopped parsley if desired, and serve with buttered
croutons.

YIELD: 6 TO 8 SERVINGS

NOTE: This soup is also good served cold.

Black Bean Soup

1 pound black beans or red
    kidney beans
2 pounds smoked-pork
    bones
12 cups water
salt and freshly ground
    pepper to taste
⅓ pound lean salt pork or
    Cajun tasso, ground
    very fine
2 cups finely chopped
    onions
1 tablespoon finely
    chopped garlic
1 tablespoon chopped fresh
    oregano or 1 teaspoon
    dried oregano
1 cup seeded and minced
    green peppers
1 cup seeded and minced
    sweet red peppers
2 cups chopped ripe fresh
    tomatoes, or 1 cup
    crushed canned
    tomatoes
1 teaspoon ground
    coriander
1 teaspoon ground cumin
2 tablespoons red wine
    vinegar
¼ cup dry sherry

YIELD: 10 SERVINGS

1. Place the beans in a bowl, add cold water and
rinse well. Some beans, as noted on the package, will
require overnight soaking

2. Place the beans in a pot, add the bones and the 12
cups water. Salt to taste. Bring to a boil and simmer
for 30 minutes.

3. Meanwhile, as the beans cook, render the salt
pork or tasso in a skillet. When the fat is rendered
(most of the fat melted away) add the onions, garlic,
oregano, green peppers, red peppers, and cook, stirring, until wilted. Add the tomatoes, coriander,
cumin. Cook about 3 minutes.

4. Scrape the mixture into the beans and continue
cooking until the beans are tender and thoroughly
cooked, stirring often.

5. Remove the bones and remove 2 cups of the
cooked beans. Mash the beans into a puree with a
potato masher. Return the beans to the pot. Add the
vinegar and the sherry wine. Blend well, bring to a
simmer and serve hot.

NOTE: For garnishing, use chopped hard-boiled eggs
and chopped fresh coriander.

Leek and Potato Soup

1. Leeks have a great deal of sand between the leaves and must be carefully cleaned. To do this trim off the root end; cut off and discard the long green stems. Split the leeks lengthwise from the stem end, then turn and slit them again. Rinse well. Separate the leaves under cold running water, shake dry, then chop them into small cubes.

2. Peel the potatoes and cut them into ¼-inch cubes, about 2 cups.

3. Melt 2 tablespoons of the butter in a saucepan, and add the onions and leeks. Cook over medium heat, stirring, until wilted. Do not brown.

4. Add the chicken broth, water, bay leaf and potatoes, and simmer for 30 minutes, uncovered.

5. Remove the soup from the heat, add the remaining butter and stir. Check for seasoning and serve hot.

NOTE: For a richer version, add ½ cup drained plain yogurt or ½ cup heavy cream.

2 large leeks
1 pound medium potatoes, such as yellow-gold, Washington or Idaho
4 tablespoons unsalted butter
1 cup finely chopped onions
3 cups fresh or canned chicken broth (see recipe page 146)
2 cups water
1 bay leaf
salt and freshly ground pepper to taste

YIELD: 4 TO 6 SERVINGS

STEWS

ℰ Pot-au-Feu with Stuffed Chicken

1 3-pound brisket of beef
    or 8 short ribs, trimmed
    of excess fat and tied
    with a string
1 beef shank bone
1 large onion, peeled and
    studded with 4 cloves
6 peppercorns
2 bay leaves
4 sprigs thyme or 1 table-
    spoon dried thyme
salt to taste
1 stuffed chicken (recipe
    follows)
8 leeks, trimmed and
    rinsed well, tied with a
    string
8 medium carrots, scraped
8 celery ribs, tied together
    with a string
2 small cabbages or 1 large
    one, cored and quar-
    tered
12 small pearl onions,
    peeled

YIELD: 8 SERVINGS

1. Place the meat and the shank bone in a deep pot. Cover with water, bring to a boil, and simmer for 1 minute to blanch. Remove the meat and bone and drain. Wipe out the pot with paper towels.

2. Return the meat and bone to the pot, and cover with water again. Add the onions, peppercorns, bay leaves, thyme and salt to taste. Bring to a boil and simmer for 1½ hours.

3. Add the whole stuffed chicken. Bring to a boil and simmer for 1 hour, until the meat is almost tender. Skim off the fat and baste often.

4. During the last half hour of cooking add the remaining vegetables and cook until tender.

5. Serve on a warm plate surrounded by the vegetables. Serve with cornichons, mustard or grated fresh horseradish.

NOTE: The broth makes an excellent soup base.

Stuffed Chicken for Pot-au-Feu

1. Place the pork sausage in a skillet and cook briefly, stirring. Add the onions and the garlic. Cook until the onions are translucent. Do not brown the garlic.

2. Add the ground chicken livers and cook briefly. Add the bread crumbs, milk and beaten egg. Cook briefly. Remove from the heat and add the parsley, thyme, salt and pepper.

3. When the mixture is cool enough to handle, stuff it in the chicken cavity and truss the chicken.

⅓ pound ground pork
    sausage
¼ cup finely chopped
    onions
1 teaspoon minced garlic
fresh livers from the
    chicken, ground
¾ cup fresh bread crumbs
¼ cup milk
1 large egg, beaten
¼ cup finely chopped fresh
    parsley
2 teaspoons fresh thyme
    leaves or 1 teaspoon
    dried thyme
salt and freshly ground
    pepper to taste
1 3-pound whole chicken

When I first came to this country, I was eager to learn as much about its culture as I could, including the food. Some of my experiments were disastrous—root beer, peanut butter—but others, like an old-fashioned New England boiled dinner, were a delight. Really, it is not that different from what the French call pot-au-feu.

In France, we might have a pot-au-feu after the New Year's celebration—which is essentially boiled lean cuts of meat, carrots, turnips, onions, leeks, celery, potatoes and parsnips. The broth yielded by this combination of ingredients is sublime. The American equivalent, the New England boiled dinner, dates to colonial days, when tough cuts of meat were tenderized through long cooking in broth.

New England Boiled Dinner

1. Remove and discard any tough outer leaves on the cabbage. Quarter the cabbage and remove the core.

2. In a large kettle, combine the pork shoulder or

1 head cabbage, about 1
    pound
1¼ pounds smoked pork
    shoulder or butt

6 medium Washington or
   Idaho potatoes, about
   1¼ pounds, peeled
6 carrots, about ½ pound,
   trimmed and scraped
2 leeks, trimmed and well
   washed (see page 151)
4 celery ribs, trimmed and
   tied
1 onion, peeled and stud-
   ded with 2 cloves
2 teaspoons allspice
2 sprigs thyme or 1 tea-
   spoon dried thyme
1 bay leaf
6 peppercorns
salt to taste
4 chicken legs and thighs

YIELD: 4 TO 6 SERVINGS

butt, potatoes, cabbage, carrots, leeks, celery, onion, allspice, thyme, bay leaf and peppercorns. Cover with water, and add salt.

3. Cover and bring to a boil; simmer for 20 minutes.

4. Add the chicken legs and thighs and simmer for 15 minutes more.

5. Serve with Dijon-style mustard, cornichons or grated fresh horseradish.

Daube, a close kin of beef Burgundy and a specialty I remember so well from child-hood, is a dish that is gaining new popularity in restaurants today. "Daube" is a term that refers to a method of braising beef or other meats. It is not really a stew, in which beef is cut into cubes, browned and braised. A daube usually has a solid piece of meat that is braised with vegetables in a red wine sauce.

Daube of Beef in Red Wine

1 6-pound center-cut
   shoulder of beef,
   trimmed and oven
   ready

MARINADE
¼ cup red wine vinegar
1 cup chopped onions
1 cup chopped carrots
1 cup chopped celery
1 cup leek greens

1. Place the meat in a large mixing bowl. Add the wine vinegar, chopped onions, carrots, celery, leek greens, parsley sprigs, garlic cloves, whole cloves, sage, rosemary, marjoram, coriander, red wine, and salt and pepper to taste. Place the mixture over and around the meat. Cover with plastic wrap and refrigerate for 12 hours.

2. Remove the meat from the marinade and pat dry. Strain the remaining liquid from the mixing bowl and set aside. Tie up the vegetables in cheesecloth.

3. Preheat the oven to 375 degrees.

4. In a large Dutch oven or cast-iron pot, place the olive oil and heat over medium-high heat. Add the meat, turning and browning on all sides. Remove the meat and set it aside. Add the shallots and the chopped garlic, and cook until wilted. Add the flour, blending well while stirring. Cook briefly, then add the reserved liquid and bring to a boil.

5. Add the meat, the reserved vegetables in the cheesecloth, and the broth. Bring to a simmer, then place the mixture in a preheated 375-degree oven. Cook for 2 hours. Remove the cheesecloth and squeeze the bundle to extract the juices.

6. Reduce the heat to 350 degrees, and add the baby carrots, pearl onions, the chestnuts and the orange peel. Cook until the meat is tender, about 1 hour.

7. Remove the meat and skim off any fat from the sauce.

8. Slice the meat and serve with the vegetables and the braising liquid.

4 sprigs parsley
2 garlic cloves, crushed
2 whole cloves
1 teaspoon fresh sage leaves
1 teaspoon dried rosemary
1 teaspoon dried marjoram
2 teaspoons coriander seeds
5 cups dry red wine, such as Côtes-du-Rhône
salt and freshly ground pepper to taste

2 tablespoons olive oil
4 tablespoons chopped shallots
1 teaspoon finely chopped garlic
¼ cup all-purpose flour
2 cups fresh or canned beef broth
12 baby carrots
12 pearl onions, peeled
12 dry chestnuts, peeled
2 ½-inch-wide orange-peel strips

YIELD: 10 TO 12 SERVINGS

Another bistro dish many Americans have known for decades is blanquette de veau, *or veal stew.*

French Veal Stew

1. Preheat the oven to 375 degrees.

2. Heat the butter in a large, deep casserole and add the veal. Sprinkle with salt and pepper to taste. Add the garlic and the onions. Cook, stirring, but not browning, for 5 minutes. Sprinkle with flour and nutmeg, add the chicken broth, water and white wine. Bring to a boil, stirring and scraping the bot-

2 tablespoons unsalted butter
4 pounds lean boneless shoulder of veal, cut into 1½-inch cubes
salt and freshly ground pepper to taste
2 teaspoons chopped garlic

1 cup finely chopped
    onions
¼ cup all-purpose flour
½ teaspoon freshly grated
    nutmeg
2 cups fresh or canned
    chicken broth (see
    recipe page 146)
1 cup water
½ cup dry white wine
1 bay leaf
4 sprigs thyme or 1 tea-
    spoon dried thyme
12 baby carrots, trimmed
    and scraped
12 pearl onions, peeled
1 cup heavy cream
1 tablespoon fresh lemon
    juice

YIELD: 8 SERVINGS

tom of the pan. Add the bay leaf and the thyme, bring to a boil and place in the oven and cover. Bake for 1 hour. If there is any fat on top, skim it off.

3. Meanwhile, add the carrots and onions to a saucepan, cover with water, bring to a boil with salt to taste and simmer for 5 minutes. Drain.

4. Remove the meat from the oven after cooking for 1 hour. Place the carrots and onions around the meat in the casserole, add the cream and lemon juice and simmer on top of the stove for 15 minutes, stirring occasionally, until the meat is tender.

Back in the 1940s and 1950s American diners, or at least those in New York City, had relatively adventuresome tastes, contrary to popular lore. Take sweet breads and tripe, for example. Tripe was served on bistro menus all over town, and many Americans enjoyed it. Even at Le Pavillon, this earthy dish was in demand. Of course, every French customer had a taste for it. I remember every Saturday a group of French executives would come to the restaurant for a long, bibulous lunch that always included tripes à la mode de Caen, *a dish that originated in Normandy. Calvados, of course, is a critical ingredient.*

Tripe à la Mode de Caen

8 pounds fresh beef tripe,
    trimmed of all fat and
    cut into 2-inch squares
2 calves' feet, cut into 3-
    inch pieces
2 cups coarsely chopped
    onions
2 cups coarsely chopped
    well-washed leeks, both
    white and green parts

1. Preheat the oven to 350 degrees.

2. Place the tripe and the calves' feet in a kettle. Add cold water to cover. Bring to a boil and simmer for 5 minutes. Drain well.

3. Tie the onions, leeks, celery, garlic, thyme, bay leaves, cloves, parsley sprigs and peppercorns in a square of cheesecloth. Bring up the ends of the cloth and tie with string to make a bundle.

4. Place the tripe, the calves'-feet pieces, the cheese-cloth bundle, the carrots, the chicken broth, water, wine and salt in a large kettle. Bring to a boil. Cover tightly and place in the oven and bake for 5 hours.

5. Remove the cheesecloth bundle, squeeze it to remove the moisture and discard. Skim off and discard most of the fat from the surface of the liquid.

6. Remove the carrots and cut them into ½-inch rounds and add them to the tripe.

7. Remove the calves'-feet pieces, cut away the gelatinous skin and discard the bones. Cut the skin and gelatin in strips and add them to the tripe. Bring to a boil, add the Calvados and serve.

NOTE: This is traditionally served with steamed parsley potatoes.

1 cup finely chopped celery
5 garlic cloves, unpeeled
6 sprigs thyme or 2 tablespoons dried thyme
2 bay leaves
4 whole cloves
8 sprigs parsley
12 black peppercorns
6 large carrots, trimmed
  and scraped
10 cups fresh or canned
  chicken broth (see recipe
  page 146)
3 cups water
3 cups dry white wine
salt to taste
¼ cup Calvados

YIELD: 12 SERVINGS OR MORE

Lamb Stew with Beans

1. Pick over the beans and soak them in water with the salt pork overnight.

2. Drain the beans and the salt pork and place them in a large kettle. Add water to cover well, add the studded onion, whole carrot, sprigs of parsley, bay leaf, salt and pepper to taste. Bring the mixture to a boil and simmer for 1 hour, or until the beans are tender. Do not overcook the beans.

3. When the beans are cooked, drain them and discard the onion, salt pork, carrot, parsley and the bay leaf.

4. Meanwhile, preheat the oven to 375 degrees. In a large cast-iron pot, heat the oil and brown the lamb

BEANS

1 pound navy beans or
  Italian white beans
¼ pound salt pork
1 small onion, studded with
  2 cloves
1 carrot, scraped
4 sprigs parsley
1 bay leaf
salt and freshly ground
  pepper to taste

STEW

1 tablespoon olive or
  peanut oil
4 pounds lean lamb, cut
  from the leg into 1½-
  inch cubes

½ cup chopped carrots
1 tablespoon finely
    chopped garlic
1 bay leaf
1 cup finely chopped
    onions
4 sprigs thyme or 1 tea-
    spoon dried thyme
¼ cup all-purpose flour
1 cup white wine
3 cups water
3 cups canned crushed
    tomatoes

YIELD: 8 SERVINGS

on all sides. When the lamb is browned, add the chopped carrots, garlic, bay leaf, onions, thyme and salt and pepper to taste. Cook and stir over high heat for about 5 minutes. Drain the excess fat.

5. Sprinkle the meat with the flour. Blend well, stirring over low heat. Add the wine, water and tomatoes. Bring to a boil, stirring. Check for seasoning.

6. Place in the oven and bake for 1½ hours.

7. Remove the lamb from the oven and skim off any fat that may appear on top. Add the beans; blend well. Return the pot to the oven and cook for a half hour. Remove the sprig of thyme if using fresh, check for seasoning and serve.

I am sometimes amused by the gastronomic debate about whether fish can be served with and cooked in red wine. In Burgundy when I was growing up, my mother reached for red wine when cooking all kinds of seafood dishes, and we would drink a light Burgundy wine with the fish course.

One of the finest Burgundian fish dishes I recall from childhood is the matelote, which is made with freshwater fish, vegetables and red wine. I have clear recollections of how we made it in my family's home. Fish and eels were cleaned, then cut up whole, on the bone. The flavor is better this way, though one must be careful when eating. Carp, pike and other freshwater fish might be added to the stew.

There are variations on matelote from region to region. In the northwest region of Touraine, for example, matelote has prunes in it. In the version here, I used a boneless fillet of monkfish, which has a firm texture that holds up well to any kind of cooking. You could substitute any nonoily fish with firm flesh.

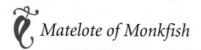

Matelote of Monkfish

2 tablespoons olive oil
12 pearl onions, peeled
16 small mushrooms
4 tablespoons finely
    chopped shallots

1. Heat the oil in a nonstick saucepan over medium-high heat. Add the onions, mushrooms, shallots, bay leaf, thyme and garlic. Cook, stirring, until wilted, about 3 minutes.

2. Add the flour and blend well. Add the wine, fish broth or clam juice, cloves, salt and pepper. Blend well with a wire whisk. Bring to a boil and simmer 10 minutes.

3. Add the fish cubes, bring to a simmer and cook about 4 minutes, or until done. Add the butter and blend well. Remove thyme sprigs if using fresh and the bay leaf. Sprinkle with the parsley and serve hot with garlic croutons (see recipe page 233) on the side.

1 bay leaf

4 sprigs thyme or ½ teaspoon dried thyme

1 tablespoon finely chopped garlic

2 tablespoons all-purpose flour

2 cups red wine, such as Côtes-du-Rhône or Cabernet Sauvignon

1 cup fresh fish broth (see recipe page 147) or bottled clam juice

2 cloves

salt and freshly ground pepper to taste

1¾ pounds monkfish fillets, cut into ½-inch cubes

2 tablespoons unsalted butter

4 tablespoons finely chopped fresh parsley

YIELD: 4 SERVINGS

SEAFOOD

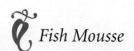 *Fish Mousse*

*1½ pounds very cold skin-
less boneless nonoily
fish, such as Dover sole,
American sole, striped
bass, pike, scallops,
salmon, cut into 1½-
inch cubes*
*salt and freshly ground
white pepper to taste*
*⅛ teaspoon freshly grated
nutmeg*
pinch cayenne pepper
1 egg
2 cups heavy cream
*2 teaspoons unsalted
butter, softened*

1. Preheat the oven to 375 degrees.

2. Place the cubed fish in the container of a food processor. Season with salt, pepper, nutmeg and cayenne pepper. Add the egg, blend for 10 seconds and continue blending while adding the cream, for about 30 seconds, or until the mixture is smooth.

3. Butter a 6-cup mold (a charlotte ring or fluted ring will do) with a pastry brush. Press the mousse mixture evenly into the mold, smoothing the top with a rubber spatula.

4. Cover the mold tightly with aluminum foil and place it in a baking pan containing enough water to cover 1½ inches up the sides of the mold.

5. Boil the water on top of the stove. Place the pan in the oven and bake for 45 minutes, or until the internal temperature of the mousse is about 140 degrees.

6. Carefully invert the mold onto a serving platter. Serve the mousse with champagne sauce (page 226).

YIELD: 8 SERVINGS AS A
MAIN COURSE OR 16 TO 20
SERVINGS AS AN APPETIZER

NOTE: This mousse also could be used to make quenelles.

One of the more labor-intensive sauces is the américaine, *the foundation for that renowned—and all but forgotten today—shellfish extravaganza called lobster* américaine. *It is surely one of the greatest creations of the French kitchen, yet, curiously, no one is certain who created the sauce or how it came by its name. It is generally agreed that it does not mean "in the American style" and that it was not created in America.*

Lobster américaine *is believed to have originated in Provence; it certainly has all the taste marks of that region, with its use of tomatoes, garlic and olive oil. Some people insist that it should be called* armoricaine, *which would mean "in the style of Brittany," but their suggestion is generally ignored by gastronomic historians.*

It is undeniably a labor of love, but the results can be sublime.

Lobster Américaine

1. To kill the lobsters, insert the tip of a heavy knife between the eyes. Cut off the claws, then separate the body and the tail. Cut the tail crosswise to make 3 medallions. Reserve the coral and the liver to bind the sauce. Split the head in two. Remove and discard the tough sac near the eyes.

2. In a large, heavy skillet, heat the oil over high heat. Add the lobster pieces and sprinkle with salt and pepper. Toss and stir the pieces until the meat is seared. Transfer the meat to a platter and keep warm.

3. Discard the oil from the skillet, add the shallots, carrots, celery and garlic. Cook, stirring, until wilted. Do not burn the garlic. Add the tomatoes, 2 tablespoons of the fresh tarragon (or 1 teaspoon dried), thyme, bay leaf, wine or clam broth, tomato paste, cayenne and salt and pepper to taste. Bring to a simmer.

4. Transfer the lobster and any liquid that has gathered around it to the mixture. Add 2 tablespoons of the cognac and bring to a boil. Cover and simmer for 10 minutes.

5. Remove the lobsters from the pan; keep them warm. Discard the sprigs of thyme, if using fresh,

4 1½-pound live lobsters
2 tablespoons olive or vegetable oil
salt and freshly ground pepper to taste

SAUCE
4 tablespoons finely chopped shallots
¼ cup finely chopped carrots
¼ cup finely chopped celery
2 teaspoons finely chopped garlic
2 cups ripe plum tomatoes, peeled and cut into ¼-inch cubes
4 tablespoons finely chopped fresh tarragon or 1 teaspoon dried tarragon
2 sprigs thyme or ½ teaspoon dried thyme
1 bay leaf
1 cup dry white wine or ½ cup clam broth and ½ cup water, mixed

2 tablespoons tomato paste
¼ teaspoon cayenne
   pepper
4 tablespoons cognac
2 tablespoons unsalted
   butter

YIELD: 4 SERVINGS

and the bay leaf. Transfer the remaining cooking liquid into the container of a food processor. Add the coral and the liver and process to a fine textured sauce.

6. Return the lobster to the pan and add the sauce. Transfer the mixture to the lobsters. Add the cognac and the butter and blend. Check for seasoning, bring to a simmer and serve immediately. Sprinkle with the 2 tablespoons of remaining fresh tarragon, if using. Serve with rice pilaf on the side.

Lobster Pavillon

4 1½-pound live lobsters
3 tablespoons olive oil
salt and freshly ground
   pepper to taste
¼ teaspoon cayenne
   pepper
3 tablespoons minced
   shallots
4 tablespoons minced
   onions
1 teaspoon chopped garlic
⅓ cup diced celery
⅓ cup diced carrots
4 sprigs tarragon or
   2 teaspoons dried
   tarragon
4 tablespoons cognac
1½ cups dry white wine
1 cup canned crushed
   tomatoes or 1½ cups
   cubed ripe fresh
   tomatoes
2 sprigs thyme or 1 tea-
   spoon dried thyme
1 bay leaf
1 cup heavy cream
2 tablespoons unsalted
   butter

1. To kill the lobsters immediately, plunge a large knife between the back of the head and the body, thereby severing the spinal cord. Using a heavy knife or cleaver, cut off the claws and separate the tail from the body of the lobsters. Split each body in half lengthwise and remove the sac near the eyes. Remove the liver and coral and refrigerate. Chop each body into roughly 1-inch pieces.

2. In a heavy saucepan heat the oil over high heat. Add the lobster pieces except the livers and coral. Cook, stirring, for about 3 minutes. Add salt, pepper, and cayenne. Add the shallots, onions, garlic, celery, carrots and tarragon, and cook, stirring, for about 3 minutes. Drain off the oil.

3. Add half the cognac and ignite it with a long kitchen match. Add the wine, tomatoes, thyme and the bay leaf. Check for seasonings. Stir, bring to a boil and simmer for 8 to 10 minutes. Do not overcook.

4. Remove the lobster claws and the tails. Set them aside to cool. Add the cream, blend well and bring to a boil. Simmer for 4 minutes. Add the livers and coral. Blend well with a wire whisk. Bring to a boil and remove from the heat.

5. Place the mixture in a food mill or large strainer. Press to extract as much liquid as possible.

6. Place the sauce through the finest strainer. It should be smooth and silken.

7. When the tails and claws are cool enough to handle, crack them and remove the meat. Cut the tails into 3 or 4 pieces. Add the lobster meat to the sauce.

8. Bring the lobsters and the sauce to a simmer. Swirl in the remaining cognac and the butter. Remove immediately from the heat and serve with rice pilaf on the side.

YIELD: 4 SERVINGS

Lobster Thermidor

1. Preheat the broiler.

2. Kill each of the lobsters by plunging a knife into the spot where the tail and body meet. Split the lobsters lengthwise and cut off the claws. Then remove and discard the tough sac near the eyes of each lobster.

3. Place each lobster half with split side up on 1 or 2 baking dishes. Sprinkle each lobster half with salt and pepper. Brush lightly with the oil. Place the lobsters on the middle rack of the oven. Broil for 10 minutes. Do not overcook.

4. Meanwhile, place the shallots, tarragon, chervil or parsley, wine and vinegar in a small saucepan. Bring to a boil. Simmer until most of the liquid has evaporated.

5. Melt 2 tablespoons of the butter in another saucepan and stir in the flour, using a wire whisk. When the mixture is blended, add the milk and cream, stirring rapidly with the whisk. Add the cayenne pepper and salt and pepper to taste. Spoon

4 1½-pound live lobsters
salt and freshly ground
*   pepper to taste*
2 tablespoons vegetable oil
4 tablespoons finely
*   chopped shallots*
2 tablespoons chopped
*   fresh tarragon or*
*   1 tablespoon dried*
*   tarragon*
2 tablespoons chopped
*   fresh chervil or parsley*
½ cup dry white wine
1 tablespoon wine vinegar
4 tablespoons unsalted
*   butter*
4 tablespoons all-purpose
*   flour*
1 cup milk
1 cup heavy cream
¼ teaspoon cayenne
*   pepper*
1 egg yolk, lightly beaten

2 tablespoons Dijon
   mustard
4 tablespoons grated
   Gruyère or Parmesan
   cheese

the herb mixture into the sauce; blend well. Add the egg yolk and stir to blend. Add the mustard and set aside.

6. When the lobster is cooked, remove the tail meat and crack the claws. Cut the meat into bite-sized pieces. Melt the remaining 2 tablespoons of butter and toss the lobster meat in it quickly. Add half of the sauce to the lobster meat and use this mixture to fill the lobster shells. Spoon equal portions of the remaining sauce over the lobsters; sprinkle with the cheese. Place the lobster about 4 to 6 inches from the source of the heat and broil for a few minutes until lightly browned. Serve immediately.

YIELD: 4 SERVINGS AS A
MAIN COURSE OR 8 SERV-
INGS AS AN APPETIZER

Brook Trout Meunière

4 10-ounce brook trout,
   with fins cut off, head
   and tail intact
¼ cup milk
salt and freshly ground
   pepper to taste
¼ cup all-purpose flour
2 tablespoons vegetable or
   peanut oil
4 lemons, thinly sliced
4 tablespoons unsalted
   butter
2 tablespoons fresh lemon
   juice
2 tablespoons finely
   chopped fresh parsley

1. Place the trout in a large pan; add the milk and salt and pepper to taste. Turn the trout in the mixture.

2. Dredge the trout, one at a time, in the flour. Shake to remove the excess flour.

3. Heat the oil in a large, heavy nonstick skillet and cook all the trout over medium-high heat for about 6 minutes, or until golden on one side. Turn the fish and cook for 6 minutes more, basting often. (The basting is vital to keep the trout moist.) Remove the trout to a warm platter and set aside. Garnish with the lemon slices.

4. Pour off the fat from the pan and wipe out the skillet. Add the butter and shake the pan over medium-high heat while stirring until the butter turns a hazelnut color. Do not let it burn. Add the lemon juice to the butter, blend well and pour the sauce over the fish. Sprinkle with the chopped parsley and serve.

YIELD: 4 SERVINGS

I have spent countless hours in restaurant kitchens assembling this glorious dish called a coulibiac *of salmon—Craig Claiborne once called it "the world's greatest dish." The* coulibiac, *a dish of Russian derivation, requires the preparation of several different recipes before it can be assembled and baked, and it cannot be completed in one day as you will see from a careful and mandatory reading of all the recipes before making the attempt.*

Once completed, the coulibiac *is a salmon pâté of sorts, but the most elegant one you might imagine, with its layers of ingredients encased in a beautiful brioche. In the interest of history, I have included an optional ingredient called vesiga, the gelatinous spinal marrow of the sturgeon. After diligent work, it yields something like an aspic that contributes a pleasant, chewy texture to the whole creation. I know there are not many readers who will try this* coulibiac *today, but I have modernized certain parts of the recipes (using a food processor, for instance) and offer it here not only because of its place in history but because I truly hope a few daring home cooks will give it a whirl.*

Coulibiac of Salmon

REQUIRED FOR ASSEMBLY AND BAKING (COMPLETE EACH OF THE INDIVIDUAL RECIPES BEFORE BEGINNING ASSEMBLY):

MAIN COMPONENTS

Brioche dough
Salmon-and-mushroom mixture
14 Crepes
Egg-and-rice filling
Vesiga (optional)

ADDITIONAL INGREDI-
ENTS FOR ASSEMBLY
2 egg yolks
2 tablespoons cold water
*2 tablespoons butter at
    room temperature*
1¾ cups hot melted butter

Brioche

1. In the container of a food processor combine 4 cups of the flour, and the sugar, milk and salt and process for several seconds.

2. Dissolve the yeast in a small cup with the warm water. Set aside.

3. With the food processor's motor running, add the butter through the feed tube. When the flour has absorbed it, add the yeast and, one by one, the egg yolks. Continue to process for 30 seconds, or until the dough forms a ball around the shaft.

*4½ cups high-protein
    bread flour*
½ teaspoon sugar
*¾ cup warm milk, at 90
    degrees*
½ teaspoon salt
*3 envelopes fast-rising
    active dry yeast*
*3 tablespoons warm water,
    at 90 degrees*

6 tablespoons unsalted
butter, cut into small
pieces, at room
temperature
6 large egg yolks

4. Dust a board as needed with remaining flour, and knead the dough, then form it into a ball.

5. Lightly butter a clean mixing bowl and add the dough. Cover the bowl with a towel and let it stand in a warm place for about 1 hour, until the dough doubles in bulk. Punch the dough down, turn it out once more onto a lightly floured board. Knead the dough for about 1 minute, then return it to the bowl. Cover tightly with plastic wrap and refrigerate overnight.

6. The next morning punch the dough down again and refrigerate it, covered, until ready to use.

Salmon-and-Mushroom Mixture with Sauce

2 1½-lb. skinless, boneless
center-cut salmon fillets
3 tablespoons unsalted
butter
2 tablespoons finely
chopped shallots
2 tablespoons finely
chopped onions
salt and freshly ground
pepper to taste
¾ pound fresh
mushrooms, thinly
sliced
2 cups dry white wine
3 tablespoons all-purpose
flour
⅛ teaspoon cayenne
pepper
3 tablespoons fresh lemon
juice
2 large egg yolks
¼ cup finely chopped fresh
dill

1. Cut each fillet on the bias into slices about ⅓-inch thick. Each fillet should produce about 12 slices.

2. Select a rectangular baking dish that is suitable for the range top and is large enough to hold all the salmon in one layer (a dish measuring 13½ by 8½ inches is adequate). Rub the bottom of the dish with 1 tablespoon of the butter and sprinkle with onions, shallots, salt and pepper. Arrange the salmon in two parallel rows, each slice slightly overlapping the next.

3. Sprinkle the salmon liberally with pepper. Scatter the mushrooms over the salmon and pour the wine over all. Cover the dish tightly with aluminum foil and, on the range top, bring the wine to a boil. As soon as the boil is reached, remove the salmon from the heat and let it stand for 5 minutes, covered.

4. Uncover the dish and carefully pour the liquid into a bowl. Gently spoon off the mushrooms and set them aside.

5. To prepare the sauce, melt the 2 remaining tablespoons of butter in a saucepan and whisk in the flour. Blend well. Add the reserved cooking liquid,

and cook the mixture for about 5 minutes at medium heat, stirring frequently. Add the mushrooms and continue to cook for another 5 minutes. Stir in the cayenne, lemon juice and pepper, along with any liquid that has continued to gather around the fish in the baking dish.

6. Meanwhile, beat the yolks with a whisk and add them and the dill to the saucepan, stirring rapidly. Cook the mixture for about 30 seconds and remove it from the heat. Check to see if the sauce requires additional salt or pepper.

7. Spoon and scrape this thick sauce evenly over the layers of salmon in the baking dish. Let it cool and then cover the dish with plastic wrap. Refrigerate until thoroughly chilled.

Crepes

1. Place the flour in the mixing bowl and make a well in the center. Add the eggs, salt and pepper. Add the milk gradually while stirring with a wire whisk. Make sure there are no lumps.

2. Add 1 tablespoon of the melted butter and the dill; blend well. (Use the remaining butter to grease the pan for each crepe.)

3. Brush a 7- or 8-inch skillet with some of the butter, and place it on the stove. When the skillet is hot but not burning, add 2 tablespoons of the batter and swirl it around neatly to completely cover the bottom of the pan. Let it cook over moderately high heat for about 30 seconds, or until browned on the bottom. Turn the crepe and cook the second side for only about 15 seconds. Place the crepe on a sheet of plastic wrap.

4. Continue making the crepes one at a time, brushing the pan lightly as needed until all the batter is used and stacking the crepes on the plastic wrap.

1½ cups all-purpose flour
3 large eggs
salt and freshly ground
pepper to taste
1¾ cups milk
2 tablespoons unsalted
butter, melted
2 tablespoons finely
chopped fresh dill

Egg-and-Rice Filling

2 large hard-boiled eggs
1¾ cups cooked rice
¼ cup finely chopped fresh
    parsley
2 tablespoons finely
    chopped fresh dill
salt and freshly ground
    pepper to taste
1½ cups chopped cooked
    vesiga (optional; see
    recipe below)

1. Chop the eggs and place them in a mixing bowl. Add the remaining ingredients and blend well.

Vesiga

½ pound vesiga
salt to taste

1. Wash the vesiga in cold water. Split it as necessary for thorough cleaning. Wash again in cold water, and drain.

2. Place it in a large saucepan; cover with lots of water and salt to taste. Simmer for 3 hours, or until tender. Replace the liquid as it evaporates. Drain the vesiga and chop it to look like chopped aspic.

NOTE: Although vesiga is an unusual ingredient, it is often available through certain fish stores.

TO ASSEMBLE THE *COULIBIAC*

1. Remove the salmon-and-mushroom mixture from refrigeration. Using a knife, cut it in half lengthwise down the center.

2. Remove the brioche dough from the bowl, and place it on a floured board. With your fingers, shape it into a thick flat pillow shape, then roll it into a rectangle measuring 21 by 18 inches. The rectangle will have somewhat rounded corners. Arrange 8 crepes, edges overlapping in a neat pattern, over the center of the rectangle, leaving a border of brioche dough.

3. Sprinkle about a third of the egg-and-rice filling lengthwise down the center of the crepes. Using a large spatula, gently pick up half of the chilled

salmon and carefully arrange it, mushroom side down, over the egg mixture. Sprinkle this with another third of the egg-and-rice mixture. Top this sandwich fashion with another layer of the salmon mixture, mushroom side up. Sprinkle with the egg-and-rice mixture, and cover with a layer of the remaining crepes.

4. Bring up one side of the brioche. Brush it liberally with a mixture of the 2 egg yolks blended with 2 tablespoons cold water, reserving the remainder for the next steps. Bring up the opposite sides of the brioche dough to enclose the filling, overlapping the 2 sides of the dough. Brush all over with the yolks. Trim off the ends of the dough to make them neat. Brush with the yolks and bring up the ends, pinching as necessary to enclose the filling.

5. Carefully turn the *coulibiac* upside down onto a buttered baking pan. This will keep the seal intact. Brush the *coulibiac* all over with the yolk mixture. Using a small, round decorative cookie cutter, cut a hole in the center of the *coulibiac*. This will allow steam to escape. Cut out another slightly larger ring of dough to surround the outline of the hole neatly. Roll out a scrap of dough and cut out strips of dough to decorate the *coulibiac*. Always brush with beaten egg before and after applying a pastry cutout.

6. Roll out a 6-foot length of aluminum foil. Fold it into thirds to make one long band about 4½ inches in height. Brush the band with ¼ cup of the melted butter. Arrange the band neatly and snugly around the loaf, buttered side against the brioche. (The purpose of this band—which creates a thin, high wall, resembling that of a terrine—is to prevent the side of the loaf from collapsing before the dough has a chance to firm up while baking.) Fasten the top of the band with a jumbo paper clip. Run a string around the center of the foil band to keep it in place.

Wrap it 3 times and tie the ends. Make certain the bottom of the loaf is securely enclosed with foil. Set the pan in a warm, draft-free place for about 30 minutes for proofing the dough.

7. Meanwhile, preheat the oven to 400 degrees.

8. Place the loaf in the oven and bake for 15 minutes. Reduce the oven temperature to 375 degrees and bake for 10 minutes. Cover with a sheet of aluminum foil to prevent excess browning. Continue baking for 30 minutes. Remove the foil and continue baking for 15 minutes more.

9. Remove the *coulibiac* from the oven. Pour ½ cup of the melted butter through the steam hole into the filling. Serve cut into 1-inch-thick slices with the remaining butter on the side.

When I was a young cook, making mousses required the forearm of a construction worker and great patience. With the advent of the food processor, mousses of all kinds can be made in minutes. In fact, they are no more challenging than poached eggs. The salmon mousse here, which has a wonderful texture and color, is a cinch for home cooks. Just remember that the salmon and the cream must be thoroughly cold so they emulsify properly.

Individual Salmon Mousses

1 pound very cold skinless
    boneless salmon fillets,
    cut in 1-inch cubes
salt and freshly ground
    pepper to taste
⅛ teaspoon freshly grated
    nutmeg
dash Tabasco or to taste
1 large egg
¾ cup half-and-half

1. Preheat the oven to 400 degrees.

2. Place the salmon in the container of a food processor. Add the salt, pepper, nutmeg and Tabasco. Add the egg and blend for 10 seconds. Combine the half-and-half and heavy cream. Add the cream mixture and continue blending for about 30 seconds, until the mixture has a fine texture.

3. Grease the inside of four 1½-inch soufflé dishes

with the butter. Spoon an equal portion of the mixture into each soufflé dish. Smooth over the tops and cover loosely with aluminum foil.

4. Place the dishes in a high-sided metal pan and pour hot water halfway up the sides of the dishes. Place the pan on top of the stove and bring the water to a boil. Transfer the pan to the bottom of the oven and bake for 20 minutes.

5. Determine the doneness by inserting a thermometer into the mousse. If the thermometer registers 140 degrees or if the end comes out clean, the mousse is done. Unmold onto a warm plate and serve with hot tomato sauce, placing a thyme sprig or coriander leaf in the center of the mousse for garnish.

¾ cup heavy cream
1 teaspoon unsalted butter, softened
tomato sauce (see following recipe)
4 sprigs thyme or fresh coriander leaves

YIELD: 4 SERVINGS

Quick Fresh Tomato Sauce

1. Melt the butter in a saucepan over medium heat. Add the shallots and garlic. Cook, stirring, until wilted; do not brown.

2. Stir in the tomatoes, tomato paste, broth, 1 thyme sprig or dried thyme, bay leaf, and salt and pepper. Cook, stirring occasionally, for about 10 minutes.

3. Discard the thyme sprig, if using fresh, and the bay leaf. Put the mixture in a food mill or food processor. Blend to a fine puree. Return the sauce to the pan and warm. Serve hot over salmon mousse.

2 tablespoons unsalted butter
1 tablespoon finely chopped shallots
¼ teaspoon minced garlic
4 ripe plum tomatoes, cored and cut in small cubes
1 tablespoon tomato paste
½ cup fresh or canned chicken broth (see recipe page 146)
1 sprig thyme or ¼ teaspoon dried thyme
1 bay leaf
salt and freshly ground pepper to taste

YIELD: 2 CUPS

Brandade de morue, *a salt-cod puree, is another country-French specialty that has been rediscovered in a big way by chefs and restaurant patrons. I say rediscovered because it was a sought-after dish at Le Pavillon in the 1940s. The version I served back then was unremittingly rich, made with heavy cream and milk, caviar and truffles. Today a lighter Provençal style is most common. I offer the original version from Le Pavillon partly for historical purposes. If you want to lighten it remove the heavy cream and add about ⅔ cup of olive oil.*

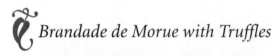

Brandade de Morue with Truffles

2 pounds boneless skinless
    salt cod
1½ pounds potatoes,
    peeled and cut into 2-
    inch cubes
2½ cups milk
1 peeled onion, studded
    with 3 cloves
4 sprigs parsley
1 bay leaf
1 cup heavy cream
2 tablespoons minced
    garlic
1 cup olive oil
½ teaspoon freshly grated
    nutmeg
⅛ teaspoon cayenne
    pepper
freshly ground white
    pepper to taste
salt to taste, optional
2 black truffles or 4 table-
    spoons caviar, optional
croutons (see recipe page
    233)

YIELD: 8 SERVINGS AS A
MAIN COURSE OR 10 TO 12
SERVINGS AS AN APPETIZER

1. Place the cod in a large bowl and cover it with cold water. Soak it for 12 hours, changing the water often.

2. Place the potatoes in a saucepan and cover them with water. Simmer for about 20 minutes, or until the potatoes are soft. Drain.

3. While the potatoes are cooking, drain the salt cod and transfer it to a large saucepan. Cover it with cold water. Add ½ cup of the milk, the onion, parsley and bay leaf. Bring to a boil, lower the heat and simmer for about 3 minutes, or until the cod is cooked. Drain well, and carefully remove any small bones or skin that remains.

4. In another saucepan blend the remaining milk and the cream. Warm the mixture over low heat.

5. Combine the potatoes and the garlic in the bowl of an electric mixer. Beat at low speed until crumbled. Then beat at a higher speed until coarsely textured.

6. Meanwhile, warm the oil in a saucepan. In the mixing bowl alternately drizzle in all of the milk-cream mixture and the oil while beating slowly until the texture is smooth. Add the nutmeg, cayenne and the freshly ground pepper. Add salt only if needed. Place on serving plates with croutons and garnish, if desired, with thinly sliced truffles or caviar.

My most famous customers from stage and screen included Errol Flynn, Marlene Die-
trich, Jean Gabin and Charles Boyer. Most were fairly well versed in food, having trav-
eled extensively, and one dish celebrities frequently called for was baked striped-bass
Pavillon. I always suspected it had something to do with the theatrical presentation.
The whole fish was brought to the table, its top skin removed and decorated with shal-
lots, onions, garlic and mushrooms. This dish was a particular favorite of Joseph
Kennedy and his family.

Baked Striped-Bass Pavillon

1. Preheat the oven to 425 degrees.

2. Rinse the bass in cold water and pat it dry with
paper towels. Coat a baking dish with 2 tablespoons
of the butter, place the fish in the center and sprinkle
with salt and pepper. Add the shallots, onions, garlic,
mushrooms, parsley sprigs, thyme and bay leaf.
Scatter this around the fish. Add the white wine.
Sprinkle the lemon juice over the fish. Place 2 tablespoons of the butter over the fish. Cover the dish
loosely with aluminum foil.

3. Bake for 45 minutes to 1 hour, depending on the
size of the fish. The fish is done when the dorsal
fin in the middle of the backbone comes out easily
and cleanly when tugged, or when the cheeks in the
head separate from the bone. Baste every 15
minutes.

4. Transfer the fish to a warm serving platter.
Remove the sprigs of parsley, thyme sprigs, if using,
and the bay leaf. Pour the liquid and solids from
the baking dish into a small saucepan. Reduce if necessary. Swirl in the remaining butter. Do not let it
boil.

5. Remove the skin from the top of the fish. (Use a
sharp paring knife or your fingers to do this.) Then
ladle the sauce over and sprinkle with chopped
parsley.

1 6-to-8-pound striped
bass, cleaned, scaled
and left whole, head
and tail intact
8 tablespoons unsalted
butter
salt and freshly ground
pepper to taste
¼ pound finely chopped
shallots
¼ cup chopped white
onions
2 teaspoons finely chopped
garlic
¼ pound sliced mush-
rooms
4 sprigs parsley
4 sprigs thyme or 1 tea-
spoon dried thyme
1 bay leaf
3 cups dry white wine
juice of 1 lemon
4 tablespoons finely
chopped fresh parsley

YIELD: 6 TO 8 SERVINGS

Quenelles de Brochet Lyonnaise

PIKE DUMPLINGS LYONNAISE STYLE

PANADE

2 large egg yolks
½ cup all-purpose flour
⅛ teaspoon freshly grated
*   nutmeg*
salt and freshly ground
*   white pepper to taste*
2 tablespoons unsalted
*   butter, melted*
½ cup milk

1½ pounds boneless skin-
*   less pike fillets, very cold*
*   and cut into 1½-inch*
*   cubes*
2 large egg whites
salt and freshly ground
*   pepper to taste*
⅛ teaspoon cayenne
*   pepper*
⅛ teaspoon freshly grated
*   nutmeg*
1½ cups heavy cream, very
*   cold*
1 tablespoon butter, very
*   cold*
4 cups salted boiling water
champagne sauce (see
*   recipe page 226)*

1. Combine the egg yolks, flour, half of the nutmeg, salt and pepper in a saucepan. Stir rapidly and add the melted butter. The mixture should be well blended.

2. Bring the milk just to the point of boiling. Place the saucepan with egg yolk mixture over medium-high heat and add the hot milk. Blend well. Continue stirring rapidly until the mixture pulls away from the sides of the saucepan. Remove the pan from the heat and let the mixture cool. This mixture is called a *panade*. Remove the *panade* from the saucepan, cover and refrigerate until thoroughly cold.

3. In the container of a food processor, combine the fish, the *panade* (cut into small pieces), the egg whites, salt, pepper, cayenne and the remaining nutmeg. Blend for about 30 seconds, stopping the blade occasionally to scrape down the mixture if necessary. Add the cold cream slowly while blending. Blend for about 50 seconds.

4. Transfer to a bowl; cover with plastic and keep cool.

5. To form the quenelles, dip a large soupspoon into a container of hot water. Spoon out a heaping portion of the mixture, enough to create the desired football shape of the quenelle. Each quenelle should measure roughly 2¾ inches long by 1¾ inches wide. Smooth the mixture with another spoon. Then, with the spoon used for shaping, scoop the mixture cleanly into a shallow pan. There should be about 20 to 24 quenelles.

6. Cut wax or parchment paper into the shape of the pan's rim. Cut a hole in the center about an inch in

diameter. Butter one side of the paper and cover the quenelles with the buttered side down.

7. Bring a large quantity of lightly salted water to a boil. Gently ladle the water over the wax or parchment paper so that it will flow gradually into the dish. Continue adding water until the quenelles are covered. Place pan over medium heat. Bring the water back to a simmer. Lower the heat and simmer gently for 5 minutes.

8. Remove the wax or parchment paper and turn the quenelles once. Cover again and turn off the heat.

9. Remove the quenelles carefully with a slotted spoon. Drain them briefly on paper towels. Serve immediately with champagne sauce (see recipe page 226).

NOTE: To make this recipe it is important that the fish, butter, *panade* and cream are very cold before they are combined.

YIELD: 6 SERVINGS AS A MAIN COURSE OR 12 SERVINGS AS AN APPETIZER

Here's the first recipe I ever did as a "60-Minute Gourmet" chef. It's my crevettes *"margarita," or shrimp with tequila. Shrimp cooks so fast that I knew this could not fail to meet the criteria of the new column.*

Shrimp with Tequila

1. Shell and devein the shrimp and butterfly them; that is, split them partly down the back and flatten them lightly. Place the shrimp in a bowl and add the lime juice and salt and pepper. Let them stand briefly until ready to cook.

2. Peel the avocado and cut it into half-inch-thick slices. Discard the pit. (Use the avocado as soon as possible or the flesh will discolor.)

3. Heat the butter in a skillet, and when it is quite hot, but not smoking, add the shrimp, stirring

¾ pound (about 20) raw shrimp
¼ cup lime juice
salt and freshly ground pepper to taste
1 small ripe unblemished avocado
2 tablespoons unsalted butter
1 tablespoon finely chopped shallots
¼ cup tequila

¾ cup heavy cream
1 tablespoon finely
   chopped fresh cilantro
   or Chinese parsley

rapidly, and cook about 2 minutes. Sprinkle with the shallots and cook, stirring, about 10 seconds. Add the tequila. Take care, for the tequila may flare up. Add the cream and cook over high heat about 1 minute. Add salt and pepper to taste. Add the avocado and cook just until the slices are piping hot, no longer. Using a slotted spoon, transfer the shrimp and avocado pieces to hot serving dishes. Bring the sauce to a full rolling boil for about 30 seconds and add the chopped cilantro or Chinese parsley. Spoon the sauce over the shrimp and avocado. Serve with rice.

YIELD: 4 SERVINGS

 ## Grilled Shrimp with Herb Butter Sauce

24 jumbo shrimp, about
   2 pounds, shelled and
   deveined
¼ teaspoon hot red pepper
   flakes
4 tablespoons Dijon
   mustard
2 tablespoons olive oil plus
   extra for brushing
2 tablespoons fresh lemon
   juice
1 tablespoon chopped fresh
   thyme or 1 teaspoon
   dried thyme
salt and freshly ground
   pepper to taste
herb butter sauce (recipe
   follows)

1. Preheat an outdoor grill or the oven broiler to high.

2. In a bowl, combine the shrimp with the red pepper, mustard, olive oil, lemon juice, thyme, salt and pepper, and blend well.

3. Arrange 6 shrimp on each of 4 skewers. Brush the sides with oil.

4. Place the shrimp on the grill or under the broiler about 4 inches from the heat source. Cook for about 2 minutes and turn; continue grilling for about 2 minutes more. Serve with herb butter sauce.

YIELD: 4 SERVINGS

Herb Butter Sauce

¼ cup minced shallots
¾ cup dry white wine
¼ cup heavy cream
8 tablespoons unsalted
   butter

Combine the shallots and the wine in a heavy saucepan. Cook over medium-high heat until the wine has almost evaporated. Add the cream and reduce by half. Add the butter quickly, 1 tablespoon at a time, whisking constantly. Remove the saucepan from the heat and stir in the salt, pepper and herbs.

salt and freshly ground pepper to taste
2 tablespoons finely chopped fresh basil
2 tablespoons finely chopped fresh chervil
2 tablespoons finely chopped fresh chives

This light and healthful dish underscores how far my cooking style has evolved since I arrived in this country. When I was cooking at Le Pavillon, my notion of yogurt was that it was a staple of certain Eastern European immigrants, but nothing our customers would eat.

It is amazing how in the last twenty years yogurt has become a tremendously popular snack food. It is only beginning to be appreciated—in Western cooking, that is—as a low-fat alternative to cream. Quality plain yogurt—not the sweet stuff that is bound with a lot of gelatin—is a fine low-fat sauce ingredient. The inspiration for the following shrimp dish comes from Russian cuisine. Lentils are an excellent complement.

Shrimp with Yogurt and Coriander

1. Shell and devein the shrimp. Rinse well and drain. Pat dry.

2. Combine the yogurt, cayenne, garlic, turmeric, salt, cumin and caraway seeds in a bowl. Add the shrimp and blend well. Cover and refrigerate until ready to use.

3. Heat the oil in a large nonstick skillet. Add the mushrooms and cook, stirring, 2 minutes. Add the shrimp mixture and coriander and cook, stirring gently, until the shrimp change color, about 2 to 3 minutes. Do not overcook. Serve hot.

1½ pounds shrimp
1 cup plain yogurt, drained for 5 minutes in cheesecloth
½ teaspoon cayenne pepper
1 tablespoon finely chopped garlic
1 teaspoon ground turmeric
salt to taste
½ teaspoon ground cumin
1 teaspoon caraway seeds
2 tablespoons mustard oil or vegetable oil
½ pound small white mushrooms
½ cup finely chopped fresh coriander

YIELD: 4 SERVINGS

The annual migration of shad to rivers in the East reaches its peak about late April. These inexhaustible fish migrate at that time of year into virtually every major river system from Florida to the Gulf of St. Lawrence. Shad has a rich, yet delicately fla-vored, flesh that is best with a sauce that has some acid: vinegar, lemon or dry white wine. In France, I remember cooks braising shad in an acidic sorrel sauce. The flesh is very bony, and the acid helped break down the bones. Although shad is usually sold boned, it should be checked carefully. Any remaining bones can be removed with tweezers. Sautéed shad can be prepared in numerous ways. A quick sauce can be made with shallots, capers, cream and lemon juice or with butter, lemon and parsley. The roe is usually sautéed and served on the side, sometimes topped with crisp bacon. The recipe here is one of my favorites. On the side, you might serve simple steamed potatoes with parsley, which can be done slightly ahead of time and reheated before serving.

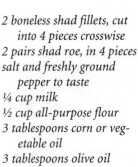

Shad and Roe with Tomatoes and Shallots

2 boneless shad fillets, cut into 4 pieces crosswise
2 pairs shad roe, in 4 pieces
salt and freshly ground pepper to taste
¼ cup milk
½ cup all-purpose flour
3 tablespoons corn or veg-etable oil
3 tablespoons olive oil
2 tablespoons unsalted butter
1 medium zucchini, cored and cut into ¼-inch cubes
6 ripe plum tomatoes, about 1 pound, cored and peeled, cut into small cubes
2 tablespoons finely chopped shallots
2 teaspoons finely chopped garlic

1. Place the fillets and the roe in a flat dish. Sprinkle with salt and pepper. Add the milk, coating the fillets and the roe.

2. Dredge the fish and the roe in the flour and remove the excess.

3. Heat the corn or vegetable oil in a nonstick skillet large enough to hold the fillets, skin side up, and the roe in one layer. Cook the fillets and the roe over medium-high heat until crisp and brown, about 4 minutes, basting occasionally. Turn and cook for 2 minutes. Transfer the fillets and roe to a warm plat-ter and keep them warm. If the pan is not large enough, cook in 2 segments.

4. Discard the cooking oil and wipe out the skillet. Add the olive oil and the butter. Add the zucchini and tomatoes, salt and pepper to taste. Cook over high heat for about 2 minutes, shaking and tossing the skillet so that the zucchini and tomatoes cook evenly. Add the shallots and garlic. Cook about a

minute more, shaking the skillet. Pour this mixture over the fish, sprinkle with parsley and serve immediately.

4 tablespoons finely chopped fresh parsley

YIELD: 4 SERVINGS

One of the great revelations to me shortly after arriving in this country was soft-shell crabs. I had never heard of such bizarre creatures in France. When spring arrived in the Northeast I would head down to the Fulton Fish Market and buy as many as I could carry. I am still addicted to them.

I was amazed to learn that when an Atlantic blue crab sheds its shell it expands by as much as a third. Blue crabs are particularly meaty at that point. They must be removed from the traps immediately or hard-shell crabs may devour them. Soft-shell crabs are a great delicacy, something I prepare at home whenever the opportunity arises. A classic and quick preparation involves sautéing them and serving them with almonds. In the recipe here, the crabs are dipped in milk that has been seasoned with salt, pepper and Tabasco (the recipe calls for ¼ teaspoon, which is mild; if you like them spicy, add a little more), then dredged in flour.

Soft-Shell Crabs with Almonds

1. To clean soft-shell crabs, first place them top side up on a cutting board and cut off the eyes. Then lift the flap on each side and remove the spongy gill tissue underneath. Rinse the crabs with cold water and pat dry with paper towels. (Seafood shops will often do the cleaning for you.)

2. In a flat dish, combine the milk, salt, pepper and Tabasco. Blend well. Add the crabs, turning them over to coat well with the milk.

3. Place the flour in a flat dish and remove the crabs from the milk. Dredge them in the flour. Shake the crabs to remove any excess flour.

4. Heat 2 tablespoons of the vegetable oil in a large nonstick skillet. Place 6 crabs in the pan and cook them over medium heat for about 3 minutes, or until lightly browned on one side. Turn and cook

12 small fresh soft-shell crabs, cleaned
½ cup milk
salt and freshly ground pepper to taste
¼ teaspoon Tabasco sauce or more to taste
¾ cup all-purpose flour
4 tablespoons vegetable oil
2 tablespoons unsalted butter
2 tablespoons olive oil
1 tablespoon finely chopped shallots
½ cup sliced almonds
2 tablespoons fresh lemon juice
4 tablespoons finely chopped fresh parsley.

until golden brown on the other side. The total cooking time is about 6 or 7 minutes, depending on the thickness of the crabs. Transfer the crabs to a warm serving platter and keep them warm. Add the remaining vegetable oil to the pan and repeat the procedure with the other crabs.

5. Pour off the fat from the skillet and wipe it clean with paper towels. Add the butter and olive oil, add the shallots and sliced almonds and cook until lightly browned, shaking the pan. When the oil is bubbling, add the lemon juice and pour the mixture over the crabs. Sprinkle with the parsley.

YIELD: 4 SERVINGS

Many home cooks have the mistaken perception that to cook foreign cuisines—in this case Moroccan—one needs special knowledge and equipment. But one can dip into the flavors of another cuisine simply by knowing the appropriate seasonings and how to blend them. Usually nothing more exotic than a sauté pan or a steamer is needed.

In the case of Moroccan food, which is well known in France, the major flavor sensations come from cumin, turmeric, sometimes coriander, ginger and cinnamon. Applying these judiciously to chicken, fish or red meat can give them a startling new dimension.

As a side dish, there is couscous with raisins and red peppers (see recipe page 232), a nice semisweet foil to the spicy fish. Quick, or precooked, couscous cuts the preparation time to under 6 minutes.

 ## Tuna Steaks Moroccan Style

1 teaspoon paprika
½ teaspoon ground cumin
1 teaspoon turmeric
¼ teaspoon ground anise
    seed
½ teaspoon ground ginger
⅛ teaspoon ground
    cinnamon
¼ teaspoon hot red pepper
    flakes

1. In a small mixing bowl, combine the paprika, cumin, turmeric, anise, ginger, cinnamon, hot red pepper flakes, salt and pepper, and blend well.

2. Place the tuna steaks on a large platter and sprinkle and rub each side with the spice mixture. Sprinkle evenly with the lemon juice and oil. Cover the fish with plastic wrap. Let stand until ready to cook.

3. If broiling, preheat broiler and arrange the steaks on a rack and place them under a very hot broiler,

about 4 inches from the heat. Broil 4 minutes with the door partly open. Turn, and continue broiling, leaving the door open, for about 3 to 4 minutes for medium rare. For rare, cook less. The steaks should be well browned.

4. For pan frying, heat a heavy cast-iron skillet, large enough to hold the steaks in one layer. Do not add fat. When the skillet is quite hot, add the tuna steaks; cook until well browned on one side, about 3 minutes. Turn and cook 3 minutes more on the second side for rare. If desired, cook longer.

5. Place the steaks on warm plates, brush them with the melted butter and sprinkle with the coriander. Serve with couscous.

salt and freshly ground white pepper to taste
4 tuna steaks, about 1½ pounds total weight, about 1½ inches thick
1 tablespoon fresh lemon juice
2 tablespoons olive oil
2 tablespoons unsalted butter, melted
4 tablespoons coarsely chopped fresh coriander

YIELD: 4 SERVINGS

Crabmeat au Gratin

1. Preheat the broiler to high.

2. Melt 2 tablespoons of the butter in a saucepan over medium heat. Add the flour and blend well. Do not brown. Add the milk and cook, stirring with a whisk, until blended and smooth. Season with cayenne pepper, nutmeg, and salt and pepper to taste.

3. Add the cream, bring to a boil and simmer briefly, stirring occasionally, about 3 to 4 minutes. Stir in half of the sherry, beat in the egg yolk and remove the sauce from the heat.

4. Melt the remaining butter in a nonstick skillet over medium-high heat. Add the shallots; cook them briefly until wilted. Add the crabmeat and cook briefly, stirring gently. Sprinkle with the remaining sherry.

5. Spoon the crabmeat into a baking dish and

3 tablespoons unsalted butter
2 tablespoons all-purpose flour
1½ cups milk
pinch cayenne pepper
⅛ teaspoon freshly grated nutmeg
salt and freshly ground white pepper to taste
¾ cup heavy cream
¼ cup dry sherry
1 large egg yolk
4 tablespoons finely chopped shallots
1 pound fresh lump crabmeat, shell and cartilage removed
4 tablespoons freshly grated Gruyère or Parmesan cheese

smooth it over with a spatula. Cover the crabmeat with the hot sauce. Sprinkle with the cheese.

6. Place the dish under the broiler and cook until golden brown and bubbling hot.

YIELD: 4 SERVINGS

Mahimahi is a large, firm-fleshed, medium-moist, flaky fish that also goes by the names dorado and dolphin. It commonly comes from Pacific waters. Mahimahi is generally less expensive than tuna, salmon and swordfish—three popular grilling fishes— and if cooked properly it can be delightful.

Broiled Mahimahi with Capers and Fresh Tomato Sauce

4 boneless 6-ounce
   mahimahi fillets, or any
   similar fish fillets, like
   halibut or swordfish
salt and freshly ground
   pepper to taste
4 teaspoons chopped thyme
   leaves or 1 tablespoon
   dried thyme
4 tablespoons olive oil
4 tablespoons finely
   chopped shallots
⅓ cup drained capers
4 ripe plum tomatoes,
   peeled and cubed
1 teaspoon finely chopped
   garlic
1 tablespoon red wine
   vinegar
4 tablespoons finely
   chopped fresh basil or
   parsley

YIELD: 4 SERVINGS

1. Preheat the broiler to high.

2. Place the mahimahi fillets in a flat ovenproof dish. Sprinkle with salt, pepper, thyme and 2 tablespoons of olive oil. Set aside and cover with plastic wrap. Let the fish stand in a cool place for 15 minutes.

3. Meanwhile, heat the remaining olive oil in a saucepan over medium-high heat. Add the shallots and the capers. Cook until wilted. Add the tomatoes, salt, pepper and the garlic. Cook, stirring, for 3 minutes. Add the vinegar; cook briefly and blend well. Remove the sauce from the heat and keep it warm.

4. Place the mahimahi fillets under the broiler, about 4 inches from the source of heat. Cook about 3 minutes. Carefully flip the fillets and cook for 3 minutes, or until the fish is slightly pink in the center. Do not overcook.

5. Transfer the fish to a warm serving plate and spoon equal portions of the tomato sauce over each fillet. Sprinkle with the basil and serve immediately.

As soon as I could walk, it seems, I was plodding around the fields of my hometown gathering escargots. Burgundy is a very humid region, making it excellent for escargots. In the rainy season we would head out early in the morning with our little boxes.

Here is a classic Burgundian recipe for escargots. Since fresh Burgundian snails are not available in this country, the recipe calls for standard canned escargots.

Escargots Burgundy Style

1. Place the shells in a saucepan, cover with water, bring to a boil and simmer for 5 minutes. Drain well and cool. Make sure all the water is removed from the shells.

2. Open the can of snails into a saucepan and add the white wine, the sliced shallots, sliced garlic, parsley sprigs, carrots, thyme and bay leaf and salt and pepper to taste. Bring the mixture to a boil and simmer for 5 minutes. Let it cool and drain. Set the snails aside and discard the rest.

3. Place the butter, bread crumbs, chopped parsley, chopped shallots, chopped garlic, and salt and pepper to taste in a mixing bowl. Blend well. Check the seasoning.

4. Spoon half a teaspoon of the butter mixture into each of the snail shells. Add 1 snail to each shell, pushing it within the shell with your finger. Fill the remaining opening with butter mixture to the top and smooth out. This may be done in advance and the snails placed in the refrigerator or freezer.

5. When ready to cook, preheat the oven to 500 degrees. Arrange the snails on 4 traditional snail dishes; bake for 5 minutes, or until sizzling hot.

6. Serve with French bread.

24 snail shells
1 7½-ounce can snails imported from France
4 tablespoons dry white wine
1 tablespoon shallots, thinly sliced
1 teaspoon sliced garlic
2 sprigs parsley
4 thinly sliced carrot rounds
1 sprig thyme or ¼ teaspoon dried thyme
½ bay leaf
salt and freshly ground pepper to taste
1½ sticks unsalted butter, at room temperature
2 tablespoons very fine fresh bread crumbs
4 tablespoons minced fresh parsley
1 tablespoon minced shallots
1 tablespoon minced garlic

YIELD: 4 SERVINGS

ℰ Frogs' Legs Provençale

24 medium fresh frogs' legs
⅓ cup milk
½ cup all-purpose flour
salt and freshly ground
    pepper to taste
4 tablespoons vegetable oil
6 tablespoons unsalted
    butter
1 tablespoon chopped
    garlic
8 ripe plum tomatoes,
    peeled, cut into small
    cubes
1 tablespoon fresh lemon
    juice
4 tablespoons chopped
    fresh parsley

YIELD: 4 SERVINGS

1. Prepare 1 pair of frogs' legs at a time. Slip 1 leg between the 2 lower muscles of the other leg. This helps keep the leg flat while it cooks. Repeat this with all the legs.

2. Soak the legs briefly in the milk. Drain the legs and then dredge them in flour that has been seasoned amply with salt and pepper. Shake off the excess.

3. In a nonstick skillet large enough to hold half of the frogs' legs, heat 2 tablespoons of the oil. Add the legs, and cook them over medium-high heat until golden on one side. Turn and cook on the other side until golden. Repeat with the remaining frogs' legs. Arrange the frogs' legs on each serving plate. Keep them warm.

4. Pour off any fat from the skillet and wipe out the skillet with paper towels. Add the butter and garlic over high heat and cook briefly; do not burn. Add the tomatoes and salt and pepper to taste. Cook over high heat. When the butter foams, add the lemon juice, stir and pour the mixture over the frogs' legs and sprinkle with parsley.

The traditional French and American way to cook flatfish like sole and flounder is sautéing. Delicate species like these can be broiled, but they tend to dry out quickly if not watched carefully. A third method I have used successfully for years is high-temperature roasting.

At a temperature of 425 to 450 degrees, four fillets of flounder will cook in five minutes. The intense heat seals in the moisture and yields a crisp exterior. The fillets can be placed in a baking dish with just a little butter, salt and pepper. I then brush them with a little white wine for extra moisture.

Fillet of Flounder with Coriander Butter Sauce

1. Preheat the oven to 475 to 500 degrees.

2. Select a baking dish large enough to hold the fillets in one layer. Grease the bottom with 1 tablespoon of the butter. Sprinkle with salt and pepper.

3. Arrange the fillets close together in the pan. Sprinkle with salt and pepper and brush the tops with 1 tablespoon of the wine.

4. Place the fish in the oven and bake 5 minutes.

5. Meanwhile, place the remaining 3 tablespoons butter in a saucepan. Add the remaining wine. Bring to a boil and cook for 1 minute. Add salt, pepper and the coriander or parsley. Blend well with a wire whisk.

6. Transfer the fish to a warm serving plate. Pour the sauce evenly over the fish and serve immediately.

4 tablespoons unsalted butter
salt and freshly ground pepper to taste
4 flounder fillets, about 1¼ pounds total
3 tablespoons dry white wine
4 tablespoons chopped fresh coriander or parsley

YIELD: 4 SERVINGS

POULTRY AND GAME

If there was one thing we had an abundance of in Burgundy when I was growing up it was rabbits. Hare could be found all over the rolling hills and vineyards. Many families, like mine, also raised rabbits.

Civet de lapin is a dish that always reminds me of the gruesome task of selecting a victim from our domestic brood and preparing it for the pot. Traditionally this recipe was made with rabbit blood. Since that is not exactly a household staple, I usually recommend a thickened red wine sauce, which yields a delicious, albeit different, flavor. Here, I offer a version that contains the blood as an optional ingredient.

Rabbit in Red Wine

1 2½- to 3-pound rabbit,
   cut into serving pieces
salt and freshly ground
   pepper to taste
4 ounces sliced salt pork,
   cut into ¼-inch strips
1 tablespoon vegetable oil
16 pearl onions, peeled
½ pound small button
   mushrooms
½ cup trimmed small
   carrot rounds
1 tablespoon chopped
   garlic
4 tablespoons all-purpose
   flour (to be used only if
   blood is not used)

1. Preheat the oven to 350 degrees.

2. Sprinkle the rabbit with salt and pepper.

3. In a small saucepan add the salt pork and cover with water. Bring to a boil; simmer for 1 minute. Remove and drain.

4. Place a heavy ovenproof skillet (with a cover) over medium-high heat and add the oil and salt pork. Cook, stirring, over medium heat until the strips are rendered of their fat and are crisp. Remove the pieces with a slotted spoon and set aside.

5. Add the rabbit and brown on all sides while stirring over medium-high heat. Add the onions and mushrooms; stir until all are lightly browned. Drain

the excess fat, then add the carrots and garlic. Cook, stirring, for 1 minute.

6. Sprinkle the rabbit pieces with the flour, and stir to coat everything evenly.

7. Tie the bay leaf, thyme and parsley sprigs in a cheesecloth bundle.

8. Add the wine and broth or water. Stir and scrape the skillet to remove the particles that cling to the bottom and sides. Add the cloves. Bring the mixture to a boil on top of the stove, then cover and place in the oven. Bake for 45 minutes, or until tender.

9. Remove the bundle of herbs. Stir in the blood mixture if available. Bring to a simmer. Do not boil. Remove at once and serve.

1 bay leaf
4 sprigs thyme or 1 teaspoon dried thyme
4 sprigs parsley
3 cups dry red Burgundy wine
1 cup fresh chicken broth (see recipe page 146) or water
2 whole cloves
¾ to 1 cup rabbit blood (if available), blended with the juice of ½ lemon to prevent coagulation
4 tablespoons chopped fresh parsley

YIELD: 6 TO 8 SERVINGS

Coq au vin, chicken in red wine, is one of the classics of French cuisine, said to have been devised by a hostelry owner in the Puy de Dôme in Auvergne during the reign of Henry IV. It was one of the first dishes I learned at my mother's side. Most chefs call for Burgundy wine in the sauce and flour as a thickener; my mother preferred chicken blood to bind the sauce, something we had an abundance of in our rural village. The recipe here follows the bloodless method.

Coq au Vin

1. Cut the salt pork into roughly ⅓-inch cubes. Place them in a skillet with the pearl onions. Cover with water and bring the mixture to a boil. Cook for about 2 minutes, then drain, and continue to cook the salt pork and the onions over medium-high heat for 5 minutes, until the cubes of pork start to brown. Discard the fat. Add the mushrooms and cook for 5 minutes longer, or until the mushrooms are lightly browned.

2. Meanwhile, heat the oil in a heavy casserole or Dutch oven over medium-high heat. Sprinkle the

¼ pound lean salt pork
1 cup pearl onions, peeled
½ pound small whole mushrooms
2 tablespoons vegetable oil
1 3-pound chicken, cut into serving pieces
salt and freshly ground pepper to taste
2 tablespoons minced shallots
2 tablespoons minced onions

2 teaspoons minced garlic
2 tablespoons all-purpose
flour
3 cups dry red wine, such
as Burgundy or Côtes-
du-Rhône
2 sprigs thyme or 1 tea-
spoon dried thyme
1 bay leaf
4 sprigs parsley

chicken with salt and pepper to taste. Place the chicken pieces in the pan skin side down and cook until golden on one side, about 4 minutes. Cook on the reverse side about 3 minutes. Drain the fat.

3. Put the shallots, minced onions and garlic into the casserole or Dutch oven with the chicken. Cook, stirring, for about 2 minutes. Blend the flour into the mixture well. Add the wine, and bring to a boil to dissolve the brown particles clinging to the bottom and sides of the casserole or Dutch oven. Add the onion–mushroom–salt pork mixture. Add the thyme, bay leaf and parsley. Check the seasoning, cover and simmer for 20 to 30 minutes, or until tender. Do not overcook. Serve with fine noodles.

NOTE: In France, sometimes a few tablespoons of Marc de Bourgogne, which is an eau-de-vie made from grape skins, is added to the pot.

YIELD: 4 SERVINGS

Poached Chicken with Rice

1 3½-pound whole chicken
2 leeks, trimmed and
washed well
3 celery ribs
4 sprigs parsley
2 sprigs thyme or 1 tea-
spoon dried thyme
1 bay leaf
3 medium carrots, scraped
1 onion, peeled and
studded with 2 cloves
6 peppercorns
salt to taste

SAUCE
2 tablespoons unsalted
butter

1. Rinse the chicken well in cold water. Place the chicken in a deep pot and nearly cover with water.

2. Tie the leeks, celery, parsley and thyme sprigs (if using) with a string to form a bouquet garni. (If dried thyme is used, sprinkle it into the pot.) Add it to the pot, then add the bay leaf, carrots, onion with cloves, peppercorns, and salt to taste. Bring the mixture to a boil, and cook until the chicken is tender (about 45 minutes). Skim the surface often to remove the fat.

3. Remove the chicken from the broth and keep it warm while preparing the sauce. Reserve the broth.

4. Melt the butter in a saucepan, add the flour, and mix well with a wire whisk over low heat. When blended, add 2 cups of the chicken broth, and stir

vigorously with the whisk. Bring to a boil and simmer for 10 minutes.

5. Strain the sauce through a sieve, if desired, for smoother texture, then add the cream, nutmeg, cayenne and the lemon juice. Bring to a boil. Check for seasoning and simmer for 5 minutes.

6. Serve one-quarter of the chicken per person, removing the skin if desired. Spoon a little of the sauce over the chicken and serve the remainder in a sauceboat. Serve with rice.

4 tablespoons all-purpose flour
1 cup heavy cream
¼ teaspoon freshly grated nutmeg
pinch cayenne pepper
2 tablespoons fresh lemon juice

YIELD: 4 SERVINGS

As the American household shrank in the 1970s and 1980s, and lifestyles changed, whereby many couples, married and unmarried, lived in small apartments without children, I tried to devise recipes that could suit such situations. The Norman Rockwell American family dinner, with two or three children eagerly watching Dad carve the turkey, has faded like a photograph left out in the sun.

The recipe here represents the kind of dish that makes sense for the new American household. It is quick, portion controlled and easy. And since relatively few families today sit down to dinner together, parents can prepare the side dishes and the hen, leaving cooking to the last minute.

Cornish hens are an American hybrid of an American fowl, the Plymouth Rock hen, and a British bird, the Cornish or bantam rooster. The term "Cornish game hen" was used earlier in this century, but because the birds are now raised commercially in large numbers under controlled conditions, their flavor is no longer gamey. Yet they are convenient to serve and can be moist and tasty when cooked properly.

Roasted Cornish Hens with Rosemary and Garlic

1. Preheat the oven to 450 degrees.

2. Rub the hens inside and out with salt and pepper and remove any excess fat inside. Place 1 sprig of rosemary (or ½ tablespoon dried) and 1 garlic clove in each cavity, and truss the hens, if desired.

3. Place the hens in a large metal roasting pan.

4 1-pound Cornish hens
salt and freshly ground pepper to taste
4 sprigs rosemary or 2 tablespoons dried rosemary
4 garlic cloves, peeled
2 tablespoons olive oil

4 1-pound Cornish hens
salt and freshly ground
   pepper to taste
4 sprigs rosemary or 2
   tablespoons dried rosemary
4 garlic cloves, peeled
2 tablespoons olive oil
1 medium onion, peeled
   and quartered
¼ cup dry white wine
¾ cup fresh or canned
   chicken broth (see
   recipe page 146)

Brush them with the oil. Arrange the birds on their sides. Scatter the necks, gizzards, hearts, livers and onion around the birds. Place the pan on top of the stove and heat until the oil is sizzling.

4. Place the pan in the oven and bake for 20 minutes, basting occasionally.

5. Turn the birds on the reverse side and cook for 15 more minutes, basting occasionally.

6. Remove all the fat from the dish and add the wine and chicken broth.

7. Reduce the heat to 425 degrees. Place the hens on their backs for a final 10 minutes of cooking. The simmering broth will deglaze the pan as the birds roast, making a gravy. Remove the pan from the oven and pour the cavity juices, including the rosemary and garlic, from the hens into the pan. Remove the rosemary and the trussing string, and let the hens rest in a warm place for 5 minutes before carving.

YIELD: 4 SERVINGS Serve with the gravy, giblets and onion, if desired.

This dish was brought to America by my coworker at the 1938 World's Fair in New York, Marius Isnard. It became one of our most popular dishes. Note how light and contemporary this chicken preparation is. The same sauce is sometimes paired with veal chops and veal scaloppine.

Chicken Beauséjour

1 2½-pound chicken, cut
   in 10 serving pieces
salt and freshly ground
   white pepper to taste
1 tablespoon olive oil
3 tablespoons unsalted
   butter
3 garlic cloves, unpeeled
3 sprigs thyme or 1 tea-
   spoon dried thyme

1. Sprinkle the chicken with salt and pepper.

2. Heat the olive oil and 1 tablespoon of the butter over medium-high heat and add the chicken pieces skin side down. Do not add the chicken liver. Cook 5 to 7 minutes until golden brown. Turn and cook 3 minutes, until lightly browned. Add the garlic, thyme, bay leaf and the liver. Cook over moderate heat for about 5 minutes more. Do not let the garlic

burn. Turn the chicken pieces so they are evenly cooked.

3. Remove the chicken pieces and the liver. Keep them warm. Drain most of the fat. Make sure the thyme, bay leaf and garlic remain in the skillet. Add the wine, and cook over high heat, stirring to dissolve the brown particles that cling to the bottom. Cook until the wine is reduced by half. Add the chicken broth or water and squeeze the garlic cloves to extract the pulp. Cook for 1 minute.

4. Add the chicken pieces; cook for 5 minutes over medium-high heat. Swirl in the remaining butter, check for seasoning and serve with mashed potatoes or buttered noodles. Sprinkle with parsley or chervil.

1 large bay leaf
½ cup dry white wine
⅓ cup fresh chicken broth (see recipe page 146) or water
chopped fresh parsley or chervil

YIELD: 4 SERVINGS

As I have said, in classic French cuisine, anything prepared in the style Véronique refers to a dish that contains fresh grapes. Most commonly this preparation is applied to chicken or fish, specifically sole. At Le Pavillon, chicken Véronique was a popular lunch entrée. It was made with suprême *of chicken, meaning a skinless, deboned breast. We always left on a little section of the wing as visual flourish. This is my lighter version.*

Chicken Breast Véronique

1. Trim all the fat and white membranes from the chicken breasts. Place the pieces on a flat surface and, with a flat mallet, pound them lightly all over. Slice the breasts into ½-inch strips. There should be about 3 cups.

2. If canned grapes are used, drain them and set aside. If fresh grapes are used, remove the stems, rinse and drain well and set aside.

3. Heat the butter in a large, heavy skillet. When the butter is hot but not brown, add the chicken breasts. Sprinkle with salt and pepper. Cook over high heat,

4 skinless boneless chicken breasts, about 1¾ pounds
½ cup seedless grapes (if fresh unavailable, use canned)
3 tablespoons unsalted butter
salt and freshly ground pepper to taste
1½ tablespoons finely chopped shallots
½ cup dry white wine
½ cup heavy cream

stirring constantly, so that the pieces cook evenly. Cook just until the chicken loses its raw look and is almost cooked through, about 3 to 5 minutes.

4. Use a slotted spoon to transfer the pieces to another skillet or platter and keep warm.

5. Add the shallots to the first skillet. Cook briefly, stirring, and add the wine. Cook over high heat while shaking the skillet and stirring the contents. As juices accumulate around the chicken pieces in the second skillet, add them to the first skillet's liquid. When the wine has reduced by half, add the cream. Cook the sauce over high heat, stirring to blend.

6. If fresh grapes are used, add them to the sauce. Cook over high heat about 4 to 5 minutes, or until the cream mixture takes on a saucelike consistency. Add salt and pepper to taste. If canned grapes are used, add them at the last minute of cooking just to heat through.

YIELD: 4 SERVINGS

7. Spoon the chicken into the sauce and heat through. Serve with rice pilaf.

Sesame-Coated Chicken Breasts

4 ⅓-pound skinless bone-
  less chicken breasts
salt and freshly ground
  pepper to taste
½ cup sesame seeds
1 teaspoon vegetable oil
1 teaspoon sesame oil
4 tablespoons unsalted
  butter
2 teaspoons freshly grated
  ginger
2 tablespoons fresh lemon
  juice

1. Place each chicken breast between sheets of plastic wrap. Pound the chicken lightly all over with a mallet. Remove from the plastic wrap.

2. Sprinkle the chicken pieces on both sides with salt and pepper. Dredge the pieces on all sides with the sesame seeds.

3. Heat the vegetable oil and sesame oil in a large nonstick skillet and add the breasts in one layer. Cook on one side over medium heat for about 5 minutes, or until lightly browned. Turn and cook on the second side, about 4 to 5 minutes more. Transfer

the chicken to a heated serving dish or platter, pour off the fat from the skillet and wipe it clean with a paper towel.

4. Melt the butter in the same skillet and add the grated ginger. Cook until the butter turns hazelnut brown. Stir in the lemon juice and the soy sauce; blend well. Pour the sauce over the chicken breasts and sprinkle with the chopped coriander.

1 tablespoon light soy sauce
3 tablespoons chopped fresh coriander

YIELD: 4 SERVINGS

When I am on an extremely tight schedule to produce a meal at home for four or more, I often reach for boneless chicken breasts. Not only do they cook quickly—whether grilled, poached, sautéed or broiled—but they also adapt to an endless variety of accompaniments.

On one such rushed occasion I bought some shiitake mushrooms in the market and built a fast meal around them. Believed to be among the oldest cultivated mushrooms, dating back two thousand years or more, shiitakes have become a favorite ingredient of contemporary restaurant chefs.

Shiitake caps are somewhat spongy in texture, decidedly less dense and chewy than many American mushrooms. They have a faint smoky flavor that enhances poultry beautifully. These fairly assertive mushrooms do not shrink when combined with strong herbs and spices.

Chicken Breasts with Shiitake Mushrooms

1. Sprinkle the chicken breasts with salt and pepper.

2. Heat the oil in a heavy skillet and add the chicken breasts, the mushrooms and the onions. Cook about 5 minutes over medium heat, until lightly browned. Turn the pieces and cook 5 minutes more, shaking the pan and turning the mushrooms and onions so they brown evenly. Remove the chicken breasts, and keep them warm. Pour off the fat from the pan.

3. Add the rosemary and shallots and cook briefly, until wilted. Add the wine and cook, stirring and

4 5-ounce skinless boneless chicken breasts
salt and freshly ground pepper to taste
2 tablespoons olive oil or vegetable oil
¼ pound shiitake or small white mushrooms, washed and dried
8 small white onions, peeled

4 sprigs rosemary or
   1 tablespoon dried
   rosemary
2 tablespoons finely
   chopped shallots
¼ cup dry white wine
¾ cup fresh or canned
   chicken broth (see
   recipe page 146)
2 tablespoons unsalted
   butter
2 tablespoons finely
   chopped fresh parsley

YIELD: 4 SERVINGS

scraping to dissolve the brown particles that cling to the skillet.

4. When the wine is reduced by almost half, blend in the chicken broth. Continue cooking for about 5 minutes, and when the sauce is reduced by half, stir in the butter. Remove the pan from the stove immediately. Pour the sauce over the chicken, sprinkle with the parsley and serve.

Turkey breast, which in my opinion is still an underused product among home cooks, is often the centerpiece of summer lunches around my house. It is every bit as lean and light as chicken breast, sometimes less expensive, and always appreciated by those who think of turkey only as a holiday staple.

When you are preparing turkey breast, as in the recipe here, it is always a good idea to slice the meat and then pound it lightly to ensure even cooking.

Sliced Turkey Breasts with Herbs

8 sliced turkey tenderloin
   steaks, about 1½
   pounds total
salt and freshly ground
   pepper to taste
2 tablespoons olive oil
2 tablespoons unsalted
   butter
4 garlic cloves, unpeeled
1 large bay leaf
4 sprigs thyme or 1 tea-
   spoon dried thyme
⅓ cup dry white wine
⅓ cup fresh or canned
   chicken broth (see
   recipe page 146)

1. Place each turkey breast steak between sheets of clear plastic wrap and pound lightly and evenly with a meat pounder or flat mallet to make the slices about ¼ inch thick.

2. Sprinkle the sliced turkey with salt and pepper.

3. Heat the olive oil and 1 tablespoon of the butter in a skillet large enough to hold the turkey in one layer, or use 2 smaller pans. Add the sliced turkey and the garlic, bay leaf and thyme. Cook over medium-high heat for about 5 minutes, turning the pieces until lightly browned on both sides. Do not overcook.

4. Remove the turkey slices to a warm platter. Leave

the garlic, bay leaf and thyme in the pan. Add the wine to the skillet and cook over high heat, stirring to dissolve the brown particles that cling to the bottom and sides of the skillet. Cook 3 to 5 minutes until the wine is reduced by half. Add the chicken broth and boil briskly 3 to 5 minutes until reduced by half.

2 tablespoons finely chopped fresh parsley

5. Swirl in the remaining butter and the parsley. Add the turkey slices and any juices that have accumulated around it, and reheat the turkey through. Remove the bay leaf, and serve with the garlic cloves and the sauce.

YIELD: 4 SERVINGS

Turkey was not something I was exposed to very much as a boy growing up in Burgundy, though it was available. The turkey was introduced to Europe in the seventeenth century, but was not part of the traditional French-cooking repertory. When turkey was brought to Europe by Jesuits, it was known as Indian chicken, or poule d'Inde, a variation of names coined by Spanish conquerors in the century before.

Until recently, Americans reserved turkey for Thanksgiving. But the bird's versatile and inexpensive meat has led to a newfound popularity. Supermarkets now carry turkey steaks and turkey parts, which are ideal for quick family cooking. The only caveat in cooking turkey meat, as all Thanksgiving chefs know, is that extra care must be taken to keep it moist.

Turkey Steaks with Prosciutto and Mushrooms

1. Place the turkey steaks between sheets of plastic wrap and pound them evenly, with a meat pounder or flat mallet, without breaking the flesh, until the fillets are about ¼ inch thick.

2. Sprinkle the turkey with salt and pepper. Dredge lightly in the flour and shake off the excess.

3. Heat the oil in a nonstick skillet large enough to

4 turkey breast steaks, total weight about 1½ pounds
salt and freshly ground pepper to taste
¼ cup all-purpose flour
2 tablespoons olive oil
¼ pound small button mushrooms, washed and drained

4 large thin slices
  prosciutto, about
  2 ounces total
2 tablespoons unsalted
  butter
1 garlic clove, peeled
1 tablespoon chopped fresh
  sage or 2 teaspoons
  dried sage
¼ cup Marsala
2 tablespoons chopped
  fresh Italian parsley

cook the turkey pieces in one layer. Scatter the mushrooms around the turkey and cook over high heat about 2 minutes, or until golden brown on one side. Turn the turkey and cook about 1 minute more on the other side. Remove the turkey and the mushrooms and place them on a warm platter. Keep the turkey warm.

4. In the same skillet, without removing the oil, sauté the prosciutto briefly, about 15 seconds. Add the butter and garlic clove to the pan. Return the turkey and the mushrooms to the pan along with any juices that have accumulated around the turkey. Place a slice of prosciutto over each turkey breast.

5. Sprinkle the sage over the prosciutto and pour the Marsala into the pan. Cover and cook for about 1 minute.

6. Remove and serve immediately. Top each serving with the turkey and mushrooms. Pour the sauce over and sprinkle with the parsley.

YIELD: 4 SERVINGS

Squab is the centerpiece of some fine dining memories for me. I have always been fond of the Moroccan squab-and-phyllo pie called pastilla. And as a boy in the Chablis region, I came to love the regional specialty known as Burgundy squab pie, made with a rich red wine sauce.

For many years it was considered an exotic game bird here, seen only in fancy restaurants. But now squabs can be found neatly lined up in supermarket butcher cases, along with guinea hens, pheasants and rabbits.

To me, squab is one of the finest of all game birds. I say game, knowing that most squabs sold in this country are cultivated on farms where they are carefully fattened. I think of them as game because they have darker flesh and tastier meat than chickens or turkeys.

Squab can be delicious grilled on a spit, roasted in the oven or baked in a pie.

Roast Squab with Apples

1. Preheat the oven to 450 degrees.

2. Peel, core, and cut the apples into quarters.

3. Season the cavities of the squabs with salt and pepper. Inside each, put a sprig or a pinch of thyme, a bay leaf and a clove of garlic.

4. Put the squabs in a large, heavy roasting pan, breasts up. Scatter the onions, potatoes, and apples around them. Brush the squabs, potatoes and onions with the olive oil. Cook 20 minutes, basting often with the pan juices.

5. Remove the fat and apples, and set the apples aside, keeping them warm. Add the wine and chicken broth. Cook 10 minutes longer, basting often and scraping the bottom of the pan. Do not overcook: the cooked squabs should be pink in the thigh.

6. Lift the squabs with a fork and let the herbs and juices flow into the pan. Put the squabs on a serving platter; untruss and keep them warm.

7. Put the roasting pan on top of the stove. Bring the gravy to a simmer, add the butter, and blend, stirring and scraping. If there is not enough gravy, add some chicken broth or water. Carve the squabs if desired and serve with the onions, potatoes, apples and pan gravy.

NOTE: Cornish hens can be substituted. Cook them 10 minutes longer.

2 tart green apples
4 ¾-pound squabs, oven-
ready and trussed
salt and freshly ground
pepper to taste
4 sprigs thyme or 4 pinches
dried thyme
4 small bay leaves
4 small garlic cloves, peeled
4 small white onions,
peeled
4 small red potatoes,
peeled
1 tablespoon olive oil
4 tablespoons dry red wine
½ cup fresh or canned
chicken broth (see
recipe page 146)
1 tablespoon unsalted
butter

YIELD: 4 SERVINGS

Quail, once an exotic bird rarely available commercially, has become as commonplace as duck. Fresh or frozen quail is available in supermarkets and specialty food shops all the time now, and cookbooks routinely give recipes for its preparation.

Today, the quail offered for sale are grown mainly on game farms. The birds are usually cleaned and partly deboned before they are shipped to market, ready to cook.

The availability and ease of preparation of farm-raised quail are only two of the reasons for their popularity. The taste is delectable, retaining some of the gamey flavor of the wild bird. Quail is also one of the quickest of all birds to cook, and one of the fastest techniques—my favorite—is broiling.

Broiled Quail with Raisin and Apple Stuffing

½ cup fresh or canned chicken broth (see recipe page 146)
¼ pound bulk sausage
½ cup chopped onions
½ cup chopped apples, cut in small cubes
¾ cup golden raisins
¼ cup quick-cooking couscous
¼ teaspoon ground cumin
⅛ teaspoon ground cinnamon
salt and freshly ground pepper to taste
4 tablespoons gin
4 tablespoons chopped fresh coriander (cilantro)
8 quail, boned, except for the wings, thighs and legs
1 tablespoon unsalted butter, melted
1 tablespoon olive oil
2 tablespoons chopped fresh thyme or 1 teaspoon dried thyme

1. Preheat the broiler to high.

2. In a saucepan, bring the chicken broth to a simmer.

3. Heat another saucepan, and add the sausage meat. Cook and stir for 2 minutes, breaking the meat into small pieces. Add the onions, and cook, stirring, until wilted. Add the apples, raisins, couscous, warmed broth, cumin, cinnamon, salt and pepper. Bring to a boil, stirring. Cover tightly, remove from the heat, and let stand for 5 minutes.

4. Add the gin and coriander, and blend well with a fork. Divide the mixture into 8 portions. Set aside.

5. Salt and pepper the cavity of each quail. Add the stuffing with your hands. Crisscross the legs, and flatten the quail so they will cook evenly.

6. Pour the butter and oil into a baking dish large enough to hold the quail in one layer. Add the quail, and sprinkle with half of the thyme. Turn the quail in the butter-and-oil mixture, and sprinkle with salt, pepper and the remaining thyme. Then turn the quail breast side down.

7. Place the quail under the broiler about 6 inches from the heat source. Leave the door partly open. Cook them about 4 minutes, until lightly browned. Turn the quail breast side up. Return them to the broiler and, basting occasionally, broil for 4 minutes longer, or until nicely browned.

8. Set the oven at 400 degrees. Place the quail on the bottom rack, and bake for 2 to 3 minutes, basting with the butter-and-oil mixture and the lemon juice. Serve immediately with the sauce.

1 tablespoon fresh lemon juice

YIELD: 4 SERVINGS

BEEF

Filet de Boeuf Périgourdine

ROAST FILLET OF BEEF WITH TRUFFLE SAUCE

1 4-pound center-cut fillet
 of beef, oven ready from
 the butcher
salt and freshly ground
 pepper to taste
2 tablespoons vegetable oil
4 tablespoons unsalted
 butter
¼ cup coarsely chopped
 shallots
¼ cup Madeira
1½ cups demiglace sauce
 (see recipe page 201)
⅓ cup chopped truffles,
 with their juices

1. Preheat the oven to 450 degrees.

2. Sprinkle the fillet of beef with salt and pepper to taste.

3. Place the meat in a heavy roasting pan and brush the fillet all over with the oil. Place in the oven and roast, turning and basting, for 25 to 30 minutes for rare. If you desire, cook 5 minutes longer or more. Transfer the meat to a dish and keep it warm.

4. Pour the fat from the roasting pan, add 1 tablespoon of the butter and the shallots. Place the pan on top of the stove and cook over medium heat, stirring, until the shallots are wilted. Add the Madeira, then stir to dissolve the brown particles that cling to the bottom and sides of the roasting pan. Add the demiglace sauce, bring to a boil and simmer for 5 minutes.

5. Pour the mixture through a fine mesh strainer into a saucepan. Press with a fork or spatula to extract all the sauce. Add the truffles and their liquid to the saucepan, bring to a boil and simmer for 5 minutes. Add any juices that accumulate around the beef fillet. Swirl in the remaining butter gently. Keep the mixture warm.

6. Carve the fillet into approximately ½-inch-thick

slices. Spoon some of the sauce on each plate. Carefully arrange the slices over the sauce and serve.

I still remember that wonderful aroma in the kitchen of my boyhood home in Burgundy. It was a soothing, familiar scent that, to me, defined home as much as anything else. It came from a big iron pot that my mother kept on the stove twenty-four hours a day. It was our stockpot, and every family at the time had one. My mother would toss into the simmering liquid meat bones, scraps of vegetables and seasonings. The delicious broth was used for soups, sauces and poaching liquid.

When she reduced the broth to a gelatinous thickness, it was called demiglace. That highly concentrated stock was the backbone for so many excellent sauces. Today I make demiglace every few months at home, pour the liquid into ice-cube trays and freeze it.

Demiglace

1. Preheat the oven to 425 degrees.

2. Scatter the bones in a large flat roasting pan, place it in the oven and bake for 1 hour. Stir and turn the bones every 15 minutes.

3. Over the bones scatter the carrots, onions and celery and add the leeks, peppercorns, bay leaves, garlic and thyme over all. Bake 15 minutes longer.

4. Transfer the contents of the roasting pan to a large stockpot. Add 2 cups of the water to the roasting pan to dissolve the particles that cling to the bottom and sides of the pan. Add this to the stockpot.

5. Add the remaining water to cover the bones; add the parsley and tomatoes. Do not add salt. Bring to a boil and simmer over low heat for about 6 hours, depending on the intensity of the heat. Be careful to simmer very gently. Skim the surface often for the first 2 hours.

6. Strain the liquid and reduce it to 8 cups by simmering further. Strain again and place the liquid in jars. This stock will keep for weeks in the refrigerator and will keep indefinitely in the freezer. The demiglace can be stored frozen in ice-cube trays and the cubes transferred to a plastic bag.

10 pounds veal bones, chopped into 3- to-4-inch pieces
2 cups chopped carrots
4 cups chopped onions
2 cups chopped celery
2 cups leek greens
10 peppercorns
2 bay leaves
4 garlic cloves, unpeeled, cut in half
4 sprigs thyme or 2 teaspoons dried thyme
8 quarts water
1 cup loosely packed fresh parsley stems
4 cups chopped tomatoes

Steak au Poivre

4 8-ounce boneless shell
   steaks, with the excess
   fat removed
salt to taste
4 tablespoons cracked
   white or black pepper-
   corns
1 tablespoon vegetable oil
2 tablespoons finely
   chopped shallots
½ cup dry red wine
½ cup demiglace (see
   recipe page 201)
2 sprigs thyme or ½ tea-
   spoon dried thyme
2 tablespoons unsalted
   butter
2 tablespoons finely
   chopped fresh parsley

YIELD: 4 SERVINGS

1. Sprinkle the steaks with salt.

2. Using a mallet or meat pounder, crush the peppercorns coarsely. Sprinkle the steaks evenly on both sides with the peppercorns. Press down with your hands so the peppercorns adhere to the meat.

3. Heat the oil in a cast-iron skillet large enough to hold the steaks in one layer. When the pan is nearly smoking, add the steaks and cook about 3 minutes. When the steaks are well browned, turn them. Cook about 2 to 3 minutes more for medium-rare. Remove to a warm platter.

4. Pour off the fat from the skillet, add the shallots and cook, stirring, until wilted. Do not brown. Add the wine, demiglace and the thyme. Reduce the mixture to half a cup. Add any liquid that may have accumulated around the steak. Bring to a simmer, add the butter and swirl in. Remove the skillet from the heat.

5. Remove the thyme sprig if using and pour the sauce over the steaks. Garnish with fresh parsley.

NOTE: If you do not have demiglace, you can make the sauce using ½ cup fresh or canned beef broth and 2 teaspoons tomato paste.

Everyone seems to be nostalgic for meatloaf these days. It is showing up on restaurant menus in all different incarnations: loaded with garlic, à la Tex-Mex, laced with cheese.

Meatloaf does not have to be made only with traditional ground beef. I like to add some pork or veal for a leaner texture. Recently, I added ground turkey to a meatloaf, and the result was excellent. The ground beef had more than enough fat to keep it moist.

Growing up in France, I was not exposed to American-style meatloaf. But we had many terrine mixtures that approximated it. The key to a good terrine or a good meatloaf is to keep it moist and well seasoned.

Meatloaf Oriental Style 🍲

1. Preheat the oven to 425 degrees.

2. Heat the oil in a nonstick skillet. Add the scallions, garlic and water chestnuts. Cook briefly till wilted. Set aside.

3. Place the beef and the turkey in a mixing bowl. Add the scallion mixture, ginger, coriander, bread crumbs, soy sauce, egg, sherry and pepper. Blend well with your hands, taking care not to overmix.

4. Divide the mixture into 4 equal portions and place into 4 individual 1½-cup soufflé dishes. Smooth over the tops.

5. Set the soufflé dishes in a large ovenproof pan with an inch of water and bring to a boil on top of the stove. Place the pan in the oven and bake for 30 minutes. Let the loaves cool about 5 minutes before unmolding. Spoon barbecue sauce over and around the loaves.

1 tablespoon vegetable oil
¾ cup finely chopped scallions, with greens included
1 teaspoon finely chopped garlic
½ cup water chestnuts, drained and chopped
¾ pound lean ground beef
¾ pound ground turkey
1 teaspoon freshly grated ginger
¼ cup loosely packed coriander leaves, chopped
½ cup fine fresh bread crumbs
3 tablespoons soy sauce
1 large egg, beaten
¼ cup dry sherry
freshly ground white pepper to taste
barbecue sauce (recipe follows)

YIELD: 4 SERVINGS

Barbecue Sauce

Combine all the ingredients in a saucepan. Blend well, bring to a boil and remove from the heat.

NOTE: This sauce is good with any barbecued meat.

3 tablespoons olive oil
1 cup ketchup
2 tablespoons fresh lemon juice
1 tablespoon chopped garlic
2 tablespoons honey
2 teaspoons freshly grated ginger
2 teaspoons soy sauce
3 thin lemon slices, seeded
1 tablespoon Dijon mustard

YIELD: ABOUT 1 CUP

The U.S. Army was a revelation for a young Frenchman in many ways, and there are so many experiences I will not forget. Most of the food, of course, I would rather never think about again, but there is one dish that bursts into my memory from time to time because it was so common and the soldiers had so much fun laughing at it with various scatological denigrations: creamed beef. Truthfully, I almost liked it. It was essentially a roux mixed with chopped beef and seasonings.

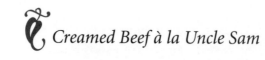

Creamed Beef à la Uncle Sam

3 tablespoons unsalted
    butter
4 tablespoons all-purpose
    flour
2 cups warm milk
½ cup evaporated milk
1 pound ground beef,
    chopped coarsely
1 cup minced onions
salt and freshly ground
    pepper to taste
½ teaspoon freshly grated
    nutmeg
1 teaspoon paprika
¼ teaspoon cayenne
    pepper
toast or crackers

YIELD: 4 TO 6 SERVINGS

1. Melt the butter in a saucepan over medium-high heat. Add the flour and blend well with a wire whisk. Add the milk and condensed milk all at once and stir vigorously with the whisk until the mixture is thick and smooth.

2. Heat a large skillet and add the ground beef. Cook, stirring, until most of the fat is melted. Do not brown the meat. Add the onions, salt and pepper, nutmeg, paprika and cayenne. Cover and cook until the onions are wilted. Drain off the excess fat.

3. Add the milk mixture to the skillet, blend well with a wire whisk and bring to a simmer. Serve hot with toast or crackers on the side.

PORK

Country pâtés were one thing families did not generally make at home in Burgundy when I was a boy, especially not the tricky pâté en croûte described earlier. I was usually dispatched to the local charcutier several times a week to buy a fresh pork or game terrine. Actually, basic terrines without the pastry cover are easy to make—not much more involved than a meatloaf. My version here has a fairly assertive liver flavor. It is delicious with rough-textured country bread and a zesty mustard.

Country Pâté

1. Preheat the oven to 375 degrees.

2. In a large mixing bowl, combine all the ingredients except the sliced fatback and the bay leaf. Blend well with your hands, cover the mixture with plastic wrap and refrigerate for 30 minutes.

3. Meanwhile, select a 10-to-12-cup rectangular or oval pâté mold or 2 smaller pâté molds. Line the mold with the sliced fatback and reserve enough to cover the pâté.

4. Using a food processor or meat grinder, grind the mixture coarsely. Return the mixture to the mixing bowl and blend well again.

5. Spoon the mixture into the mold and smooth the top. Lay the fatback over the meat so it hangs over the edges of the mold. To cover and seal the meat

2½ pounds pork liver, with sinew removed, finely ground
2½ pounds boneless skinless pork butt, both lean and fatty parts, cut into ½-inch cubes
1 cup chopped onions
½ cup chopped shallots
2 teaspoons chopped garlic
2 teaspoons chopped fresh thyme or 1 teaspoon dried thyme
1 cup flour
½ teaspoon saltpeter, optional (this gives the meat an attractive cured tint)
salt to taste

*1 teaspoon freshly ground
   pepper*
⅛ teaspoon ground cloves
⅛ teaspoon ground allspice
*¼ teaspoon freshly grated
   nutmeg*
½ cup dry white wine
1 large egg, beaten
*12 strips unsalted fatback,
   thinly sliced (the strips
   should span the mold
   used)*
1 bay leaf

*cornichons or pickled
   onions*
country bread
mustard

YIELD: 18 OR MORE SERVINGS

securely, press the edge of the fatback down into the mold, securing it all around the rim.

6. Set the mold in a large pan, and pour boiling water around it several inches deep. Cover the mold loosely with aluminum foil and bake for 1½ to 2 hours, or until the internal temperature reaches 160 degrees. Remove the mold from the water bath, cover again with foil and place some weights— plates, cutting boards and so on—on top to pack the pâté down. Let it stand until cool, then refrigerate.

7. Serve with cornichons or pickled onions, country bread and mustard.

🦪 Roast Pork Family Style

*1 2½-to-3-pound center-
   cut pork loin, with bone*
*2 garlic cloves, cut into
   8 slivers*
1 tablespoon vegetable oil
*salt and freshly ground
   pepper to taste*
*2 tablespoons chopped fresh
   thyme or 1 teaspoon
   dried thyme*
1 bay leaf
1 large onion, peeled
*12 medium red potatoes,
   peeled*
½ cup water
*4 tablespoons chopped fresh
   parsley*

1. Preheat the oven to 400 degrees.

2. Make 8 gashes in the fat of the pork. Insert slivers of garlic in the gashes.

3. Place the pork in a heavy roasting pan and brush the meat with the oil. Sprinkle with salt and pepper and the thyme. Add bay leaf and the onion. Place the meat in the oven and bake for 30 minutes, basting every 10 minutes.

4. Turn the roast, add the potatoes around the meat, and coat them with the cooking juices. Bake for 15 minutes, or until the potatoes are browned.

5. Remove most of the fat from the pan with a large spoon, add the water and cover with aluminum foil. Reduce the heat to 350 degrees and bake for 45 minutes, basting occasionally.

6. To serve, discard the bay leaf, remove the meat from the oven, and slice the roast in the pan. Present the meat on a platter surrounded by the potatoes and the onion. Pour the pan juices over everything. Sprinkle with the chopped parsley.

YIELD: 6 TO 8 SERVINGS

Pork was the most popular meat in my family when I was a boy. As I described earlier, the ritualistic killing of a pig was somewhat like the Fourth of July for us. Yet I never thought of making burgers from pork until a few years ago when I was looking for lean alternatives to beef. It works splendidly, especially with lots of black pepper, caraway seeds and some ground cumin.

Pork Burgers with Caraway

1. Place the pork in a mixing bowl. Add the caraway seeds, cumin, salt and pepper. Blend with your fingers. Do not overmix.

2. Divide the mixture into 8 portions of equal size. Using your fingers, shape the portions into neat round flat patties about ½ inch thick.

3. Heat the vegetable oil in a nonstick skillet over medium heat and add the patties. Cook on one side about 5 minutes. Turn and cook for 5 minutes more, or until well done. Remove to a warm serving platter. Cover with foil and keep warm.

4. Pour off the fat from the skillet and add the olive oil, onions and garlic. Cook until wilted. Do not brown the garlic. Add the vinegar, tomatoes, sage, salt and pepper. Cook, stirring, about 3 minutes. Pour over the patties and serve.

1½ pounds lean ground
 pork
1 teaspoon caraway seeds
½ teaspoon ground cumin
salt and freshly ground
 pepper to taste
1 tablespoon vegetable oil
1 tablespoon olive oil
½ cup finely chopped
 onions
1 teaspoon finely chopped
 garlic
1 tablespoon red wine
 vinegar
4 ripe plum tomatoes, cut
 into ¼-inch cubes
1 tablespoon chopped fresh
 sage or 2 teaspoons
 dried sage

YIELD: 4 SERVINGS

This Alsatian sauerkraut specialty has almost universal appeal. There are regional variations of it in France, and this one is my particular favorite, using thyme, juniper berries and pork meatballs. Sauerkraut has a very strong flavor, so it is important to rinse it thoroughly before cooking.

Choucroute Garnie

8 pounds sauerkraut
2 tablespoons lard
½ cup sliced onions
1 cup sliced carrots
4 sprigs thyme or 1 teaspoon
    dried thyme
2 bay leaves
12 juniper berries
1 tablespoon chopped garlic
6 fresh pig knuckles
½ pound smoked salt pork,
    cut into 12 slices
2 cups dry white wine
2 cups fresh or canned
    chicken broth (see recipe
    page 146)
salt and freshly ground
    pepper to taste
12 small potatoes, peeled
12 pork meatballs (recipe
    follows)
2 kielbasas
12 frankfurters
12 thin slices baked ham

YIELD: 10 TO 12 SERVINGS

1. Soak the sauerkraut in cold water for 5 minutes. Drain well. Squeeze it with your hands to extract the liquid, then loosen the sauerkraut with your fingers.

2. Preheat the oven to 400 degrees.

3. Melt the lard in a Dutch oven or heavy-gauge kettle and add the onions, carrots, thyme, bay leaves, juniper berries and garlic. Stir and cook over medium heat until wilted. Add the pig knuckles, salt pork, wine and broth.

4. Place the loosened sauerkraut on top and add salt and pepper to taste. Bring to a boil on top of the stove, then cover and place in the oven to bake for 30 minutes.

5. Add the potatoes and the meatballs over the sauerkraut and bake for 30 minutes longer.

6. Place the kielbasas and the frankfurters on top. Bake for 10 minutes.

7. Add the sliced ham and bake for 10 minutes more. Serve with mustard.

Pork Meatballs

1½ pounds lean ground pork
½ teaspoon ground cumin
1 teaspoon crushed caraway
    seeds
¼ cup dry white wine
4 tablespoons chopped fresh
    parsley
salt and freshly ground
    pepper to taste
mustard

YIELD: 12 MEATBALLS

1. Place the pork in a mixing bowl with all the remaining ingredients. Blend well.

2. Shape the mixture into 12 large meatballs. Cook as directed in *choucroute garnie* recipe.

LAMB

Roast Leg of Lamb with Pan Gravy

1. Preheat the oven to 400 degrees.

2. Prepare the lamb for roasting by cutting away the hipbone and excess fat.

3. With a paring knife make small incisions in the meat and insert the garlic slivers.

4. Rub the lamb with the oil and place it in a roasting pan, fat side down, along with the onion and the hipbone (with most of its fat removed). Sprinkle the meat with salt and pepper.

5. Roast the lamb on the floor of the oven (or the lowest rack if in an electric oven), basting every 15 to 20 minutes. Turn the fat side up after a half hour. After 1 hour of cooking time, remove and discard all the liquid from the pan, and pour the water into the pan.

6. Continue roasting the lamb for 15 minutes. The internal temperature should reach at least 140 degrees (for rare).

7. Remove the pan from the oven and place the bone under the roast to serve as a rack in the pan, then let the lamb rest for 20 minutes as dripping juices enrich the gravy. Carve and serve with the pan gravy.

1 6-to-7-pound leg of lamb
6 garlic cloves, slivered
1 tablespoon vegetable oil
1 medium onion, cut in
*   half crosswise*
salt and freshly ground
*   pepper to taste*
¾ cup water

YIELD: 6 TO 8 SERVINGS

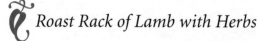 Roast Rack of Lamb with Herbs

2 racks of lamb, with shin-
bones removed (the flat
continuous bone on top
of the ribs)
salt and freshly ground
pepper to taste
2 tablespoons olive oil
½ cup fine fresh bread
crumbs
2 tablespoons chopped
fresh parsley
2 teaspoons finely chopped
garlic
2 tablespoons finely
chopped shallots
2 teaspoons chopped fresh
thyme leaves or 1 tea-
spoon dried thyme
2 tablespoons unsalted
butter, melted
2 tablespoons dry white
wine
⅓ cup fresh or canned
chicken broth (see
recipe page 146)

1. Preheat the oven to 500 degrees or more.

2. Using your fingers and a sharp knife, remove the thick top layer of fat from each rack of lamb. The loins and the ribs should be almost clean of fat. Hack off the ends of the rib bones, leaving about 2 inches of the ribs intact. Sprinkle with salt and pepper.

3. The baking pan should be large enough to hold the racks in one layer, side by side. Place the racks, meat side down, in the pan and brush with 1 table-spoon of the olive oil.

4. Meanwhile, combine the bread crumbs, parsley, garlic, shallots, thyme and the remaining tablespoon of olive oil in a bowl. Set aside.

5. Place the racks of lamb on the bottom rack of the oven. Cook for 10 minutes, turning and basting occasionally.

6. Remove the lamb and sprinkle the meaty side of the ribs with the bread-crumb mixture. Pour the melted butter over the topping. Place in the oven and bake for additional 8 minutes for medium-rare. The topping should be lightly browned. Remove the racks onto a platter and keep them warm.

7. Remove any melted fat from the pan. If there is any bread-crumb mixture in the pan, leave it. Add the white wine and the broth. Place the pan on top of the stove, and bring the liquids to a boil, scraping the bottom to remove the brown particles from the pan. Add any juices that accumulate on the platter around the racks. Bring to a simmer and cook for 2 to 3 minutes. Serve with the carved racks.

YIELD: 6 TO 8 SERVINGS

Côtes d'agneau champvallon *was a particular favorite of J. Edgar Hoover and Cole Porter, two frequent patrons at Le Pavillon. Sometimes they didn't even look at the menu and simply asked the captain if* champvallon *was available.*

I can't blame them, for it is indeed a wonderful assemblage, and easy to make. Many cooks in my day made it with mutton chops. My version calls for more delicate rib lamb chops.

Côtes d'Agneau Champvallon

BAKED LAMB CHOPS WITH POTATOES AND ONIONS

1. Preheat the oven to 375 degrees.

2. Trim off all of the fat from the chops and prepare them French style by trimming off the meat from the base of the chops. Cut off the bone about 2 inches from the main part of the chop. Sprinkle the chops with salt and pepper.

3. Peel the potatoes, then cut them into thin slices about ⅛ inch thick. There should be about 4 to 5 cups. Drop the slices immediately in cold water to avoid discoloration. Drain just before using them.

4. Cut the onions in half and slice them as thinly as possible. There should be about 2 to 3 cups. Set aside.

5. Heat the butter in a heavy skillet and brown the chops lightly on one side. Do not cook through. Turn them and cook until they are lightly browned on the other side.

6. Place all the lamb chops in a large baking dish also suitable for the range top. Scatter the onions over the chops and add the crushed garlic in the center. Lay the sliced potatoes over the chops evenly. Sprinkle with salt and pepper to taste, pour the chicken broth over everything and add the thyme and bay leaf. Cover with aluminum foil.

7. Bring the liquid to a boil on top of the stove, then

12 rib lamb chops, about 2½ pounds total weight
salt and freshly ground pepper to taste
6 medium Idaho or Washington potatoes, about 2¼ pounds
2 medium white onions, about ½ pound
2 tablespoons unsalted butter
2 peeled cloves, crushed
1½ cups fresh or canned chicken broth (see recipe page 146)
2 sprigs thyme or 1 teaspoon dried thyme
1 bay leaf

place the dish on the bottom rack of the oven. Bake about 20 minutes, remove the foil and continue cooking, basting often, for 50 minutes or 1 hour, or until the chops are fork tender and the potatoes are lightly browned. If you want the potatoes browned further, place the dish under the broiler for a minute or so.

YIELD: 6 SERVINGS

Marinades can make the difference between great barbecued food and something that is just acceptable. One can have lots of fun adding different flavors with various combinations of oils, vinegars, fruits and herbs, especially at peak season for produce.

Marinades also serve a tenderizing function. There are two ways to tenderize a piece of meat. One is to damage it physically: pounding, piercing, grinding, cutting. All of these break down fibers.

Another way is to introduce a chemical compound that does the same thing. Indians in pre-Columbian Mexico wrapped meat in papaya leaves before cooking to make it easier to chew. Vinegar and oil, the common household marinade base, breaks down fibers, too, but only on the surface of the meat. I usually recommend marination of about 15 minutes, as in this lamb dish. After that the meat becomes mushy. The best a marinade can do is impart some flavor to the surface of the meat, not tenderize the entire piece.

Marinated Brochettes of Lamb with Honey

1½ pounds skinless boneless loin or leg of lamb
4 tablespoons fresh lemon juice
4 tablespoons olive oil
½ cup dry red wine
⅓ cup honey
1 tablespoon chopped fresh rosemary or 2 teaspoons dried rosemary
1 tablespoon finely chopped garlic

1. Cut the lamb into 16 2-inch cubes.

2. Combine the lamb with the lemon juice, olive oil, wine, honey, rosemary, garlic, cumin, salt and pepper. Blend well, cover with plastic wrap and marinate for 15 minutes.

3. Preheat the oven broiler or a charcoal grill. If wooden skewers are being used, soak them in cold water until ready to use.

4. Drain the meat, reserving the marinade, and

arrange the meat on 4 skewers, alternating with red pepper, onion and eggplant squares.

5. Broil under high heat, 3 minutes on each side for rare, brushing with the reserved marinade. Garnish with parsley or coriander.

NOTE: This recipe works well with pork or chicken.

2 teaspoons ground cumin
salt and freshly ground
pepper to taste
2 large sweet red peppers,
cut into 16 2-inch
squares
2 large white onions, cut
into 16 2-inch squares
1 medium eggplant, cut
into 16 2-inch squares,
½ inch thick
8 tablespoons coarsely
chopped fresh coriander
or parsley

YIELD: 4 SERVINGS

VEAL

The crucial element in cooking this dish is speed and high heat. Ideally the paillard should be cooked on a hot grill, but a very hot cast-iron skillet will do. This recipe is for 1 serving because a paillard must be prepared individually. Simply repeat the process.

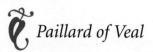 *Paillard of Veal*

*6-ounce veal steak, thinly sliced and cut from the top round of the leg
salt and freshly ground pepper to taste
vegetable oil
1 teaspoon unsalted butter
1 lemon wedge*

1. Place the veal between sheets of plastic wrap and pound it with a flat mallet or meat pounder until it is about ¼ inch thick or less.

2. Sprinkle the meat with salt and pepper and brush lightly with oil on both sides.

3. Meanwhile, if a grill is to be used, it should be very hot. Or heat a heavy iron skillet that is large enough to hold the meat so that it cooks quickly and evenly.

4. If a grill is used, it should be very clean. Place the steak diagonally on the grill. Cook for about 10 seconds on one side. Turn the meat 30 degrees in order to give it a diamond pattern. Cook 10 seconds and turn the meat over. Cook 10 seconds and give it a half turn again. Cook for 10 seconds.

5. If a skillet is used, add the meat when the pan is

very hot and cook about 20 seconds. Turn the meat over and cook 15 seconds on the other side.

6. Place the meat on a hot plate and rub the butter over it. Serve it with a lemon wedge.

NOTE: This can also be made with beef sirloin.

YIELD: 1 SERVING

Two aspects of the classic French restaurants of earlier generations were the opulence and showmanship. There was a lot of tableside service in those days—lots of elaborate carving, deboning, flambéing—and customers loved it. At Le Pavillon so many dishes came with a sideshow. Even kidneys. We used to send out roasted veal kidneys with mustard sauce on a big platter. The captain drenched them with cognac or another liqueur and ignited it. Of course, this wasn't just restaurant fireworks; the cognac did add a lovely sweetness to the dish.

Roasted Veal Kidneys in Mustard Cream Sauce

1. Preheat the oven to 425 degrees.

2. Sprinkle the kidneys with salt and pepper. Heat the oil in an ovenproof skillet large enough to hold the kidneys in one layer. Over medium-high heat add the kidneys and brown quickly all over.

3. Place the kidneys in the oven and bake for 10 minutes. Remove the kidneys and keep them warm. Pour off the fat and any liquid that may have accumulated in the pan. In the same skillet add the butter and the shallots. Cook briefly until wilted. Add the cognac or Armagnac and the demiglace. Simmer for 1 minute. Add the cream and cook over high heat until reduced by half. Add the mustard and salt and pepper to taste. Stir the mixture and remove it from the heat. Do not cook further.

4. Slice the kidneys crosswise, cutting them into ½-inch pieces. Spoon the sauce over them and serve.

2 veal kidneys, trimmed of all fat
salt and freshly ground pepper to taste
1 tablespoon vegetable or corn oil
1 tablespoon unsalted butter
2 tablespoons finely chopped shallots
1 tablespoon cognac or Armagnac
2 tablespoons demiglace (see recipe page 201)
½ cup heavy cream
1 tablespoon regular or coarse Dijon mustard

YIELD: 4 SERVINGS

This recipe, a staple of the dinner menu at Le Pavillon for many years, is more or less a veal version of the chicken beauséjour *described on page 190. Red wine vinegar gives it a pleasant sharp edge.*

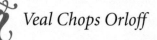 Veal Chops Pavillon

4 ½-pound center-cut
    veal chops from the
    rack or loin
salt and freshly ground
    pepper to taste
2 tablespoons unsalted
    butter
1 tablespoon olive oil
4 garlic cloves, peeled
4 small bay leaves
4 sprigs thyme or 1 tea-
    spoon dried thyme
1 tablespoon red wine
    vinegar
½ cup fresh or canned
    chicken broth (see
    recipe page 146)

YIELD: 4 SERVINGS

1. Sprinkle the chops on both sides with salt and pepper. Heat 1 tablespoon of the butter and the olive oil in a skillet over medium heat. Add the chops and brown evenly on both sides. Cook about 5 minutes on each side, then add the garlic, bay leaves and thyme. Cook for about 3 minutes, shaking the pan frequently.

2. Pour the vinegar around the chops and turn the heat up to medium-high. Add the broth, cover closely and simmer for about 15 minutes. Swirl in the remaining butter. Serve immediately.

This regal-looking preparation, said to have been invented by the French chef Urbain Dubois, who cooked for a nineteenth-century Russian prince named Orloff, was a showcase at Le Pavillon. I carefully arranged a whole saddle of veal on a gueridon, and the dining room captains carved it at tableside. This was a particular favorite of Joseph Kennedy and his family. (They also often ordered striped bass, which we presented whole at the table.)

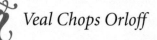 Veal Chops Orloff

4 center-cut veal chops
    from the rack or loin,
    maximum about ½
    pound each, with most
    of the fat removed

1. Preheat the oven to 425 degrees.

2. Chop the mushrooms on a flat surface with a heavy knife.

3. Melt 2 tablespoons of the butter in a skillet. Add

the onions and cook, stirring, until wilted. Add the mushrooms, lemon juice, and salt and pepper to taste. Cook, stirring, over medium-high heat until the mushrooms become fairly dry. Set the mixture aside.

4. Melt 1 tablespoon of the butter in a saucepan and add the flour. Cook, stirring briefly, without browning. Add the milk, stirring rapidly with a whisk. When all is blended and smooth, add the cream, nutmeg, cayenne, and taste for seasonings. Bring to a boil and simmer for 5 minutes while stirring. Remove from the heat and add the grated cheese. Set the cheese sauce aside and keep warm.

5. Sprinkle the chops with salt and pepper. Melt the remaining 2 tablespoons of butter in a large heavy skillet. Add the chops and cook over medium-high heat for about 6 minutes, or until nicely browned. Turn and cook 6 more minutes.

6. Transfer the chops to a baking dish that can hold them in one layer. Spoon equal portions of the mushroom mixture over each chop. Smooth it over.

7. Meanwhile, pour off the fat from the skillet and add the shallots to the pan. Cook briefly, stirring, then add the wine and the chicken broth. Bring to a boil, and stir to dissolve the brown particles that cling to the bottom of the skillet. Reduce by half, pour the sauce into a small saucepan and set aside.

8. Add the beaten egg yolk to the cheese sauce and stir to blend. Spoon equal portions of the sauce over the chops. Place the chops in the oven and bake for 10 minutes. Put the chops under the broiler just until all are nicely browned.

9. To serve, reheat the pan sauce, place each chop on a plate, and pour the sauce around the meat.

⅓ pound fresh mushrooms
5 tablespoons unsalted butter
½ cup (about 1 large) finely chopped onions
2 tablespoons fresh lemon juice
salt and freshly ground pepper to taste
2 tablespoons all-purpose flour
1 cup milk
¼ cup heavy cream
½ teaspoon freshly grated nutmeg
pinch cayenne pepper
2 tablespoons grated Parmesan or Gruyère cheese
2 tablespoons finely chopped shallots
⅓ cup dry white wine
⅓ cup fresh or canned chicken broth (see recipe page 146)
1 egg yolk, lightly beaten

YIELD: 4 SERVINGS

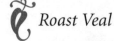

Roast Veal

1 3½-pound veal roast from
the leg, rolled and
boned, with bone
reserved
salt and freshly ground
white pepper to taste
2 tablespoons vegetable oil
½ cup sliced carrots
1 cup sliced onions
¼ cup diced celery
3 sprigs thyme or 1 tea-
spoon dried thyme
1 bay leaf
½ cup dry white wine
1 cup water
½ cup crushed canned
tomatoes

YIELD: 6 TO 8 SERVINGS

1. Preheat the oven to 350 degrees.

2. Sprinkle the meat with salt and pepper; heat the
oil in a Dutch oven large enough to hold the veal
comfortably. Brown the veal evenly all over. Add the
bone, the carrots, onions and celery. Scatter the vegetables around the meat. Add the thyme and the bay
leaf.

3. Cover the meat with aluminum foil and place it in
the oven for ½ hour. Remove the excess fat from the
pan, add the wine, water, and the tomatoes. Cook,
basting often, for 1 more hour. The internal temperature should be 170 degrees.

4. Remove the meat from the oven and place it on a
warm serving platter. Carve the veal into ¼-inch
slices. Strain the sauce and serve with the meat.

Veal Marengo was another semipermanent resident on the menu at Le Pavillon. Its
origins go back to Napoleon's enterprising chef at the Battle of Marengo, in Italy. With
provisions running low, Napoleon ordered him to come up with something. He saved
the day, and maybe his life, by concocting chicken Marengo. The veal version has
become favored in nonbellicose times.

Sautéed Veal Marengo

3 pounds veal from the leg,
cut into 1½-inch cubes
salt and freshly ground
pepper to taste
2 tablespoons olive oil
1 cup finely chopped onions
1 tablespoon finely chopped
garlic
¼ cup all-purpose flour
2 cups fresh or canned
chicken broth (see recipe
page 146)
1 cup dry white wine

1. Sprinkle the meat with salt and pepper. Heat the
oil in a skillet over high heat. Add the veal, a few
pieces at a time, stirring over high heat until well
browned on all sides. Drain the fat.

2. Add the onions and garlic, and cook over
medium heat until wilted. Stir in the flour until
lightly browned. Add the chicken broth and the
white wine, and bring to a boil, scraping and stirring
the bottom. Add the tomatoes, parsley sprigs, celery,
bay leaf and the thyme. Cover, bring to a boil and
simmer over low heat for 1 hour.

3. Add the pearl onions, cover and cook for 45 minutes longer, or until the meat is tender. Remove the parsley sprigs, bay leaf and the thyme sprigs, if using.

4. Sprinkle with chopped parsley and serve with buttered noodles or buttered parsley potatoes.

1 cup canned crushed
   tomatoes
4 sprigs parsley
½ cup chopped celery
1 bay leaf
2 sprigs thyme or ½ tea-
   spoon dried thyme
18 pearl onions, peeled
2 tablespoons chopped
   fresh parsley

YIELD: 6 TO 8 SERVINGS

Veal Kidneys in Red Wine Sauce

1. Combine the coarsely chopped shallots, wine, bay leaf, thyme, peppercorns and parsley in a saucepan. Bring to a boil for about 5 minutes over high heat until reduced by half. Add the demiglace and simmer for 10 minutes. Add salt and pepper to taste. Strain in a fine mesh and set aside.

2. Meanwhile, remove the fat and the sinews from the kidneys. Split the kidneys in half and cut away the white center core. Slice the kidneys crosswise into thin slices and sprinkle them with salt and pepper.

3. Heat the oil in a large skillet over high heat. Add the kidneys, shaking the skillet and stirring for about 2 to 3 minutes, no longer. Transfer the kidneys to a colander and let them stand for 5 minutes to drain thoroughly.

4. Remove the fat from the skillet. Add 1 tablespoon of the butter and the mushrooms, salt and pepper to taste. Cook over high heat until the mushrooms give up their juice and until the liquid is evaporated.

5. Add the finely chopped shallots and the drained kidneys to the mushrooms. Cook briefly, tossing and stirring, about 30 seconds. Add the demiglace mixture, bring to a simmer and swirl in the remaining butter. Check for seasoning and serve hot.

2 tablespoons coarsely
   chopped shallots
1 cup dry red wine, such as
   Burgundy or Cabernet
1 bay leaf
3 sprigs thyme or 1 tea-
   spoon dried thyme
6 peppercorns
2 sprigs parsley
1 cup demiglace (see recipe
   page 201)
salt and freshly ground
   pepper to taste
3 veal kidneys, about 1¾
   pounds total weight
2 tablespoons vegetable or
   corn oil
3 tablespoons unsalted
   butter
¼ pound fresh button
   mushrooms, cleaned
1 tablespoon finely
   chopped shallots

YIELD: 4 TO 6 SERVINGS

Juniper berries have a distinctive, sharp quality that enhances so many dishes. Choucroute garnie, for example, comes to life when juniper berries are added to the sauerkraut. I have always liked them with veal kidneys, for they cut the richness and complement their assertive flavor. Kidneys were a staple on French menus in this country after World War II, especially in the family-run bistros on Manhattan's West Side.

At Le Pavillon, we always had kidneys on the lunch menu. Not only were they popular, but inexpensive kidneys also yielded a high profit for the restaurant. Making good money on kidneys allowed us to keep down our veal prices. The recipe for veal kidneys with juniper berries, always a big seller, uses Madeira as a sweetener.

Veal Kidneys with Juniper Berries

4 veal kidneys, with most
of the fat removed
salt and freshly ground
pepper to taste
4 tablespoons unsalted
butter
¼ pound sliced mush-
rooms
18 juniper berries
½ cup Madeira
¾ cup demiglace (see
recipe page 201)
2 tablespoons finely
chopped fresh parsley

1. Place the kidneys on a flat surface and split them in half lengthwise. Remove all the white core that runs down the center of each kidney. Cut the kidneys crosswise into ¾-inch lengths; sprinkle with salt and pepper.

2. In a large skillet melt 2 tablespoons of the butter. When the butter is very hot add the kidney pieces. Cook over high heat, turning the pieces as they brown. Brown well, about 5 minutes. Do not overcook. The pieces must remain a bit rare or they will be dry. Remove the kidneys to a warm plate.

3. In the same skillet heat the remaining butter and add the mushrooms. Cook about 3 minutes over high heat, stirring often.

4. Add the juniper berries and cook over high heat for 1 minute. Add the Madeira and the demiglace. Cook over high heat and reduce by half. Add the drained kidneys and bring to a boil. Serve immediately, sprinkled with parsley.

YIELD: 4 TO 6 SERVINGS

The rather odd name "stuffed veal birds" derives from the shape of these stuffed veal packets. This was a big lunch favorite at Le Pavillon. I remember well, for as chef, it was my job to assemble the stuffing and the veal and make the dish look vaguely ornithological.

Stuffed Veal Birds

1. Cut away and discard any tough spinach stems and blemished leaves. Wash in clean water and drain.

2. Place the spinach in a saucepan, cover and cook in the water that clings to the leaves. Stir often until wilted. Drain and cool. Press the spinach between your hands to remove excess moisture. Coarsely chop the spinach and set it aside.

3. Heat 1 tablespoon of the butter in a skillet and add 2 tablespoons of the shallots, 1 teaspoon of the garlic, 1 cup chopped mushrooms and salt and pepper to taste. Cook over medium-high heat, stirring, for about 3 minutes. Add the spinach and stir to blend. Cook until all the moisture has evaporated.

4. Place the pork in a mixing bowl and add the egg, bread crumbs, nutmeg, Parmesan, spinach mixture and salt and pepper to taste. Blend well.

5. Pound the veal slices evenly with a meat pounder or a flat mallet. They should be a little more than ⅛ inch thick.

6. Spoon equal parts of the spinach-pork filling over the center of each slice. Roll up each paupiette like a jelly roll and tie it with twine at 2 places so it holds its shape while cooking. Sprinkle with salt and pepper and dredge lightly in flour.

7. Heat the remaining butter in a large skillet and add the veal rolls. Brown over medium-high heat on one side, then turn and brown on the other side.

SPINACH-PORK FILLING
1 pound loose spinach leaves
4 tablespoons unsalted butter
4 tablespoons minced shallots
2 teaspoons minced garlic
1 cup chopped fresh mushrooms, about ¼ pound (for spinach mixture)
salt and freshly ground pepper to taste
½ pound lean ground pork
1 large egg
½ cup fresh bread crumbs
⅛ teaspoon freshly grated nutmeg
2 tablespoons freshly grated Parmesan cheese

8 thin slices veal, about 2 ounces each
all-purpose flour
½ pound thinly sliced mushrooms
1 cup dry white wine
2 cups chopped fresh tomatoes or 1 cup canned crushed tomatoes
4 sprigs thyme or 1 teaspoon dried thyme
4 tablespoons finely chopped fresh parsley

Scatter the sliced mushrooms, the remaining shallots and the remaining garlic around the skillet. Cook, stirring, for 5 minutes. Add the wine, tomatoes and thyme. Bring to a boil. Cover and cook over medium-high heat for 30 minutes, or until the veal is tender.

8. To serve, remove the twine and spoon the sauce over the paupiettes. Sprinkle with the parsley. Serve with buttered noodles or mashed potatoes.

YIELD: 4 SERVINGS AS A
MAIN COURSE, OR 8 SERV-
INGS AS AN APPETIZER

NOTE: Slices of turkey breast can be substituted for the veal in this recipe.

As the story goes, the dish veal Pojarski was originally made with beef and was a favorite dish of Czar Nicholas I. One day the czar arrived at an inn and the owner, one Mr. Pojarski, hastily prepared the patties with veal instead of beef, which greatly pleased the czar.

This has always been a favorite dish of mine. The veal should be very lean. The option of cream is offered, but my recommendation for those watching their fat intake is to use plain drained yogurt instead. Yogurt works splendidly as a binder. At Le Pavillon we made a wonderful version of this dish with fresh salmon.

Veal Pojarski

1 pound lean veal,
    trimmed of all gristle
⅛ teaspoon freshly grated
    nutmeg
salt and freshly ground
    white pepper to taste
1 cup heavy cream or ½
    cup heavy cream plus ½
    cup plain yogurt
1½ cups fine fresh bread
    crumbs
4 tablespoons unsalted
    butter
1 tablespoon corn oil

1. Ask a butcher to grind the veal twice to give it a finer texture, or use a food processor to achieve a fine consistency.

2. Place the veal in a mixing bowl and refrigerate it until very cold.

3. Remove the chilled veal from the refrigerator and add the nutmeg, salt, pepper, cream or cream and yogurt and ¾ cup of the bread crumbs. Blend well. Beat briskly in a circular fashion with a wooden spoon until well blended and smooth.

4. Divide the mixture into 4 equal portions. Shape

into patties about ¾ inch thick. Coat all over with the remaining bread crumbs.

1 tablespoon fresh lemon juice

5. Heat 1 tablespoon of the butter and the oil in a nonstick skillet large enough to hold the patties in one layer without crowding. Brown the patties lightly over medium heat for about 5 minutes, then turn them. Continue cooking and browning on the other side until the meat is cooked through. Do not overcook or it will dry out.

6. Transfer the patties to a warm plate; wipe out the skillet. Add the remaining butter. Cook until foamy. Continue cooking until the butter is a hazelnut color. Add the lemon juice, stir, and pour lemon butter over each of the patties.

YIELD: 4 SERVINGS

I have always admired calf's liver for its tenderness and ease of preparation. This is one of my favorite approaches.

Calf's Liver with Capers

1. Sprinkle each slice of liver on both sides with salt and pepper. Dredge them in flour on both sides and shake off the excess.

2. In a nonstick skillet large enough to hold all the liver slices, heat the oil over high heat. Add the liver and cook on one side for about 2 minutes. Flip and cook for another 2 minutes for rare.

3. Transfer the liver to warm plates. Discard the fat from the skillet.

4. Add the butter to the skillet and let it melt. Add the capers and cook over high heat until browned, shaking the pan often. Add both vinegars to the skillet and bring them to a boil while swirling them. Pour this liquid immediately over the liver and sprinkle with parsley.

1¼ pounds calf's liver, cut into 4 slices
salt and freshly ground pepper to taste
⅓ cup all-purpose flour
2 tablespoons vegetable oil
4 tablespoons unsalted butter
4 tablespoons capers, drained
2 tablespoons red wine vinegar
1 teaspoon balsamic vinegar
4 tablespoons chopped fresh parsley

YIELD: 4 SERVINGS

Braised Sweetbreads with Green Peas

3 pairs sweetbreads, about
　1½ pounds total
3 tablespoons unsalted
　butter
½ cup thinly sliced carrots
½ cup sliced onions
½ cup coarsely chopped
　celery
1 medium garlic clove,
　peeled
4 sprigs thyme or 1 tea-
　spoon dried thyme
1 bay leaf
4 sprigs parsley
salt and freshly ground
　pepper to taste
½ cup dry white wine
½ cup fresh or canned
　chicken broth (see
　recipe page 146)
¼ pound lean salt pork
1 cup very small white
　onions, peeled
1 teaspoon sugar, optional
2 cups fresh shelled peas or
　2 cups frozen peas

1. Pull off and discard any tough membranes from the sweetbreads. Place the sweetbreads in cold water and refrigerate for several hours.

2. Drain the sweetbreads and place them in a saucepan. Add cold water to cover. Bring to a boil. Simmer for 5 minutes, drain immediately and run under cold water.

3. Weigh down the sweetbreads to improve their texture. To do this, place them on a wire rack over a deep plate. Cover with a baking dish and add weights to the dish. Let stand for at least 2 hours in a cool place. This will extract the excess moisture.

4. Preheat the oven to 400 degrees. Select a baking dish large enough to hold the sweetbreads in one layer. Rub the bottom with 1 tablespoon of the butter. Scatter the sliced carrots, onions, celery, garlic, thyme, bay leaf, and parsley sprigs over the bottom of the baking dish. Arrange the sweetbreads over the vegetables and sprinkle them with salt and pepper. Dot with 1 tablespoon butter, then add the wine and broth. Cover and bring the mixture to a boil on top of the stove. Place the dish in the oven and bake for 20 minutes.

5. Meanwhile, cut the salt pork into small strips. Place the pieces in a saucepan and add the small white onions. Add water to cover, bring to a boil and simmer for 2 minutes.

6. Drain the salt pork and place it in a small pan along with the small white onions. Sauté over medium heat, stirring, until the pork is rendered of its fat and is golden. Drain the fat, add the remaining butter, salt and pepper to taste and sugar if desired.

Cover tightly and cook over low heat for about 10 minutes, stirring often.

7. When the sweetbreads have baked for about 20 minutes, uncover the pan. Cook, basting occasionally, for about 10 minutes.

8. Transfer the sweetbreads to a heavy skillet, drain the liquid from the baking dish, and discard it along with the vegetables. Add the peas and salt pork mixture. Cover and cook for 5 minutes on top of the stove over low heat. Uncover and cook about 5 minutes longer, basting occasionally.   YIELD: 6 SERVINGS

SAUCES

I have often been asked by home cooks if using champagne in a sauce really makes a difference. I always tell the story that involves a professional friend, Gérard Boyer, the owner and chef of Les Crayères in Reims, in the Champagne region. A few years ago Boyer conducted a little experiment in his kitchen in which he prepared three beurre blanc sauces that were identical, except that one was made with still white wine, one with a regional sparkling wine and one with champagne. Five of us tasted the sauces without knowing which was which. We all voted for the champagne sauce, which was unmistakably lighter and more distinctive. The sparkling wine sauce was good, too, but just not as refined.

 Champagne Sauce for Fish

6 tablespoons unsalted
    butter
1 cup sliced mushroom
    stems
1½ cups thinly sliced
    shallots
2 cups dry champagne
2½ cups fresh fish broth
    (see recipe page 147)
4 tablespoons all-purpose
    flour
2 cups heavy cream
1 tablespoon fresh lemon
    juice
salt and freshly ground
    pepper to taste, optional

1. Melt 1 tablespoon of the butter in a saucepan, then add the mushrooms and the shallots. Cook, stirring, until wilted, about 1 minute. Add the champagne and 1 cup of the fish broth. Simmer until the liquid is reduced by half.

2. Melt 3 tablespoons of the remaining butter in another saucepan. Add the flour while stirring with a wire whisk. Be careful not to burn it. When the mixture is well blended, add the remaining 1½ cups of the fish broth. Blend well, bring to a boil and simmer for 10 minutes. Add the sauce to the mushroom mixture. Stir well and simmer for 10 minutes.

3. Add the cream, bring to a boil and simmer for 10

minutes, stirring frequently. Pass the sauce through a fine wire strainer. Return the strained sauce to the saucepan. Add the lemon juice and salt and pepper if needed. Swirl in the remaining butter. Serve very hot over a mousse, quenelles or poached fish.

YIELD: 2 CUPS

Classic Sauce Béarnaise

(FOR BROILED STEAKS, CHOPS OR FISH)

¾ pound unsalted butter
4 tablespoons red wine vinegar
2 tablespoons chopped shallots
2 tablespoons chopped tarragon stems or 1 teaspoon dried tarragon
1 teaspoon black peppercorns, crushed (use the bottom of a heavy saucepan)
3 tablespoons water
2 large egg yolks
salt and cayenne pepper to taste
2 tablespoons chopped tarragon leaves

1. Place the butter in a 2-quart glass measuring cup. Place the measuring cup in a shallow saucepan holding enough boiling water to reach 2 inches up the side of the cup. When the butter melts, remove the cup from the water but leave the water simmering. Ladle any foam from the surface of the butter. Let the butter cool to about 120 degrees.

2. Place the vinegar, shallots, tarragon and peppercorns in a small slanted saucepan (called a *fait-tout*). Reduce the liquid until evaporated. Let cool.

3. Add the water and yolks to the shallot-and-tarragon mixture. Place the saucepan in the pot of simmering water. Stir rapidly with a flexible wire whisk in a controlled fashion so that all of the mixture is agitated (a figure-8 motion is best, occasionally extending outward toward the edges). As the mixture begins to thicken, remove it from the heat for the last seconds of whisking. The mixture is done when it is thickened to a pastelike consistency.

4. While the pan is off the heat, drizzle the clarified butter into the egg mixture, beating continuously with the whisk to form an emulsion, as in mayonnaise.

5. Add salt and cayenne to taste, then the tarragon leaves. Blend well with a whisk.

YIELD: 1½ CUPS

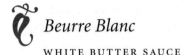

Beurre Blanc

WHITE BUTTER SAUCE

8 tablespoons cold unsalted
    butter, cut into small
    pieces
4 tablespoons finely
    chopped shallots
1 cup dry white wine
2 tablespoons white wine
    vinegar
4 tablespoons heavy cream
salt and freshly ground
    white pepper to taste

YIELD: ABOUT 1 CUP

1. Place 1 tablespoon of the butter in a saucepan, melt it over medium-high heat, and add the shallots. Cook the shallots briefly until wilted. Do not brown. Add the wine and the vinegar. Cook over medium heat until the liquid is reduced by half.

2. Add the cream. Bring to a boil. Turn the heat to low and whisk in the remaining butter, one piece at a time. Remove the sauce from the heat, add salt and pepper to taste, and blend well. Keep warm.

PASTA, COUSCOUS AND BREAD

The relentless pasta craze in America has compelled me to devise many quick and healthful Italian dishes. Here is one that was particularly popular with readers of "The 60-Minute Gourmet."

Pasta with Eggplant and Zucchini

1. Heat 1 tablespoon of the olive oil in a saucepan and add the garlic. Cook and stir without browning. Add the tomatoes, parsley, oregano, pepper flakes, salt and pepper. Stir to blend, bring to a boil, and simmer for 15 minutes.

2. Meanwhile, cut off the ends of the eggplant and peel. Cut it into 1-inch cubes.

3. Cut the ends off the zucchini and slice it into 1-inch-thick slices.

4. Heat the remaining olive oil in a large skillet. When the oil is very hot, add the eggplant, zucchini, and salt and pepper. Cook, tossing, until nicely browned and tender. Add to the tomato sauce. Mix well and cook for 15 minutes.

5. Drop the pasta into salted boiling water and cook to the desired degree of doneness. Drain and reserve ½ cup of the cooking liquid.

6. Return the pasta to the pot, add the reserved cooking liquid, vegetable-and-sauce mixture, basil and Parmesan cheese. Toss and serve hot.

4 tablespoons olive oil
1 tablespoon finely chopped garlic
1 28-ounce can crushed tomatoes
4 tablespoons chopped fresh Italian parsley
2 teaspoons dried oregano
⅛ teaspoon hot red pepper flakes, optional
salt and freshly ground pepper to taste
1 pound eggplant
½ pound zucchini
¾ pound dry pasta, such as ziti, fusilli, shells or rigatoni
4 tablespoons coarsely chopped fresh basil
4 tablespoons grated Parmesan cheese

YIELD: 4 SERVINGS

I learned a little trick years ago concerning pasta from my friend Luigi Nanni. He always undercooks the pasta and finishes it in a pan with the sauce. If extra liquid is needed, use the leftover water from the pasta pot. This technique infuses the pasta with flavor.

 ## Shrimp and Pasta Medley

½ pound dry egg noodles
  or fettuccine
4 tablespoons olive oil
1 cup coarsely chopped red
  onions
1 pound small zucchini,
  cut into 1-inch-thick
  slices, about 3 cups
2 sweet red peppers, cored
  and seeded, cut into
  ½-inch cubes
salt and freshly ground
  pepper to taste
1¼ pounds medium
  shrimp, shelled and
  deveined
6 ripe plum tomatoes, cut
  into ½-inch cubes
1 tablespoon finely
  chopped garlic
1 tablespoon finely
  chopped ginger
¼ teaspoon hot red pepper
  flakes
¼ cup pitted small green
  olives
½ teaspoon saffron stems
4 tablespoons chopped
  fresh coriander or basil
1 tablespoon red wine
  vinegar

YIELD: 4 SERVINGS

1. Bring salted water to a boil; add the noodles; stir and cook according to package instructions. The pasta should be al dente. Drain and reserve ¼ cup of the cooking liquid.

2. Meanwhile, heat 2 tablespoons of the olive oil in a large skillet or wok. Add the onions, zucchini, red peppers, salt and pepper. Cook, stirring, over high heat until wilted, about 3 minutes.

3. Add the shrimp, tomatoes, garlic, ginger, pepper flakes, olives and saffron. Cook and stir about 3 minutes longer over high heat.

4. Add the remaining 2 tablespoons of olive oil, the drained noodles, the coriander or basil, the vinegar and, if needed, the reserved cooking liquid. Toss and stir well. Bring to a simmer and cook for 2 minutes. Serve immediately.

Over the years I have devised numerous pasta dishes using scallops. The addition of seasonal vegetables and herbs lends color, texture and variety.

Pasta with Scallops and Green Beans

1. Trim and cut the green beans into 1¼-inch lengths. Drop them into salted boiling water and cook them for 7 minutes, or until slightly crisp and tender. Drain immediately and reserve ½ cup of the cooking liquid.

2. Heat 2 tablespoons of the olive oil in a saucepan over medium heat and add 1 tablespoon of the garlic. Cook briefly without letting it brown. Add the tomatoes, tomato paste, marjoram, basil, oregano, red pepper flakes, salt and pepper. Cook, stirring well, for about 5 minutes. Set aside.

3. Bring 3 quarts salted water to a boil. Add the pasta, return to a boil and cook, stirring, for about 12 minutes or according to package instructions. The pasta should be al dente.

4. Meanwhile, heat the 2 remaining tablespoons of olive oil in a large saucepan over medium-high heat. Add the scallops, the remaining garlic and salt and pepper to taste. Cook, stirring, for about 1 minute, then add the tomato sauce, green beans and reserved liquid to the pan. Bring to a boil, then lower the heat to a simmer. Cook for 1 minute, stirring.

5. Drain the pasta and add it to the tomato-scallop mixture. Add basil, toss, and serve.

½ pound green beans
4 tablespoons olive oil
2 tablespoons finely chopped garlic
3 cups ripe fresh tomatoes, cored, peeled and cut into small cubes
2 tablespoons tomato paste
1 tablespoon chopped fresh marjoram or 1 teaspoon dried marjoram
¼ cup coarsely chopped fresh basil
2 teaspoons chopped fresh oregano or ½ teaspoon dried oregano
¼ teaspoon hot red pepper flakes
salt and freshly ground pepper
¾ pound farfalle or bow-tie pasta
1 pound sea scallops (if sea scallops are very large, cut them in half)

YIELD: 4 SERVINGS

Couscous with Raisins and Red Peppers

1 tablespoon olive oil
⅓ cup finely chopped onions
½ cup cubed sweet red
 peppers
1¼ cups boiling water
⅓ cup raisins
⅛ teaspoon ground
 cinnamon
¼ teaspoon ground cumin
½ teaspoon grated orange
 rind
salt and freshly ground
 pepper to taste
1 cup quick-cooking couscous
1 tablespoon unsalted butter

YIELD: 4 SERVINGS

1. In a saucepan with a tight lid, heat the olive oil. Add the onions and red peppers and cook, stirring, until wilted. Do not brown. Add the water, raisins, cinnamon, cumin, orange rind, salt and pepper. Bring to a boil.

2. Remove the mixture from the heat; add the couscous and stir well. Cover and let stand for 5 minutes. Uncover, add the butter and fluff well with a fork. Serve with tuna steaks Moroccan style (see recipe page 180).

Technology has taken away so much of the tedium in bread baking that I knew growing up. With a food processor at home, anyone can make quality bread with relatively little effort. This basic French bread recipe is the one I follow two or three times a week at home.

Quick French Country Bread

2 envelopes fast-rising dry
 yeast
2⅓ cups warm water (90
 degrees)
5 cups unbleached bread
 flour
1 cup whole wheat flour
1 tablespoon salt
6 ice cubes

1. Preheat the oven to 400 degrees.

2. Place the chopping blade of a food processor in its bowl. Make sure the machine is unplugged. Add the yeast and ⅓ cup of the water to the bowl. Grabbing the plastic top of the chopping blade with your hand, turn the blade slowly to mix the yeast and water. Remove your hand, plug in the machine, and add the flours. Blend for 10 seconds. Add the salt and blend another 10 seconds. While the blade rotates, add the remaining warm water. Blend until the batter begins to form a large ball (about 30 seconds).

3. Flour a board lightly and knead the dough for a minute, forming a ball when you are through. Flour

a large mixing bowl and place the ball of dough in it. Sprinkle with flour and cover with a dish towel. Let the dough rise in a warm place until it doubles in size. The time required varies with environmental conditions. At a room temperature of about 72 degrees, it should take at least 30 minutes.

4. Turn the dough onto a lightly floured board and punch it down. Divide the dough into 2 equal-sized loaves.

5. Place the loaves on a cookie sheet with room between them for expansion. Cover them with a towel and let them rise until they nearly double in size.

6. Use a razor blade to score the surface of each loaf several times. Each incision should be about ½ inch deep.

7. Place the cookie sheet on the bottom rack of the oven and throw the ice cubes onto the oven floor. (The ice cubes add steam, which helps produce a thin, crisp crust.) Bake for 40 minutes, or until the loaves are golden brown. Transfer the bread to a rack and let the loaves cool.

NOTE: This bread freezes very well if wrapped tightly in plastic.

YIELD: 2 LOAVES

Garlic Croutons

1. Preheat the broiler.

2. Rub the bread's crust all over with the garlic cloves. Cut the bread into ½-inch-thick slices and sprinkle one side with the olive oil and pepper.

3. Place the bread slices on a baking sheet under the broiler until they are golden. Turn and broil on the other side until brown.

1 loaf French bread
2 garlic cloves, peeled
2 tablespoons olive oil
freshly ground pepper
   to taste

VEGETABLES AND EGGS

Certain vegetable dishes were bistro staples, none more than the celery remoulade.

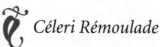 *Céleri Rémoulade*

3 or 4 bulbs knob celery,
  enough to make 3 to
  4 cups when shredded
1 large egg yolk
1 tablespoon white wine
  vinegar
2 tablespoons Dijon
  mustard
¼ teaspoon cayenne
  pepper
1¼ cups vegetable or olive
  oil
1 tablespoon fresh lemon
  juice
salt and freshly ground
  pepper to taste

YIELD: 8 TO 10 SERVINGS

1. Peel the celery and drop it in cold water. Remove one bulb at a time, trim off all the dark spots; slice the celery as thinly as possible using a mandoline or a food processor or even a sharp knife.

2. Stack the slices and cut them into the finest julienne strips. There should be about 3 to 4 cups.

3. In a large mixing bowl place the egg yolk and add the vinegar, mustard, cayenne. Start beating with a wire whisk or an electric beater, gradually adding the oil. Continue beating until all the oil is used and the mayonnaise is thick. Add the lemon juice and salt and pepper to taste. If too thick, add a little water.

4. Place the julienne strips in the mayonnaise mixture and blend well. Check for seasoning and chill. Serve cold as an appetizer or a first course. This is particularly good when served with garlic sausage or any cold meat or seafood.

Braised Celery

1. Cut each heart into halves lengthwise. Wash thoroughly and drain.

2. Heat the oil and butter in a skillet large enough to hold the celery in one layer. Arrange the celery flat side down in the skillet and cook until wilted, then add the chicken broth, and salt and pepper to taste. Cover, bring to a boil and cook until the celery is tender, about 10 minutes. Remove the celery to a warm plate and reduce the cooking liquid by half. Spoon some over the celery.

4 celery hearts
1 tablespoon olive oil
1 tablespoon unsalted butter
½ cup fresh or canned chicken broth (see recipe page 146)
salt and freshly ground pepper to taste

YIELD: 4 TO 8 SERVINGS

Mashed Potatoes with Chives

1. Peel the potatoes and cut them into 2-inch cubes.

2. Put the potatoes in a saucepan and cover them with water. Add salt and bring to a boil. Simmer 20 minutes, or until the potatoes are tender. Do not overcook them.

3. Meanwhile, heat the milk until it is hot.

4. Drain the potatoes and put them through a food mill or ricer or mash them well with a potato masher. Return them to the saucepan. Using a wooden spatula, add the butter and chives and blend well. Mix in the milk and keep warm until ready to serve.

1½ pounds russet potatoes
salt to taste
1 cup milk
4 tablespoons unsalted butter
4 tablespoons chopped chives

YIELD: 4 SERVINGS

Pan-Fried Zucchini with Fresh Corn

4 medium zucchini, about
    1¼ pounds
2 ears fresh corn
2 tablespoons olive oil
salt and freshly ground
    pepper to taste
¼ teaspoon ground cumin
½ cup coarsely chopped
    scallions
3 tablespoons finely
    chopped fresh parsley

YIELD: 4 SERVINGS

1. Trim the ends of the zucchini, and slice the vegetable into thin rounds. Cut the kernels of corn off the ears.

2. Heat the oil over medium-high heat in a large nonstick skillet. Place the zucchini, salt and pepper and the cumin in the skillet. Cook, tossing and stirring, for about 3 minutes.

3. Add the corn and the scallions. Cook and stir for 2 more minutes and blend well. Sprinkle with parsley and serve.

Puree of Knob Celery

1 pound firm knob celery
1 pound yellow-gold
    Washington or Idaho
    potatoes
salt to taste
1 cup milk
3 tablespoons unsalted
    butter
¼ teaspoon or less freshly
    grated nutmeg

YIELD: 6 SERVINGS

1. Peel the knob celery and cut it into 1-inch cubes.

2. Peel the potatoes and rinse them well. Quarter the potatoes and place them in a saucepan. Add the celery, cover with water and salt to taste. Bring to a boil. Simmer for 20 minutes, or until the celery is tender. Drain.

3. Meanwhile bring the milk to warm.

4. Place the celery and potatoes through a fine food mill or potato ricer. Add the butter and beat it in with a wooden spatula. Add the nutmeg and gradually add the hot milk. Beat with a spatula. Serve immediately or place in a dish over simmering water to keep warm.

This recipe calls for flageolets, the pale, tender French kidney beans that are mostly sold dried in the United States. Even dried they have a delicate flavor. If you cannot find flageolets, dried white kidney beans serve quite well.

White Beans à la Bretonne

1. Place the flageolets or white beans in a pot and add water to cover by about 1 inch. Soak them overnight.

2. Drain the beans and return them to the pot. Add 2 quarts of water, the clove-studded onion, salt pork, carrot, thyme, bay leaf and salt to taste. Bring to a boil and simmer 45 minutes to 1 hour.

3. Remove the salt pork and cut it into small cubes. Set aside. Cook the beans 30 minutes longer, or until tender. (Different varieties require different cooking times.)

4. Melt the butter in a skillet and sauté the salt pork cubes until golden brown, stirring occasionally. Add the chopped onions, shallot, garlic and thyme. When the onions are wilted, add the tomatoes and cook, stirring frequently, until the mixture thickens.

5. Remove the carrot, onion and bay leaf, and drain the beans. Reserve the bean liquid. Add the beans to the tomato sauce and stir gently. If the mixture seems too dry, use a little of the reserved bean liquid. Serve the beans hot, sprinkled with chopped parsley.

2 cups flageolets or dried white kidney beans
1 onion studded with 1 clove
¼ pound salt pork
1 large carrot, cleaned and halved
2 sprigs thyme or ½ teaspoon dried thyme for the beans
1 bay leaf
salt to taste
2 tablespoons unsalted butter
1¼ cups chopped onions
1 shallot, diced
1 teaspoon diced garlic
1 teaspoon diced fresh thyme for the sauce
3 cups drained and chopped fresh peeled tomatoes or canned tomatoes
2 tablespoons chopped fresh parsley

YIELD: 8 TO 10 SERVINGS

Omelette with Mixed Herbs

1 tablespoon chopped fresh
   tarragon
2 tablespoons chopped
   fresh parsley
2 tablespoons chopped
   fresh basil
2 tablespoons chopped
   chives
6 large eggs
salt and freshly ground
   pepper to taste
2 tablespoons unsalted
   butter

1. Blend all the herbs.

2. Place the eggs, salt and pepper and herbs except for 1 tablespoon of the herb mixture (reserve for garnish) into a mixing bowl and beat well with a fork.

3. In a prewarmed 11-inch black steel frying pan, melt the butter and pour in the omelette mixture.

4. Stir the mixture over high heat with the rounded base of a fork and at the same time push the edges of the mixture toward the center. When the mixture has solidified, stop stirring and let it set for a few seconds.

5. Holding the pan so that it is tilted away from you, use the fork to fold the near side of the omelette halfway to the other side.

6. Firmly grasping the handle with one hand, lift the pan off the range, still tilted away from you, and strike the base of the handle 2 or 3 times with the side of the fist of your other hand. This will cause the far edge of the omelette to fold back on itself, completing the envelope. Use the fork to press the omelette closed at the seam. Roll out onto a warm platter, seam side down. Sprinkle the remaining herbs on the top of the omelette.

YIELD: 2 SERVINGS

One of the first tests for young cooks seeking employment at Le Pavillon was to make an omelette, the perfect omelette—smooth and lightly browned outside, moist and well seasoned within. Italians have their own delicious version of the omelette, the frittata, and the strategy for making a superior frittata is similar to that used in making an omelette.

The fundamental difference between the two is that an omelette is made with eggs and seasonings, then filled with sundry ingredients, whereas the frittata mixture *incorporates the ingredients, and the result is thicker and slightly drier. Moreover, the omelette is cooked in an open pan, while the* frittata, *at least the way I make it, is covered.*

Frittata with Peppers and Potatoes

1. Wash the potatoes and cut them, unpeeled, into thin slices. Drop the slices into cold water to prevent discoloration. Drain and dry on paper towels.

2. Heat the oil in a large nonstick skillet and add the potatoes. Cook over medium heat, shaking the skillet and tossing or stirring the potatoes, about 4 minutes. Add the peppers and the onions. Cook, shaking the skillet and stirring, about 5 minutes.

3. In a bowl, beat the eggs with the basil or parsley, add salt and pepper and beat in the cheese.

4. Over high heat, add the olive oil and the egg mixture to the potatoes and cook, stirring gently but firmly with a plastic spatula, about 1 minute. Cover tightly and reduce to medium heat. Cook about 2 minutes. Run a spatula or knife around the outside of the frittata. Invert a large round plate over the skillet and turn over the skillet and plate quickly, letting the frittata fall onto the plate. It should be golden brown on top. Serve immediately

4 small red waxy potatoes, about ½ pound
2 tablespoons vegetable oil
1½ cups sweet red pepper, cut into ½-inch cubes
1½ cups green pepper, cut into ½-inch cubes
½ cup thinly sliced white onions
8 large eggs
2 tablespoons finely chopped fresh basil or parsley
salt and freshly ground pepper to taste
¼ pound cheese, preferably Gruyère, cut into small cubes
2 tablespoons olive oil

YIELD: 4 SERVINGS

Gruyère Soufflés

1. Preheat the oven to 425 degrees.

2. Chill four 1½-cup soufflé dishes.

3. Separate the eggs, placing the yolks in one bowl and the whites in a larger bowl.

4. With 1 tablespoon of the butter grease the bot-

6 large eggs
4 tablespoons unsalted butter
3 tablespoons all-purpose flour
2 cups milk

*salt and freshly ground
    white pepper to taste*
*⅛ teaspoon freshly grated
    nutmeg*
pinch cayenne pepper
2 tablespoons cornstarch
3 tablespoons water
*⅓ pound Gruyère or Swiss
    cheese, cut into small
    cubes*
*2 tablespoons grated
    Gruyère cheese*

tom and sides of each soufflé dish, paying special attention to the sides.

5. Melt the remaining butter in a saucepan and add the flour, stirring with a wire whisk. Blend well; do not brown the flour. Add the milk, stirring rapidly with the whisk; add the salt and pepper, nutmeg and cayenne. Bring to a boil, and cook at medium heat for 30 seconds, stirring.

6. Blend the cornstarch and water and add this to the bubbling sauce. Stir and cook for about 2 minutes. Add the yolks, stirring vigorously. Cook, stirring, for about 1 minute.

7. Spoon and scrape the mixture into a large mixing bowl. Add the cubed Gruyère or Swiss, and blend well with a wire whisk. Set aside.

8. Beat the egg whites in a mixing bowl, preferably copper. With a balloon wire whisk, beat them until they are stiff and thick. Add half of the whites to the soufflé mixture and mix thoroughly. Add the remaining whites and fold them in quickly but gently with a rubber spatula.

9. Spoon and scrape even amounts of the mixture into each soufflé dish. The mixture should fit inside the dish about ¼ inch from the top. Using your thumb, create a shallow channel around the periphery of the dish to allow for expansion. Sprinkle the top with the grated Gruyère.

10. Place the dishes on a baking sheet on the bottom rack of the oven and bake for 12 to 15 minutes. Serve immediately.

YIELD: 4 SERVINGS

DESSERTS

Chocolate Mousse

1. Select a 2-quart stainless-steel bowl and a sauce-pan large enough so that the bowl can snugly fit into it.

2. Add 1 inch of boiling water to the saucepan and set the bowl in the saucepan. Bring the water to a simmer. Add the chocolate to the bowl and stir. When it starts to melt, add the butter. Continue stirring until the mixture is well blended, and remove the bowl from the pan. Add the egg yolks and liqueur if desired, and stir until thoroughly blended.

3. Place the bowl in the refrigerator until the mixture is slightly cooler than lukewarm. If it becomes too chilled, it will harden.

4. Beat the egg whites until they form soft peaks. Gradually add the sugar, beating briskly. Continue beating until the whites are stiff. Fold the whites into the chocolate mixture. Spoon the mousse into 4 serving dishes. Chill briefly until ready to serve.

2 ounces semisweet chocolate
2 ounces sweet chocolate
¼ pound unsalted butter, cut into small pieces
3 large eggs, separated
¼ cup dark rum or Grand Marnier, optional
¼ cup sugar

YIELD: 4 SERVINGS

Oeufs à la Neige

FLOATING ISLANDS

4 cups milk
1½ cups sugar
1 vanilla bean or 2 tea-
   spoons pure vanilla
   extract
8 large egg whites
1 teaspoon cornstarch
pinch salt
English custard (recipe
   follows)

1. Bring the milk to a simmer in a large pot. Add 6 tablespoons of the sugar and the vanilla bean or vanilla extract. Mix well and set aside.

2. For the meringue: In a copper bowl, beat the egg whites until stiff with a balloon whisk or an electric mixer. While beating, add 8 tablespoons of the sugar, the cornstarch and the salt.

3. When the meringue is stiff, take a pastry bag with a number-4 tube attached and fill it with the meringue. Pipe it out onto a baking sheet into a 2½-inch circle. Continue piping out the meringue to make layer upon layer over the bottom circle until it is about 2½ inches high. This will produce a small, roundish beehive pattern. Continue making these rosettes until all the meringue is used. This should make 16 to 18 rosettes.

4. Using a spatula, transfer as many rosettes as possible to the simmered milk.

5. Simmer the meringues for about 30 seconds on one side, then gently flip them with a spatula. Poach for 30 seconds.

6. Drain the rosettes, which should be firm, on paper towels. Let them cool.

7. Strain the milk. Remove the vanilla bean if one was used.

8. To serve, place the chilled custard in a large serving bowl and carefully place the rosettes over the custard.

YIELD: 10 OR MORE SERVINGS

English Custard

⅓ cup sugar
3 large egg yolks
1½ cups milk

1. Combine the sugar and the yolks in a saucepan and beat with a wire whisk until thickened and pale yellow. Set aside.

2. Heat the milk to lukewarm. Add the milk to the yolk mixture, stirring rapidly with a whisk.

3. Place the mixture over medium heat, and cook, stirring constantly with a wooden spatula. Scrape the bottom. Mix well, but do not allow the milk to boil. When the custard coats the back of the wooden spatula, remove the pan from the heat immediately. Strain, then let cool.

Cherry Tart

1. Place the flour, salt, sugar and almonds in a food processor. Cut the butter into small pieces and add to the flour. Add the yolk, blend briefly and add the water. Blend until the pastry pulls away from the sides and forms a ball.

2. Using a rolling pin, roll out the dough into a circle 13 inches in diameter. Immediately line a 10½-inch pie tin equipped with a removable bottom with the pastry. Trim off the excess dough and place the pastry in the refrigerator until ready to use.

3. Preheat the oven to 400 degrees.

4. With a fork prick the bottom of the pastry. Blend 1 tablespoon of the sugar with 2 tablespoons flour. Sprinkle the bottom of the shell evenly with the mixture. Place the cherries in the shell evenly in one layer. Sprinkle with the 2 remaining tablespoons of sugar. Bake for 45 minutes.

NOTE: This technique also works with pitted and sliced plums, apricots, peaches and other fruits. Use the same quantity of ingredients.

PASTRY

2 cups all-purpose flour
¼ teaspoon salt
2 tablespoons sugar
¼ cup coarsely chopped almonds
10 tablespoons unsalted butter, very cold
1 large egg yolk
2 tablespoons ice water

FILLING

3 tablespoons sugar
2 tablespoons all-purpose flour
2 pounds fresh cherries, pitted

YIELD: 8 SERVINGS

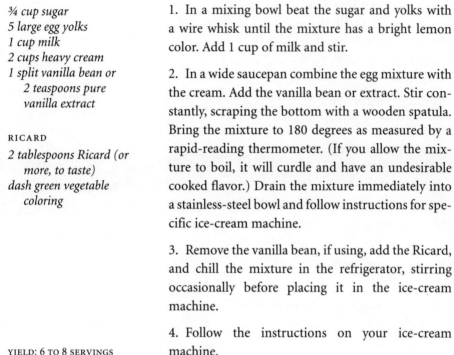

French Ice Cream with Ricard

BASE

¾ cup sugar
5 large egg yolks
1 cup milk
2 cups heavy cream
1 split vanilla bean or
   2 teaspoons pure
   vanilla extract

RICARD

2 tablespoons Ricard (or
   more, to taste)
dash green vegetable
   coloring

1. In a mixing bowl beat the sugar and yolks with a wire whisk until the mixture has a bright lemon color. Add 1 cup of milk and stir.

2. In a wide saucepan combine the egg mixture with the cream. Add the vanilla bean or extract. Stir constantly, scraping the bottom with a wooden spatula. Bring the mixture to 180 degrees as measured by a rapid-reading thermometer. (If you allow the mixture to boil, it will curdle and have an undesirable cooked flavor.) Drain the mixture immediately into a stainless-steel bowl and follow instructions for specific ice-cream machine.

3. Remove the vanilla bean, if using, add the Ricard, and chill the mixture in the refrigerator, stirring occasionally before placing it in the ice-cream machine.

4. Follow the instructions on your ice-cream machine.

YIELD: 6 TO 8 SERVINGS

It seems that any eating establishment more ambitious than a diner serves crème brûlée these days. Most of the renditions are silly and have nothing to do with the real thing. The keys to a good one are a well-made custard and a perfectly caramelized surface.

Crème Brûlée

2 cups half-and-half
2 cups heavy cream
½ cup granulated sugar
8 large egg yolks
pinch salt
2 teaspoons pure vanilla
   extract

1. Preheat the oven to 300 degrees.

2. Place the half-and-half and the cream in a double boiler. Heat, but do not boil. Add the granulated sugar and stir until dissolved.

3. Beat the egg yolks well and add the salt and

vanilla extract. Stir the hot cream mixture into the egg mixture.

4. Pour the crème into individual crème brûlée baking dishes. The custard should be about 1 inch thick. Place the dishes into a larger pan and pour boiling water around them.

5. Place the pan in the oven and bake for 30 minutes, or until the custard is set. Remove the crème brûlée from the oven and let stand until cool. Refrigerate until thoroughly chilled.

6. Remove the custard from the refrigerator and sprinkle it evenly with the brown sugar or superfine sugar, about a ⅛-inch-thick layer.

7. Preheat the broiler. Place the sugar-topped custard under the broiler. Cook quickly just until the sugar browns. Return the crème brûlée to the refrigerator until thoroughly chilled, or serve at room temperature.

½ cup sifted light brown sugar or ½ cup superfine sugar

YIELD: 8 TO 10 SERVINGS

Dessert Crepes with Orange Sauce

1. In a mixing bowl blend the eggs, flour, sugar, salt, vanilla and milk.

2. Melt 2 tablespoons of the butter in a small saucepan and add it to the batter, whisking briefly. Pour the mixture through a fine mesh strainer, pushing through the solids with a rubber spatula. The finest mesh is required to ensure a thin, smooth batter. Let the batter rest about 20 minutes before using.

3. Melt the remaining butter and use to brush the crepe pan as necessary. If a black-steel crepe pan is well seasoned, it will need little or no butter before

2 large eggs
1 cup all-purpose flour
2 teaspoons sugar
pinch salt
⅓ teaspoon pure vanilla extract
1¼ cups milk
4 tablespoons unsalted butter
1¼ cups orange sauce (recipe follows)

receiving the batter. If it is not well seasoned, brush it thoroughly with butter before its use.

4. Using a ladle, pour about 1 ounce of batter into a very hot crepe pan, rapidly dipping and moving the pan in a figure-8 motion so that the batter spreads thinly and evenly over the surface.

5. Brown the crepe on one side about 40 seconds; turn with a narrow spatula to brown the other side. Repeat with the rest of the batter.

6. Crepes can be stacked and wrapped and refrigerated until needed. Serve with the orange sauce.

NOTE: The crepes can be made satisfactorily in a nonstick pan if desired.

YIELD: ABOUT 24 CREPES

Orange Sauce

Combine all the ingredients in a skillet and stir over low heat until slightly thickened.

½ cup unsalted butter
juice of 2 oranges
¾ cup confectioners' sugar
grated rind of 1 orange
3 tablespoons Grand
    Marnier or Cointreau
    or liqueur of your
    choice

YIELD: ABOUT 1¼ CUPS

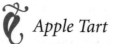 ### Apple Tart

1. Preheat the oven to 400 degrees.

2. Core and peel 3 of the apples. Slice them into eighths. Slice these pieces into thin crescents. There should be about 2 cups.

3. Heat 1 tablespoon of the butter in a small saucepan and add the apple slices. Sprinkle them with the lemon rind and ¼ cup of the sugar. Cook, shaking the pan and stirring, for about 10 minutes. Mash the

6 or 7 firm unblemished
    apples, about 2½
    pounds
2 tablespoons unsalted
    butter
grated rind of 1 lemon
½ cup sugar
½ cup apple jelly
prepared 10-inch pie shell

apples lightly with a fork. Remove them from the heat and chill.

4. Core and peel the remaining apples, and neatly slice them about ⅛ inch thick.

5. Spoon the mashed, cooked apples over the bottom of the prepared shell. Arrange the raw apple slices in a circular pattern over the cooked pulp. Sprinkle with the remaining ¼ cup sugar and dot with the remaining tablespoon of butter.

6. Bake for 40 to 45 minutes, or until the apples are soft and the pastry is browned.

7. Heat the jelly and pass it through a sieve. Brush this over the tart.

YIELD: 6 TO 8 SERVINGS

Crêpes soufflé Pavillon was one of those showstopping desserts at Le Pavillon, the kind of dish that would be ordered by one table, admired by those sitting nearby, then ordered by everyone else. We made a rainbow of different fillings for the puffed crepes, and we often had a hard time keeping up with orders.

Crêpes Soufflé Pavillon

1. Preheat the oven to 425 degrees.

2. Melt the solid butter in a saucepan. Add the flour and the cornstarch and stir with a wire whisk. When the mixture is blended, add the milk, stirring constantly with the whisk. When the mixture is thickened and smooth and bubbling, add the vanilla.

3. Beat the egg yolks and add them to the sauce, beating constantly and rapidly with the whisk. (Do not boil or the sauce will curdle.) When the sauce has thickened, remove it from the heat immediately and add the orange rind. Spoon the custard into a large mixing bowl; cool slightly.

4. Beat the egg whites until they are stiff and form peaks. Add about a third of the whites to the custard

2 tablespoons unsalted butter
2 tablespoons all-purpose flour
1 tablespoon cornstarch
2 cups milk
¼ teaspoon vanilla extract
4 large eggs, separated
1 tablespoon grated orange rind
2 tablespoons unsalted butter, melted
12 dessert crepes (see recipe page 245 but exclude orange sauce)

2 tablespoons confectioners'
  sugar
1½ cups English custard
  (see recipe page 242)
2 tablespoons dark rum

mixture. Blend them quickly with a whisk. Add the remaining egg whites and fold them in with a rubber spatula.

5. With 1 tablespoon of the melted butter, grease a baking dish large enough to hold 12 filled crepes.

6. Arrange the crepes on a flat surface, fill them with the custard mixture and roll them up.

7. Arrange the filled crepes in the baking dish, seams down. Leave a little room between each crepe for expansion. Brush with the remaining tablespoon of butter. Sprinkle 1 tablespoon confectioners' sugar over the crepes.

8. Place the crepes in the oven and bake for 10 minutes, or until puffed or slightly browned on top. Remove from the oven and sprinkle with the remaining tablespoon of confectioners' sugar. Serve one or two per person with the English custard, flavored with the dark rum, on the side.

YIELD: 6 TO 12 SERVINGS

Bread pudding in all of its variations is so au courant today. Yet it was also popular in France decades ago when mothers made it with French baguettes and prodigious quantities of eggs and cream. At Le Pavillon bread-and-butter pudding was offered every day. It was the favorite dessert of the Duchess of Windsor, who came to the restaurant unfailingly whenever she was in New York. I have lightened this rich dessert ever so slightly by substituting half-and-half for some of the heavy cream.

Bread-and-Butter Pudding Pavillon

1 cup dried white raisins
4 tablespoons unsalted
  butter, melted
12 thinly sliced rounds
  from a French baguette
2 cups half-and-half
2 cups milk
1 cup heavy cream

1. Preheat the oven to 375 degrees.

2. Place the raisins in a small bowl, add boiling water to cover, and let them stand 5 minutes. Drain.

3. Butter one side of the bread slices and set them aside.

4. Combine the half-and-half, milk, and cream in a saucepan. Bring to a boil. Immediately remove the

mixture from the heat. Add the granulated sugar and stir to dissolve. In a small bowl combine the eggs and egg yolks. Beat lightly and add them to the milk-and-cream mixture. Stir in the vanilla extract.

5. Butter a 2-quart oval baking dish. Sprinkle the bottom with the raisins.

6. Arrange the bread slices, buttered sides up, over the raisins. Strain the custard over the bread. Place the baking dish in a larger pan and pour boiling water around it, about halfway up the sides. Put the pan in the oven and bake 40 minutes, or just until the custard is set. Let it cool, and serve at room temperature with a sprinkling of confectioners' sugar.

1 cup granulated sugar
5 large eggs
4 large egg yolks
1 teaspoon pure vanilla extract
confectioners' sugar

YIELD: 6 SERVINGS

Note: Page numbers in *italics* refer to illustrations.

A Note on the Type

This book was set in Minion, a typeface
produced by the Adobe Corporation specifically
for the Macintosh personal computer, and
released in 1990. Designed by Robert Slimbach,
Minion combines the classic characteristics of old style
faces with the full complement of weights required
for modern typesetting.

Composed by North Market Street Graphics,
Lancaster, Pennsylvania
Printed and bound by Arcata Graphics/Martinsburg,
Martinsburg, West Virginia
Designed by Anthea Lingeman

Le Pavillon

MENU

Jambon de Bayonne 2.25	Melon 1.50	Grapefruit .90
Caviar Malossol 7.50	Pate Maison 3.50	Foie Gras Truffé 5.00
Saumon Fumé 2.75	Cherrystone 1.25	Anguille Fumée 2.25
Cocktails: Shrimps 2.50		Crab Meat 3.00'

Oeufs

Omelette Pavillon 4.75	Omelette aux Champignons 3.25	Poché Mornay 3.00
Poché Bourguignonne 3.00	Brouillés aux Foies de Volaille 3.25	Froid à la Gelée 1.25

Plats du Jour

MOUSSAKA D'AGNEAU PAVILLON 5.50

VOLAILLE POËLÉE AU AROMATES (P. P.) 5.00

NOIX DE VEAU FERMIÈRE 4.25

STEAK AU POIVRE. CÉLERI BRAISÉ 7.50

FOIE DE VEAU AU BACON 4.00

PIGEON GRILLÉ. POMMES SOUFFLEES 5.00

SOLE IMPORTÉE VÉRONIQUE 6.50

TRUITE SAUTE NORMANDIE 4.50

Légumes

Haricots Verts au Beurre 1.50	Epinards à la Crème 1.50	Courgettes Provençale 1.50
Céleris au Jus 2.00	Petits Pois Française 1.50	Carottes au Beurre 1.50

Entremets

Patisserie Pavillon 2.00	Soufflée Tous Parfums 3.00	Crêpes Pavillon 3.00
Macedoine de Fruits aux Liqueurs 2.50	Coupe aux Marrons 1.75	Pêche Melba 2.50

Glaces: Vanille 1.00   Chocolat 1.00   Framboise 1.00   Moka 1.00   Citron 1.00   Fraise 1.00

Café .70	Demi-Tasse .60	Bread and Butter .75